The Power of Cities in International Relations

"By addressing the political dimension to cities in globalization, this book can be viewed as long overdue, but this does not mean that it lacks maturity in the way its themes are researched. Building upon the largely economic work on global cities, the chapters show how cities are not just actors in current international politics but that they have become integral to both old ('high') politics such as security and new politics such as environment. The Power of Cities in International Relations should become a benchmark for understanding twenty-first century international relations."
—**Peter Taylor,** Northumbria University

Cities have become increasingly important to global politics but have largely occupied a peripheral place in the academic study of International Relations (IR). This is a notable oversight for the discipline, although one which may be explained by IR's traditional state centrism, the subjugation of the city to the demands of the territorial state in the modern period, and a lack of conceptual and analytical frameworks that can allow scholars to include the impact of cities within their work.

Presenting case-specific scholarship from leading experts in the field, each contribution guides the reader through the changing nature of cities in the international system and their increasing prominence in global governance outcomes. The book features case studies on the financial power of cities, city action in the security domain, collaboration of cities in coping with environmental problems, transnational urban regions, and mayors as international actors to illustrate if the relationship between the city and the state has changed in profound ways, and how cities are empowered by structural changes in world politics.

The multidisciplinary and global focus in *The Power of Cities in International Relations* sheds much-needed light on the significance of the reemergence of cities from the long shadow of the nation-state. Only by examining the mechanisms that have empowered cities in the last few decades can we understand their new functions and capabilities in global politics.

Simon Curtis is Lecturer in International Politics at the University of East Anglia. He was previously Michael Leifer Scholar in International Relations at the London School of Economics and Political Science. His research interests are in international theory and international history.

Cities and Global Governance

Edited by Noah J. Toly, Wheaton College

The Routledge series *Cities and Global Governance* is composed of contributed volumes covering key areas of study at the intersection of urbanism and global governance. Each title explores dimensions of the relationship between the local and the global, between urban landscapes and global dynamics. Authors in the series make empirical and theoretical contributions that advance our understanding of the role of cities as sites and actors in global governance.

1 **Cities, Networks, and Global Environmental Governance**
Spaces of Innovation, Places of Leadership
Sofie Bouteligier

2 **The Power of Cities in International Relations**
Edited by Simon Curtis

The Power of Cities in International Relations

Edited by Simon Curtis

Routledge
Taylor & Francis Group

LONDON AND NEW YORK

First published 2014
by Routledge

2 Park Square, Milton Park, Abingdon, Oxon OX14 4RN
711 Third Avenue, New York, NY 10017, USA

*Routledge is an imprint of the Taylor & Francis Group,
an informa business*

First issued in paperback 2016

Library of Congress Cataloging-in-Publication Data

The power of cities in international relations / edited by Simon Curtis.
        pages cm. — (Cities and global governance)
  1. Subnational governments—Foreign relations.   2. International
relations   3. Municipal government—International cooperation.
4. Globalization—Political aspects.   I. Curtis, Simon.
    JZ4059.P68 2014
    327.091732—dc23
    2013044581

ISBN 978-0-415-72877-5 (hbk)
ISBN 978-1-138-69686-0 (pbk)

Typeset in Sabon
by Apex CoVantage, LLC

Contents

Series Editor Foreword by Noah J. Toly   vii

Introduction: Empowering Cities   1
SIMON CURTIS

1 The Meaning of Global Cities: Rethinking the
   Relationship between Cities, States, and International Order   16
   SIMON CURTIS

2 The Global City: From Strategic Site to Global Actor   32
   KRISTIN LJUNGKVIST

3 A Networked Urban World: Empowering Cities
   to Tackle Environmental Challenges   57
   SOFIE BOUTELIGIER

4 An Urban Affair: How Mayors Shape Cities
   for World Politics   69
   MICHELE ACUTO

5 Globalization, Governance, and Renaturing the
   Industrial City: Chicago, IL, and Seattle, WA   89
   NIK JANOS AND CORINA McKENDRY

6 The International Activities of Canadian Cities: Are
   Canadian Cities Challenging the Gatekeeper Position
   of the Federal Executive in International Affairs?   107
   IAN MADISON AND EMMANUEL BRUNET-JAILLY

7 Municipal Bonds and Global Power: Theorizing
   the Role of Norms   132
   MARK AMEN

8   **Johannesburg: Financial 'Gateway' to Africa**   151
    ELIZABETH COBBETT

    References and Further Reading   165
    Contributors   185
    Index   189

Series Editor Foreword

"Nations talk, cities act." Despite the hyperbole, this statement by Robert Doyle, Lord Mayor of Melbourne, Australia, is an aptly chosen epigraph for *The Power of Cities in International Relations*. Editor Simon Curtis has brought together eight creative and rigorous analyses to describe and theorize the agency of cities and transnational municipal networks in global affairs. This volume engages not only the importance of cities as sites for the instantiation of global politics or the role of urban agglomerations as command and control centers in the global economy, but also it focuses on the significance of municipalities as actors on the global stage.

The contributors to this volume give careful attention to three questions: What are the global dynamics that potentiate municipal agency? What are the capabilities and limitations of municipal agency in global politics? Is the relationship between cities and states changing and, if so, how? This volume also asks what light international relations theory can shed upon these developments.

Just as importantly, *The Power of Cities in International Relations* also begins to interrogate the limitations of international relations theory in accounting for these developments. In doing so, the authors of this volume not only illuminate the agency of cities in global affairs, but also suggest the power of cities to remodel theoretical formulations about the basic conditions for and processes of the global political dynamics in which cities play an increasing role.

—Noah J. Toly

Introduction
Empowering Cities

Simon Curtis

Nations Talk, Cities Act.

I

Some of the world's most important cities have been empowered in recent decades. Their empowerment is a reflection of a shift in the nature of world politics. A political form long predating the modern territorial state, the reemergence of the city also indicates that the nature of the state is changing in the contemporary period, as its relationships with other entities undergo profound transformations. Since the era of modern state formation, cities, with few exceptions, have tended to be internalised within the national space and harnessed to the growth of national economies. At the same time, the power of nationalism reoriented older ideas of citizenship away from the original setting of the urban polis to the larger scaled 'imagined community' of the state. Now the direction of these dynamics appears to have been reversed, to some extent at least, as certain cities have emerged from the cage of bounded state space to exhibit novel transnational networked forms and a remarkable vertical and horizontal stretching of urban morphology unmatched at any time in the historical record.

The study of urban change has, in the more spatially oriented academic disciplines, led to valuable insights into contemporary social life. But in International Relations (IR) scholarship, cities rarely appear in the leading research programmes. In many ways, this is a consequence of the historical development of IR as an academic field: Arising in the heyday of the nation-state, its primary concern was with interstate relations, and particularly the state's monopoly on legitimate violence and its consequences. But international society has changed, and the complex interdependence between states, first registered in the late 20th century, has gathered pace since the end of the Cold War. IR scholars have recognised this, and the state-centric bias of the discipline has been amended to include the study of many nonstate actors. It seems essential now that if IR is to retain its relevance for the 21st century, it must focus not just on state interactions, but also on the processes that are challenging the bounded spaces of the nation-state, and the consequences of such processes. These include the empowerment of cities, and yet cities have rarely been included in this broadening of the research field. It is an aim of this volume to make the case for bringing cities back in to our narratives of world politics.

Recent developments showing the greater impact of cities on international affairs demand this attention, and there has been a steady, if still modest, increase in the number of books (Amen, Archer, & Bosman, 2006; Amen, 2011; Bouteligier, 2013; Acuto, 2013) and articles (Acuto, 2011; Brütsch, 2012) published on cities in IR. The study of the international activities of cities is not wholly new, and there is a long-standing literature on paradiplomacy (Aldecoa and Keating 1999; Lecours 2002; van der Pluijm 2007; Criekemans 2010). Cities have also long been involved in various forms of transnational cooperation. During the 20th century, a great variety of urban organisations were developed in every continent, some addressing regional issues, others scaling up to the global. The oldest of these, in the modern period, may be the International Union of Local Authorities, formed in Ghent, Belgium, in 1913, and based from then on in The Hague (Alger 2011:135). Since then, a plethora of organisational forms have emerged to network cities internationally, and many of the more recent influential networks of this kind are analysed in this volume. Cities and municipal governments increasingly play a role in the United Nations (UN) system, both as participants seeking to influence the agenda of the UN system, and also as objects of study and concern. Chadwick Alger (2011) has shown via meticulous research that cities have woven an increasingly complex web when it comes to participation in global governance. Cities and local governments have been developing the organisations that allow them to have the global reach that they need to bridge the various scales at which the global issues that affect them operate. Alger sees cities as a vital component of the evolution of democratic forms of governance in a multiscalar world and essential for the possibility of the diffusion of democratic practices across overlapping and interrelated political systems.

However, despite this literature having been around for a while, what seems to have recently attracted the attention of IR scholars is the increasing impact of cities in global governance outcomes: in particular, the contributions made by cities to the governance of climate change. All of this is very important, but, as this volume also shows, the significance of the reemergence of cities from the centuries long shadow of the nation-state is deeper and more far reaching still. Only by examining the mechanisms by which cities have become empowered in the last few decades can we understand the meaning of their new functions and capabilities for global politics.

As valuable work in urban sociology and political geography have shown us, the world's great cities have undergone remarkable transformations in form and function across the last four decades, coterminous with great structural transformations in the global economy, often discussed under the rubric of 'globalisation'. At the same time, the 20th century has witnessed an intense urbanisation of the planet. Around the world, people have vacated the land, seeking the opportunity that cities promise. A wave of humanity of unprecedented size has broken on today's teeming metropolises. Ours is now an urban age—and one that looks very different from, and contains very different social dynamics to, the world of the early 20th century in which the study of IR was born: a world now of yesterday, where only around one tenth of the global population lived in cities.

The impact of this recent global urbanisation bears comparison to that great growth of cities that accompanied the industrial revolution, although contemporary changes are occurring at an intensified pace and greatly expanded scale and bring with them the potential for even greater damaging environmental consequences. Concentrated into just 2% of the world's surface, these great urban hubs now hold half of the world's population. (This trend is accelerating: UN-HABITAT (2011:10) estimates that by 2050, over 75% of the world's population will live in cities.) Already, over 80% of global economic output is generated by cities, and the concentration is even greater in certain areas within cities, such as the central business district. Taking a systemic perspective, it is clear that cities are the points at which productivity, innovation, and wealth converge, and there is an increasingly influential analysis of the economic generative power of cities, often taking renewed inspiration from the long-unfashionable but now resurgent iconoclastic insights of the great urbanist Jane Jacobs. But another systemic feature of contemporary cities is that such dynamism and prosperity are accompanied by poverty and immiseration for an expanding urban poor, as the great migration to the city has brought with it the growth of vast slums and shantytowns. Figures from UN-HABITAT tell us that over one third of the world's population lives in some form of slum housing (p. 11). Clear as it is that today's global cities are dynamic economic growth engines, they are also set to struggle with pressing questions of social justice on a scale that the citizens of the first industrial cities in Europe could never have imagined. The Urban Age Project (Burdett and Sudjic 2007, 2011), an investigation into contemporary urban dynamics led by the London School of Economics and funded by Deutsche Bank's Alfred Herrhausen Society, has found that the forms that cities are taking around the world are often not encouraging in this regard: 'Cities are becoming spatially fragmented, more socially divisive and environmentally destructive'(Burdett and Sudjic 2011:8).

This theme of spatial fragmentation is one that recurs in contemporary writings on cities, a facet of the multiple processes of complex spatial restructurings that are underway in the contemporary international system. In addition to the horizontal and vertical stretching of urban space, the entwined rescaling of the city with technological change has brought about novel urban spatial forms that offer a transnational reach, leading some theorists to speak of 'world city networks' or 'transnational municipal networks'. This extension of the city's capabilities and influence allows them a new functionality within the international system, including the power to engage in novel forms of global governance.

Perhaps the most prominent example of this new urban capability is the C40 Cities Climate Change Leadership network, which is covered extensively by a number of the contributors to this volume. The activities of this network bring into stark relief the challenge that newly empowered cities hold for our established state-centric understandings of governance within the international system. What the C40 shows is that cities can have and are having an impact on the governance of pressing global issues. And one of the key drivers for the emergence of this nascent transnational urban networked governance is the growing conviction that states have failed to tackle some of the most pressing governance issues of the day, most significantly climate change. If the unedifying outcome of the recent climate summit diplomacy of states is a reliable indication here, it seems increasingly likely that the very structure of the international society of states is incapable of dealing with problems of collective action. And it is here, in this governance vacuum, that cities have found the motivation and capability to act in ways in which states either cannot or will not. In this respect, cities have certain advantages: they are nimbler and closer to their people, to local issues, and to the everyday. As Robert Doyle, Lord Mayor of Melbourne, Australia, pithily remarks, 'Nations talk, cities act'. These sentiments are echoed by Robert Zoellick, the former president of the World Bank, a key strategic partner of the C40 group, who argued at the C40 Sao Paulo 2011 Summit that 'when the world's largest cities pledge to work together on energy efficiency, clean energy programs, adaptation, and mitigation strategies, they can be a powerful force for change'. Here are two themes that this volume examines at length: cities as actors and city power. Cities *are* acting, and the C40 example shows that they can have an impact on global governance outcomes. But what type of actors are they? What is the nature of their actor quality? And just how powerful are cities? What forms does their power take?

In this introduction, I look at three issues surrounding the empowerment of cities. First, some context is necessary to understand the renaissance of cities. What are the forces that are drawing such large numbers of people into cities? What conditions are necessary to animate the processes that are allowing the new transnational municipal networks to form? Second, this introduction examines the characteristics and capabilities of contemporary cities in the wake of these processes. In doing so, it questions the limits of the existing literature on 'global' or 'world' cities and argues the case for bringing to bear the theoretical resources of IR onto this analytical terrain. The conviction here is that these literatures, while seminal in bringing analytic clarity to urban transformation, fall short in drawing out the political implications of new urban forms. And just as IR scholarship can bring important insights to understanding the transformative impact on the international system of urban change and state rescaling, so too may the discipline of IR emerge in a different light when it takes into account the phenomenon of urban transformation. Finally, by way of introduction to the contributions to this volume, we briefly consider the implications of these developments. Has the relationship between the city and the state shifted in profound ways? How are cities being empowered by structural changes in world politics?

II

There is a tradition of thinking about the nature of cities that sees them as the embodiment of the social. In this view, the historical forms that cities take, their morphological characteristics, are inseparably entangled with the historically situated societies they give shape to. As societies change over time, as dominant ideas, technologies, and social formations shift, so too does the form of the city. *Cityspace*, to borrow a term from the critical geographer Edward Soja,[1] is both a spatial expression of these social relations and an established and stabilised socio-spatial structure with which new agency must contend. In this sense, to study the transformation of cities in the contemporary moment is to study the transformation of social life. The remarkable metamorphosis of the materiality of cities over the last four decades cannot be divorced from broader shifts in the patterns of social life, perhaps the most important of which has been a mutation in the operations of capitalism and a far-reaching restructuring of the world economy.

Soja (2000) has argued that the changes taking place to contemporary cities are indicative of a revolution perhaps as significant as three earlier epoch-marking urban transformations: the emergence of the first settled human communities in the Levant and the Anatolian peninsular around 9,000 years ago; the creation of the first large-scale cities, beginning in Mesopotamia around the 4th century BC, and repeated around the world, supported by the new technologies of irrigation and the fertile soils along some of the world's great rivers; and, after a gap of some two millennia, the creation of the industrial metropolis of the 19th century. Soja argues that we are now witnessing, in the emergence of a distinctively new form of cityspace in the early 21st century, the coming of the 'postmetropolis', another distinctive iteration of socio-spatial relations.

One of the functions of the multiple 'posts' in Soja's postmetropolis is to connect the new form of cityspace to the intellectual currents of postmodernism, to the analysis of what Ernst Mandel (1978) called 'late-capitalism' and, to some extent, the discourses of postfordism and postindustrialism. And just as postmodern thought is not so much a rejection or transcendence of modernism as a radicalised and reflective modernity, conscious of itself, yet retaining many of its former characteristics, so too for Soja (2000):

> The new urbanization processes are not entirely new. In many ways, the postmetropolis can be seen as a distinctive variation on the themes of

crisis-generated restructuring and geohistorically uneven development that have been shaping (and reshaping) city spaces since the origins of urban-industrial capitalism. . . . The post-metropolis thus represents, in large part, an outgrowth, or better, an extension of the modern and modernist urbanism, a still partial and incomplete metamorphosis that will always bear the traces of earlier cityspaces. (p. 148)

If every historical society finds its spatial expressions in the urban, as the great French philosopher of urban life, Henri Lefebvre (1991), insisted they must, what historically distinctive forms have contemporary cities taken? We have already discussed their unprecedented demographic characteristics: but just what are the distinctive spatial configurations of the post-metropolis hinted at above, and how do we account for them?

As mentioned, the sheer size of the new urban formations is significant. Cities have grown. In just the decade between 1990 and 2000 there was a 30% increase in the size of urban settlements in the developed world and a 50% increase in the developing world (UN-HABITAT 2008:11). The central business districts of leading cities are increasingly packed with skyscrapers, as maximum value from these premium spaces is extracted. The flight from the inner cities of the developed world that accompanied deindustrialisation and grabbed the attention of the media, policymakers, and academics in the 1960s, 1970s, and 1980s, has been reversed in many cities, and the inner city reinvigorated and gentrified. The central business district offers great concentrations of wealth and power and the crucial capacity needed to direct the flows of the global economy.

Contemporary cities are also characterised by their colonisation of ever-greater proportions of their hinterlands, spreading and sprawling, cannibalising other smaller urban formations, linking with other cities in polycentric conurbations to create immense urban regions. These urban regions are made into functional economic units by the development of affordable high-speed rail and air travel, technologies now stitching together supraterritorial regions in a 21st-century equivalent of the ways in which networks of canals and roads unified nation-states. Over 20 global city regions have been identified with populations of over 10 million; some arranged around a core city, such as London or Mexico City, others taking polycentric form, such as the Dutch Randstad (Scott 2000). Recently UN-HABITAT has begun to map and describe these novel urban forms, under the categories of mega-region, city-region, and urban corridor:

> Mega-regions are natural economic units that result from the growth, convergence and spatial spread of geographically linked metropolitan areas. . . . Urban corridors, on the other hand, are characterized by linear systems of urban spaces linked through transportation networks. . . . These are emerging in various parts of the world, turning into spatial units that are territorially and functionally bound by economic,

political, socio-cultural, and ecological systems. [They] are becoming the new engines of both global and regional economies. (UN-HABITAT 2008:8)

The mega-region is human settlement on a historically unprecedented scale: Hong Kong-Shenzhen-Guangzhou has around 120 million people, Tokyo-Osaka-Kyoto-Kobe may have 60 million by 2015, Sao Paulo-Rio de Janeiro, 40 million. With their vast populations, these geographic formations far surpass the size and scale of most of the world's nation-states, a fact that alone should alert us to the transformative potential of these developments and shake the IR scholar from his or her state-centric vision of the world (as, too, should the fact that some of these new urban regions cut across state boundaries). These urban regions are another result of the great migratory flows of the 20th century, which have swelled urban regions and brought with them complex mixtures of cultural and ethnic diversity. In London, where one third of the urban population were born in countries outside of the United Kingdom, over 300 languages are spoken—an extreme case, perhaps, but indicative of the diversity of the modern metropolis. This diversification of population has the potential to problematise some of the complex issues of identity to which the unified national state was a solution. Such heterogeneity may bring in its wake new or reawakened ethnic and religious tensions and the formation of new political identities beyond the modern nation. Such cultural and demographic heterogeneity has also contributed to the wealth polarisation effect that tends to peak in global city regions (Sassen 1991).

Driving the growth of these dense economic clusters, it is argued, is the heightened competition that has accompanied economic globalisation. It is urban clustering that brings with it greater operational flexibility and enhanced learning and innovation. Urban economies have special characteristics that generate growth. Urbanisation has proceeded step-by-step with economic development: There is a fundamental complementarity between urbanism and the creation of social and economic capital (Polèse 2011). City economies differentiate themselves from the rural, from agricultural-based economies, by the economies of scale that result from market density (including reduced transport costs and the viability of infrastructure investments that accrue from agglomeration), their more complex division of labour, their superior productivity, access to services and education, and the creativity that results from proximity of people with a variety of ideas, knowledge bases, skills, and problems.

The notion of transnational urban regions, although capturing one aspect of the changing urban morphology, remains rooted in contiguous territoriality. An alternative, although complementary, perspective is to view these developments through the prism of the network. The growth in network connections between global cities has been enabled by the information technology revolution. The development of the Internet, in addition to the transport technologies already mentioned, has allowed distant, noncontiguous city spaces to develop patterned and durable interactions of a density and scope previously unavailable. Recent ongoing work has attempted to map empirically the types and intensity of network interactions between different cities and sets of cities (Taylor 2004). These two different features of the new urban form—global city regions and global city networks—are both dependent upon new technological developments, and, in this sense, represent fundamental novelty in urban form.

But the figure of the network is also, it might be argued, at the heart of emerging divisions in urban societies, as new forms of inclusion and exclusion take on networked form. Castells (1996), for example, describes in his analysis of the morphology of the network society, black holes of poverty and disconnection existing within both cities and states. This, he argues, can be characterised as the emergence of a fourth world, distinguished from the territorial inequality that separates the old third world from the more prosperous nations. These black holes of poverty very often exist physically just blocks away from areas of cities that are home to firms centrally involved in global flows of power. Members of these firms are likely to identify, culturally, more closely with others located in similar parts of other global cities: Within the space of flows forms a novel type of transnational class identity. In this sense, Castells's formulation offers something qualitatively new from earlier forms of neoimperialist theory that have influenced IR, such as that of Johan Galtung (1971), for example, who examined the core-periphery model that seemed to be emerging in the late 1960s and early 1970s. Instead, Castells focuses on how technology has created a qualitatively new global social space, where disconnection and connection are expressed through noncontiguous networks that operate at different scales. This also raises questions about the privatisation and citadelisation of corporate space, the decline of the public sphere, the integrity of the national territory, and of social justice. It is also likely that the wealth and power that accumulates within particular networks will result in a form of path dependency: a lock-in effect that continues to reproduce and accentuate patterns of uneven development and self-reinforcing cumulative growth.

III

If such are the new spatial forms, how do we account for their emergence? A technological determinism that would see them as the outcome of new machines, such as the bullet train or the Internet, is clearly insufficient. The strongest explanation for the emergence of these new characteristics of cities remains the economic one: They are enabled by, and are an expression of, crisis-generated restructuring of the world economy that took place in the 1970s. This includes the processes familiar to scholars of international political economy: the breakdown of the Bretton Woods system that had characterised the long boom since the end of World War II, the relaxing of capital controls and the formation of global financial markets, deregulation of formerly state-controlled industries, the formation of offshore economic spaces such as export processing zones, the inexorable rise of the transnational corporation, and the emergence of a new international division of labour.

This crisis-generated restructuring finds its expression at all scales of the international system—and has wrought transformative effects on both the state and the city. It was John Freidmann (1986) who first connected the emergence of the global economy with urban change, sparking the 'world cities' literature that emerged at the beginning of the 1980s. He noted how a select group of cities in the developed world, which had formerly been suffering from the impact of deindustrialisation and the onset of urban decay, were being visibly restructured by global economic flows. The core argument that has developed to explain the rise of such global cities is that the decentralised and dispersed global economic system created by neoliberal economic restructuring requires nodes of command and control to direct global capital and commodity flows. As Saskia Sassen (1991) argued in her pioneering thesis, focusing on London, New York, and Tokyo, it is global cities, acting as strategic hubs, which provide this control. The vertical concentrations of state-of-the art offices and corporate facilities that accumulate in the downtowns of global cities are the physical manifestation of this functional requirement. For Sassen, global cities represent a new form of *territorial centralisation*. The very technological infrastructure that underpins much of the activity of globalisation is tied geographically to global cities: The material supports of the information age can be seen to run through global cities, and global cities are the sites in which the information and communication sector of the economy is produced (see Castells, 2001, for a treatment of this subject).

This offers a fundamentally new type of social and economic space: at once digitalised and dematerialised, yet also reliant upon an extremely concentrated localised material infrastructure. Dematerialisation, although essential to the processes of the renegotiation of scale taking place, requires the construction and maintenance of the 'state-of-the-art built environment' that has formed at the core of global city nodes. This trend has the effect of redefining the *context* of these valued physical sites. For example,

> Financial districts in most cities have infrastructures for digital networks that are confined to those districts: they do not spread across the city, but they do span the globe and connect those districts to one another. (Sassen 2007:230–231)

Neoliberal ideas about moving investment decisions into the hands of private finance have thus resulted in valued privatised global spatial fragments being linked together, while devalued physical spaces within the same cities are often left to decay. Thus the 'neoliberal', 'market', or 'competition' state is directly implicated in a renegotiation of scale (from national to local/global connections), as both an investor and a facilitator of investment in global city infrastructure. Global city formation and state rescaling can, argues Neil Brenner (1998:1), be read as 'dialectically intertwined moments of a single dynamic of global capitalist restructuring'. States are both complicit in this rescaling but also increasingly constrained by it, as global cities and their regions emerge as one way in which the dialectic of territoriality and capital accumulation is simultaneously transcended yet preserved in new spatial forms. What we have here is a 'splintering' of the national space and the reconstitution of the fragments into novel spatial forms (Graham and Marvin 2001).

The historiography of this literature is outlined at greater length in the opening chapter of this volume, 'The Meaning of Global Cities: Rethinking the Relationship between Cities, States, and International Order'. One of the questions animating this book, however, is the extent to which the economistic bias of much of the existing global cities literature may be obscuring our understanding of the political conditions allowing for these developments, and thus the nature of their political consequences. One of the themes that emerges from the shape of the literature on global cities is that the significance of such cities is seen to derive primarily from economic processes, so that cities play a role in global governance outcomes only as a result of their particular standing vis-à-vis the global economy. If this argument is accepted, it would seem to be the case that all cultural, political, social, environmental, and ideological processes linked to global governance must 'pass through' economic processes if they are to have any bearing on global governance results. In many ways, the activities of cities described in this volume bear this out—the dominant activities of leading cities appears to be very much within the gravitational pull of neoliberal thought, including the emphasis on private expertise and market-driven urban solutions to global problems. This question of the primacy of economic processes forms a fulcrum of the current volume. Mark Amen, in his chapter 'Municipal Bonds and Global Power: Theorizing the Role of Norms', argues that economic processes do have primacy. But the early contributions of Kristin Ljungkvist and I are designed to shift the emphasis somewhat. My chapter seeks to focus attention on the prior political struggles that were a necessary condition of the emergence of global city regions and networks. It builds bridges between the cities literature and work on international systems and global order. Ljungkvist, in a related vein, places emphasis on the end of the Cold War in pushing the international system into a new security dynamic where cities are both crucial sites but also now strategic global actors in their own right.

In the opening chapter of this volume, I seek to place the emergence of global cities into a longer historical perspective than that in which it is often set. The chapter discusses, in more detail, the emergence of global cities and the literature that sought to explain them within political geography and urban sociology. But it also seeks to broaden the horizons of this debate to discuss the type of power that shapes an international system in which it is possible for transnational urban regions and networks to develop as they have. It is, in short, concerned with the conditions of possibility for such a social formation to emerge and endure. As I argue, without consideration of the victory of a hegemonic set of liberal ideas, backed by a U.S.-dominated balance of power, the global cities literature is 'doomed to float freely, untethered to the forms of international or global order that are the very conditions of its possibility'. I argue that the new form of global order in which global cities are taking their place, as key functional units within the world economy, but also as actors in global governance, is itself a response to the political history of the 20th century, and in particular the crisis of various forms of statism (by which I mean political systems where the state has significant centralised control over social and economic life). The emergence of global cities is bound up with the neoliberal solution to this crisis of statism, and the global city form is a manifestation of principles of deregulation, decentralisation, and the empowerment of private actors to move into spaces vacated by the centralised state.

In her chapter, 'The Global City: From Strategic Site to Global Actor', Kristin Ljungkvist is concerned with how cities are now appropriating responsibilities previously reserved to the domain of states in the international system. In this sense, cities are displaying just the kind of behaviour that makes them actors in the international system, and not just in areas traditionally considered not to be 'high' politics. As Ljungkvist demonstrates, with reference to issues such as global terrorism, global health, and climate change, urban policy has become crucial to governing the new security agenda. She argues that, despite the burgeoning literature on cities in global governance, little has yet been done to theorise their international political agency. One of the claims that Ljungkvist makes is that the power of global cities is to be found in the dominant discourses that they both reflect and shape. In effect, it is a shift in the dominant security discourse in the post–Cold War world that gives cities their possibility to act. New 'security imaginaries' have formed, and the militarisation of cities is one of their effects. The increasing salience of discourses of terror; the shift to a 'risk society'; the growth of surveillance, monitoring, and new legislations; the global political economies of organised crime, gangs, drugs, and weapons trading, as well as the looming impact of environmental change, mean that 'fear is reshaping the geography and politics of urban space'. Perhaps the clearest example of this security trend is the creeping militarisation of the New York Police Department in the wake of the events of September 11, 2001. But, despite the darker currents of much of this analysis, there is also the hope that cities, in their ability to unite the global and local scales, can be solutions to some of these pressing security issues.

This theme of cities containing within their resources the potential to solve pressing global concerns is also an aspect of Sofie Bouteligier's analysis in her chapter, 'A Networked Urban World: Empowering Cities to Tackle Environmental Challenges'. Again, there is the suggestion here that cities are being empowered by the inability of states to tackle transnational problems. Bouteligier argues that cities experience disproportionately the costs of climate change, especially low-lying coastal cities that are at risk from potential rises in sea levels. Yet, in attempting to act to mitigate these costs, the unique generative properties of cities give them a capacity to innovate, while their closeness to their populations allows them to implement such innovations efficiently. She demonstrates this with reference to her research on the C40 Cities Climate Leadership Group, which includes direct observations of the regular workshops, conferences, summits, and meetings that allow this transnational municipal network to endure, as well as a series of interviews with key officials. She also traces the networked links between cities and the partners, both private and public, that they have enrolled in their nascent form of networked global governance, such as the Clinton Climate Initiative, the World Bank (which began to give funds directly to cities in the 1980s), financial institutions, and transnational firms operating in sectors such as engineering and software design. One of the key themes to emerge from Bouteligier's chapter is that the growing power of cities in global governance is derived from the organisational form of the network. Being included within a network like the C40 offers participants the chance to access information, knowledge, resources, and partnerships that those outside of the network would be excluded from. This is a source of social power. Additionally, some nodes in the network are more powerful than others, in the sense that they can shape the direction of the network, its goals and activities. Within the C40, it is clear that some cities have more network power than others—although, at the same time, Bouteligier argues, smaller cities are also deriving power from these relationships. However, the extent to which states are included within these emerging networks remains a question in need of further analysis: In many ways states are still crucial in regulating access to resources for cities.

In another contribution to thinking through the nature of the agentic capabilities arising from contemporary cities, Michele Acuto argues in his chapter entitled 'An Urban Affair: How Mayors Shape Cities for World Politics' that IR scholars have so far ignored the increasingly significant role of city mayors as international actors. Mayors have always had great political influence at the domestic level, but now this influence seems to be being extended to the international arena. Arguing that the urban is increasingly central to the agenda of international politics, and a 'locus for the future of humanity', Acuto holds out the possibility that city mayors may have catalytic effects on the shape of international diplomacy in crucial areas such as water management, climate change, migration, gender equality, and social justice. Again, stress is placed on the multiscalar reach and dynamics of the city. This ability to act simultaneously at the local and global levels, to be 'gateways' for global governance, is seen as a key driver of the empowerment of cities. Indeed, as Acuto argues, part of the power of cities is to be found in their shaping of the 'everyday'. Acuto argues that the dominant discourses underpinning urban policies are key to any analysis of city agency. He finds that the dominant discourse to be found in the policy statements of city mayors is one of 'green growth', linking issues of sustainability to human security and economic stability, and of 'hybridity', emphasising networks of public/private partnerships.

This 'greening' of cities is picked up in Nik Janos and Corina McKendry's study of two U.S. cities that have sought to emerge from postindustrial malaise in recent decades: Chicago and Seattle. In their chapter 'Globalization, Governance, and Renaturing the Industrial City', Janos and McKendry focus their attention on how the emergence of urban global environmental governance is related to the structural changes to the global economy discussed in this introduction. As industrial production has relocated to the global south, strategies to 'renature' the city have played a central role in reviving these postindustrial spaces by attracting both global capital and labour. The consumption of nature becomes a key driver of growth and capital investment, in what the authors call the creation of a new 'postindustrial regime of accumulation'. Indeed, they identify that there has been something of a transfer of environmental responsibilities from the state level to the municipal level, which is traced through in the transfer of funds from national to municipal government.

Janos and McKendry identify a tension between nature, social justice, and capital accumulation, which they argue will be either harmonised or exacerbated by the choices of urban policymakers. There is here, however, an optimistic note. In their case study of the Duwamish River Valley in Seattle, such tensions mobilised the urban population to claim their 'right to the city', and to assert their right to participate in the renaturing process. Even if the consumption of nature has been a key driver of urban economic development, there is here the emerging outline of a possible new configuration of local governance, participatory democracy, and economic growth. However, a key question that emerges from this chapter, although beyond its scope, is the extent to which this greening of the postindustrial metropolis in the developed world is now dependent upon the parts of the developing world to which these industrial activities have been displaced. The emphasis on elite consumption, recreational activities, and services that is directing the policy of these postindustrial cities is made possible by the shifting of the problems of heavy industry to other regions, and the analysis of this dynamic will require a systemic perspective, which IR scholars are well placed to offer. If the future of the green, weightless, knowledge economy of the developed world depends on an increasingly polluted global south, then there are serious questions about the sustainability of this form of postindustrial life.

Ian Madison and Emmanuel Brunet-Jailly further investigate the relationship between the state and the city in their study of the relationship between

Canadian cities and the federal executive in their chapter entitled 'The International Activities of Canadian Cities: Are Canadian Cities Challenging the Gatekeeper Position of the Federal Executive in International Affairs?' Taking as their starting point the widespread assumption that state power is being devolved into subnational entities, Madison and Brunet-Jailly are skeptical as to the extent to which cities are becoming more autonomous and independent as actors on the international stage in their own right. The chapter is a study of the interaction of urban change with constitutional structures in Canada. As with some of the other pieces in this volume, they find that there is some evidence that the statutory powers of cities, and the capacity to exercise them, have been strengthened. However, they argue that this does not mean that the role of 'statutory gatekeeper' is shifting away from the state. Madison and Brunet-Jailly's key finding is that there has been no great evolution in the legal status of cities pertaining to their ability to act on the international stage, because the international relations activities of Canadian municipalities have never been the subject of restriction. Tracing this legal culture back to the colonial period, they argue that federal and provincial governments in Canada have never had the legal power to control or coordinate the international activities of cities.

In his chapter 'Municipal Bonds and Global Power', Mark Amen seeks to clarify the nature of the financial power of cities, focusing on the 4 trillion dollar U.S. municipal bond market. Amen shows how, under conditions of globalisation, the ability of cities to raise funds by issuing bonds becomes a critical source of social power. Cycles of bond issues and reissues have allowed cities to derive power from first the national and then the global economy. Amen argues that the capacity to command credit is a key component of contemporary city power. He also, however, traces the evolution of the historical struggle between the city and the state in relation to the rights of cities to issue bonds. In the United States, the federal government has, since the 1980s, made efforts to make city bonds less attractive to investors by limiting their tax-exempt status. In return, cities have invented 'special purpose' government institutions to get around state efforts to limit city indebtedness. Again, as with Madison and Brunet-Jailly's chapter, it remains clear that states retain constitutional primacy in the relationship with their cities. But the relative empowerment of cities within international affairs is made visible in this ongoing struggle between state and city. What also comes through in this piece is that the history of the municipal bond market in the United States highlights, in much the same way as Janos and McKendry's chapter on the greening of U.S. cities does, the ongoing tension between public interest and private gain that is such a feature of contemporary cityspace.

Finally, we close the volume with an examination of the crucial role that cities are playing in regional politics of the global south and how they are a vital consideration if we are to understand shifting patterns of power in the international system. In her chapter 'Johannesburg: Financial "Gateway" to Africa', Elizabeth Cobbett examines the development of a key city in the global south: One that is using its capacities as a financial centre (drawing on the historic ties to global capital networks put in place during the period of British Imperialism) to occupy a strategic nodal position as a gateway to the African continent. In the process, Johannesburg becomes a vital component of the South African state's rise to power as a regional hegemon—further demonstrating the tight linkage between the fortunes of states and their leading cities.

The study of the cities of the global south is going to be crucial for the kinds of research projects that map the shifting contours of the global political economy, as new financial centres emerge outside of the historic economic core of the international system. Drawing on the work of the historian Fernand Braudel, Cobbett argues that the study of such regional gateway cities can help us to analytically disaggregate the global political economy and enable us to view it not as a single functional unit, but as a set of interlocking networks, which contain a variety of forms of social order. She further argues that we must see the development of cities in the global south in their own terms: identifying their own distinctive contributions to the global economy, and the unexpected ways in which they may be supplanting the older urban centres of the postindustrial core.

The literature on the globalising of cities has, we believe, laid strong foundations for an understanding of the meaning of cities in the contemporary moment. But the next stage of this research programme will need to situate these developments in the wider context of the evolution of international society and the system of states, in order to truly appreciate the wider political significance of urban transformation. This volume is intended as a step in that direction.

NOTE

1. Soja (2000:8) develops the concept of *cityspace* as a general category that can be used to differentiate between particular configurations of historical-social-spatial arrangements. Soja refers to the concrete forms that city space has taken over time as the *spatial specificity of urbanism,* by which he means

    the particular configuration of social relations, built forms, and human activity in a city and its geographical sphere of influence. It actively arises from the social production of city space as a distinctive material and symbolic context or habitat for human life. It thus has both formal or morphological as well as processual or dynamic aspects.

    In this sense, social change can be captured in the dynamic shaping and reshaping of city space.

1 The Meaning of Global Cities
Rethinking the Relationship between Cities, States, and International Order

Simon Curtis

For much of its development, the global cities literature was largely confined to fields outside of International Relations (IR), such as urban studies or political geography. It made little impression on scholars of IR, who had ceased to see cities as relevant objects of analysis after their long embedding within the territory of the modern state. And, of course, for much of the modern period this assumption held true: Cities had been dominated by states, which hobbled their political independence, internalised them within the national space, and harnessed them as economic growth engines.

However, an extensive global cities literature emerged with the increasing realization that profound changes have occurred to many cities around the world over the past four decades, altering their relationships with the states in which they are embedded, allowing them to play a more visible role on the international stage, and leading to their increasingly frequent appearance in media discourses. Much has been done to analyse the meaning of the reversal in city fortunes since the dark days of the 1970s, which had seen urban poverty and inner-city crime reach combustible levels, with debt crises and race riots flaring against the backdrop of postindustrial decline. The bankruptcy of the city of New York in 1975, London's urban unrest of the early 1980s and the subsequent swing to the hard left in its municipal council, Hong Kong's stock market crash of 1982, may all be read as signals of an exhaustion of the logics of the old system. Yet, in the intervening decades the fortunes of these cities have been transformed, and any decline seemingly reversed, as people and wealth were drawn into them from around the globe. London and New York have been reborn as gleaming nodes in a worldwide network of cities that some have argued is the harbinger of a nascent form of global governance that challenges the very core logics of the international society of states. All this has occurred against the backdrop of an urban demographic explosion. We should note also that this urban transformation has not been confined to the developed world—over the last four decades, waves of migration have swelled cities to sizes unprecedented in the historical record. Vast numbers have moved internationally, while in the developing world there has been an immense transfer from the countryside to the 'mega-cities' that have also begun to attract the media's attention.

These developments are not unconnected: The same dynamics that have resurrected New York and London also operate on the cities of the developing world, albeit in different ways. The glass and steel verticality and global connectivity of the central business district is not unrelated to the global production of an endless vista of slums and shanties (Davis 2006).

Much has been done to analyse the nature of this transformation in urban morphology and function, but this is a large and difficult task and much more analysis is necessary if we are to understand the meaning of the rise of what has come to be known as the 'global city'. Much of the literature has focused upon the economic function of cities in the global economy and, crucial although this work has been, the next stage must be to draw out the political implications of both the emergence of global cities and their potentialities. In particular, a fuller investigation into the changing relationship between cities and states seems particularly pressing. This is where the IR community can add real value: a perspective on the key structures and mechanisms of the international system that is often lacking in this literature. But just as importantly, the emergence of a new urban form related to changes to the nature of capitalism in the 1970s and penetrating a variety of scales, from the local to the global, can tell IR scholars much about the nature of the contemporary state, and thus the state-system, in the contemporary moment.

In this opening chapter, I contribute to placing cities squarely on the IR agenda by offering an interpretation of the global city debate that runs slightly counter to some of the dominant themes in the literature. Although some of the contributions of urban theorists, political geographers, and world-systems theorists have been crucial in getting to grips with city transformation and its meaning, there is an excessive focus on economic and market-driven imperatives and explanations at the expense of broader considerations of the nature of contemporary international order. It is this perspective that I wish to recover here. While accepting that global cities derive their historically unique form from a mutation in the economy under late-capitalism, I foreground the role that political praxis, the state, and the state-system play in underpinning the possibility of such a transformation. Without this missing perspective, the global cities literature is doomed to float freely, untethered to the forms of international or global order that are the very conditions of its possibility.

In this sense, any analysis of the significance of global cities must rest not only on their standing in relation to circuits of production and exchange within the global economy, but also must penetrate to deeper currents, such as the problematisation of the nature of sovereignty at the contemporary conjuncture, the continuing dialectical tension between a capitalist transnational logic and the logic of a territorial state-system, and the nature of international transformation. It is only by placing the global cities debates in the context of these issues that we can see that they represent a symptom of a profound shift in the nature of global politics.

In this chapter, I pursue this intuition along a number of interconnected avenues. First, I examine the ways in which the origins and historiography of the formation of the global city concept and subsequent evolution of the debate has predisposed scholarship in this area towards economistic theoretical frameworks. This has had the result of making the global city discourse a primarily market-driven one (Amen et al. 2006:3). And indeed, historically, cities have often been viewed as entities that are symbiotically attached to markets and the generative force of exchange (Jacobs 1984). However, what often gets lost here is that this way of viewing cities must always be accompanied by an ideological move that pushes from view the need for markets to be undergirded by power and coercive force (Polanyi 1957). We must recognise, in the case of a network of global cities, spanning the globe with a fragile web of material infrastructure, lacking the capacity of the medieval city to defend itself in our world of states, that the power that sustains such a possibility resides in the state and the state-system (and a state-system with historically particular characteristics at that). It is here that we must bring the state back in and recognise the folly of trying to understand the meaning of global cities in isolation from their conditions of possibility.

Second, in this respect we might then begin to link the emergence of global cities to the crisis of statism (by which I mean political systems where the state has significant centralised control over social and economic life) in the late 20th century, which led to a variety of responses, the dominant strand of which has been the rollback of embedded liberalism and welfare capitalism and the rise to power of neoliberal social and economic philosophy in a number of key states in the international system. Concomitant to the capture of the state apparatus by the neoliberal project has been a fragmentation, commodification, and parcelisation of the national space, in ways that mirror the nature and morphology of global cities (Graham and Marvin 2001). Global cities are at one with the mutation in capitalism wrought by neoliberalism in this period and exist only in relation to the emergence of the competition or market state that emerged from the ruins of the old welfare or Keynesian model. We must recognise that it is state policy that has reshaped declining and crisis-wracked industrial metropolises such as London, New York, and Chicago, and has provided them the means and space to emerge as beacons of networked postindustrial might. We must link transformation in urban form and function to transformation in the state and the international system.

Finally, this restructuring of state space, and related redefinition of city form and function, is beginning to have significant, quite possibly unforeseen and emergent, outcomes (although we might suggest that these outcomes derive logically from a neoliberal philosophy that stresses decentralisation and bottom-up dynamics, even as it underwrites them with state power). For global cities, in the last few years, have started to realize their potential as networked and multiscalar entities, to participate in, even lead, nascent forms of global governance. The C40 initiative on climate change, for example, covered in detail in later chapters of this volume, aims to confront a critical global issue at a speed and at scales that the state and state-system have proven themselves unable to match. Such global governance initiatives by cities must pose a profound set of questions about global order and authority today.

THE ORIGINS AND SHAPE OF THE GLOBAL CITIES DISCOURSE

In this section, I argue that the particular origins of the global cities literature and its disciplinary history has given it a slant that has worked to obscure the very conditions that underpin both changes in urban form and the discourse surrounding it. Rather than focus purely on the role that global cities undoubtedly play in articulating localities into global markets, it is important to take a longer systemic view, which will ultimately lead us to discover the dynamics of global cities in the 20th-century crisis of statism. This is a problem, of course, that is very much still with us, as attempts to grapple with the problem of the correct configuration of states and markets continues to dominate the political agenda in the wake of the ongoing financial crisis.

Although there has long been an appreciation of the vital role of certain cities in world civilisation, the contemporary variant of the literature on global cities has its origins in an argument made by John Friedmann in 1986, where he put forward his 'world city hypothesis'. This was the first real linkage of a new type of city morphology to the restructuring of the global economy in the wake of the collapse of the Bretton Woods settlement in the previous decade. This economic restructuring brought with it a set of emerging processes: the formation of global financial markets, the emergence of offshore banking and export processing zones, the rise of the multinational corporation as an organizational form, and the emergence of a new international division of labour, with manufacturing jobs moving from the developed core into the developing world.

At its heart, the research programme developed by Friedmann (and pursued by others in the 'invisible college' of global city scholars; see Acuto 2011) is about the changing nature of capitalism in the late-modern period and the reconstitution of the relationship between national states, cities, and the global economy. Friedmann argued that it was no longer adequate to seek to understand cities as simply being part of national urban systems, as urban studies had previously sought to do in a period in which the nation-state was at its zenith. Instead, cities have become the places of articulation that underpin globalisation, where people and products link themselves to the wider world and its markets. The originality of Friedmann's contribution lies in his description of how the form that a city takes under globalisation, its morphology, its built environment, is shaped by the *functions* that it fulfils within the world economy. Rather than cities responding to their own internal dynamics, or to the smaller national systems of which they are also a part, they adapt to, and are shaped by, external economic forces. Friedmann's approach viewed the world economy as a globally integrated market, and it refused to recognise the national economies of single states as distinct economic units. Here, the global city becomes the *spatial expression* of a fundamentally new form of global capitalism.

Friedmann added the insight that global economic processes are *organized* through cities and, for Friedmann, such cities still formed a spatial hierarchy. He had retained from his urban school roots the hierarchical elements of national urban studies, transposing it to the larger canvas of the world economic system. From these building blocks, a number of key insights and refinements developed, including research on urban specialisation (Rodriguez and Feagin 1986), the crucial command and control functions cities play in the paradoxical dispersal and fragmentation inherent to the integration of global markets (Sassen 1996), and the empirical mapping of specific global city networks and hierarchies of global connectivity (Taylor 2004). These research projects have been essential to a deeper understanding of the phenomenon that Friedmann grappled with, but they have also replicated many of the limiting theoretical biases of Friedmann's approach. This was a discernable trend as the global cities literature multiplied with the globalisation discourses of the 1990s, where cities were seen as the key sites through which global processes flowed.

Friedmann's argument was the hybrid creation of an urban studies hierarchical thesis linked to a world systems framework. Drawing upon the work of Immanuel Wallerstein (1974) gave it a very different lineage to much IR scholarship on international systems. Friedmann's work was indeed a seminal insight, but it has also had the effects of skewing the literature in a certain economistic direction and of directing our focus to the symbiosis between global cities and the global economy, at the expense of the prior question of what type of international order generates such global economic conditions. Its reliance on world systems theory, with all the problems of its rigid and rather monocausal framework, has also not been conducive to marrying IR with the cities literature. In this way, the genealogy of the global cities concept has been an impediment to the creation of a research programme that allows IR scholars to apply their insights to these very important questions—and has maintained an undesirable academic divide between the scholarship on cities and the scholarship on states and state-systems (Curtis 2011).

This is not to say that it is not now being recognised that the global city concept is itself problematic. The literature has come in for criticism for its preoccupation with the economic construction and function of global cities at the expense of other global flows and networks, be they demographic, cultural, epidemiological, or ecological (Massey 2007). Here I take a broad view of the global city phenomenon, encompassing the wider set of effects accompanying the new urban form. This would also include the dark side of an often sanitised discourse, such as the unprecedented growth of global slum production (Davis 2006), which is as much a part of the production of the new social spaces as are the networked business districts of glass and steel that control and direct the vast financial flows of the global economy.

Indeed, there is uncertainty over the very nature of global cities: Should we view them as sites or locales, as actors or as structures, as networks or nodes? Is the global city a real object or a conceptual device? There is a clear danger in reifying cities as bounded entities and giving them a coherence that is ontologically unsustainable. There has also been a hijacking of the term by cities looking to boost their competiveness in global circuits of capital and labour. The 'global city' works very nicely as a media buzzword—witness the work of the many newspapers and magazines, consultants and think tanks that are perpetually ranking cities in terms of quality of life or business environment. These tell us nothing very profound about the deeper meaning of global cities. Michael Smith (2001:49) has argued that it is unlikely that any such entity as the global city can be identified empirically to any satisfactory degree: 'There is no solid object known as the "global city", but an interplay of networks, practices and power relations'. Such a perspective would view all cities as globalising to some extent, for the processes altering the urban fabric are uneven, lifting some areas and districts from their local context and plugging them into global networks, while neighbourhoods that may be physically contiguous to these valued spaces get disconnected. And yet, many attempts have been made to develop hierarchies of global cities, suggesting an exclusive set to which nonglobal cities might aspire. In the view adopted here, it is perhaps better to understand the global city as a conceptual tool or heuristic device that has been specially designed to shed light on important processes that are redrawing urban form in the wake of globalisation and postfordist capitalism. It is also better to understand all cities as globalising in some sense, although this is a necessarily uneven and noncitywide process, as Sassen (2007) has repeatedly stressed in her later work.

A further noteworthy strand of the global cities literature is the move to conceptualise cities and their networks as combining material and ideational elements. Global cities and their associated transnational spaces are seen as intrinsically bound up with the creation of the technological infrastructure that underpins what Manuel Castells (1996) has termed a *'space of flows'*.[1] Global cities are seen as crucial nodal points that form part of the material infrastructure of this space of flows. They are the physical sites and locations that link the space of flows to the material world. They provide the place-specific and nonsubstitutable enabling socio-technological infrastructure that forms the backbone for globalisation. The association of global cities with informational capitalism, as command and control centres and as the location of advanced producer service firms, is necessarily founded upon the material infrastructure that facilitates an economy where value is increasingly derived from information. This type of infrastructural paradigm is, furthermore, intrinsically bound up with the social context in which it developed. In this case, it has become imbued with a particular set of *political* ideas that contrast strikingly with the model of integrated national infrastructure that characterised modernity and its territorial national states. This interaction of social context and technological development is referred to by historians and sociologists of technology as the 'social shaping of technology', and consideration of the particular interplay of social context and technology informs an important part of the discussion here. This technological paradigm, first emerging in the early 1970s, was shaped by the rise of neoliberal ideas and values. The subsequent emergence and refinement of a transnational space of flows, connecting distant parts of the globe together in new configurations, while necessarily dislocating and fragmenting national spaces, is at the heart of a reconfiguring of the relationship between territory, cities, and states in the contemporary international system.

What I want to stress is that the founding moment of the new technological paradigm that gives global cities their particular qualities was underpinned by *state* agency, and that such agency successfully mobilised a political project that saw the state and its future in very specific ways. The implication of this is that the true meaning of global cities is political: It is to the political history of the 20th century that we must look to understand their emergence and the implications they hold for the future.

THE CRISES OF STATISM AND
THE NEOLIBERAL SOLUTION

Global cities must, then, be read as a further manifestation of state strategies to deal with the tensions that have recurred as a result of two contradictory logics: that of the modern territorial system of states, and of the fundamentally transnational form of the capitalist economic system. They are conditioned by the embrace of a political philosophy that favours bottom-up self-organizing dynamics to the various statist-centralised economic and political systems of the 20th century. It is the repeated failure of such statist models, from the perversities of the fascist and communist variants, to the inability of the Keynesian social democratic welfare model to sustain itself, which has provided the backdrop to the neoliberal experiment and the networked dynamics that support it. In this sense, as Neil Brenner (2004) has argued, global cities are a product and outcome of state restructuring in the late 20th century. In this section, I focus on the interconnections between dominant ideologies, state form, and international order, and suggest that global cities emerge as a result of a particular configuration of this relationship in the late 20th century.

One way to think about this variable relationship is via the work of Henri Lefebvre, which is undergoing something of a revival in its application to questions of the international.[2] Lefebvre describes how, throughout modern history, states have developed a variety of strategies to manage the crisis tendencies within capitalism by producing different forms of space in successive incarnations of modernity. This process Lefebvre names the State Mode of Production (SMP). Imperial, fascist, social democratic, and embedded liberal variants each have represented varying mixtures of coercion/repression, bureaucracy, administration, and centralisation (Lefebvre 2009:358–360). These successive historical SMPs have sought various strategic fixes during the crisis-prone history of capitalism, in attempts to master or manage the contradictions inherent within the territory/capital dialectic (the urban expression of this trend is captured by David Harvey's [1982] notion of a 'spatial-fix'). Lefebvre argues that capitalism owes its survival to the spatial interventions of the state. Only the state has been able to provide a hospitable environment for capital, and the means to extend this environment, to enlarge its space.

Lefebvre's work on SMPs coincides temporally with the period when the project of neoliberalism was beginning to take control of the state apparatus in the United States and the United Kingdom, and one important task for scholars today might be to take this project forward by outlining the features of a distinctive *neoliberal SMP*. It has since become clear that the crisis-induced restructuring of the 1970s marks a distinctive break with Fordism and ushered in a new period of flexible accumulation. State power, in the service of neoliberal ideas, has been activated to reshape the local, national, and global scales, resulting in the production of novel spaces that instantiate neoliberal principles such as decentralisation and self-organization. Acting as a supply-side entrepreneur in this processes, investing heavily in premium spaces (such as global city central business districts) designed to attract deregulated global capital into its territory (Brenner 1998), states have been essential to the growth of the new forms of city space we are discussing here.

These developments must be viewed in the context of a response to the exhaustion of statist models of organizing economy and society in the 1970s. The working out of the relationship between state form and economic system may be said to represent the fulcrum of the ideological conflicts of the 20th century, which, with the fall of the Soviet Union, seemed to be settled decisively. The high-water mark of the expansion of neoliberal ideas coincided with the United States' unipolar moment (Ikenberry 2011) as a hegemonic orthodoxy emerged, shaping states, governance institutions, and global order. It is this moment that coincided with the great expansion in the global cities discourse, and I now turn to some of the reasons why this may be so. I outline an argument in relation to three key areas: the content of neoliberal political philosophy, the central role of a new technological paradigm in providing the necessary material supports for these ideas, and the relationship between markets and global governance.

As is well known, Thatcher's and Reagan's tenures were built on the implementation of neoliberal principles. By the end of their time in office, they had managed to neuter the power of trade unions, deregulate most industry sectors and place many formerly public assets into private hands, empower finance both domestically and globally, and make reliance upon market exchange so pervasive a feature of social life, through the work of universities, think tanks, and international institutions, that it had come to be a hegemonic discourse. David Harvey (2003:12–15) has shown how there were alternatives to neoliberalism in the 1970s, such as socialist solutions based upon the national community, including the worker/share owner democracy, and also widespread urban social movements. But these alternative paths, which seemed incompatible with renewed capital accumulation, were broken by neoliberalism's political success, and the memory of their possibility as real political choices has been largely effaced. Against a renewed solidarism of the national community, the project of neoliberalism has been to 'unbundle' the territorial state, and to 'disembed' the social and regulatory framework of the previous socio-economic regime. It is this 'territorial unbundling', and subsequent restructuring at a global scale, which underpins the emergence of new spatial forms such as global cities.

The tenets of this political philosophy are important if we are to consider the relationship of the idea to its inscription in the material world. At the centre of neoliberal philosophy is the desire to limit the state to a minimal role in social life (as a constraint against the concentration of power in centralised institutions, a repeated feature of the 20th-century SMPs). Neoliberal states would provide and enforce the legal structures that allow for and protect private property rights, guarantee the integrity of money, and underpin (creating where necessary) a variety of markets. Beyond these minimal functions, the state should not play much of a role, the argument being that it can never possess the amount of information necessary to read market signals correctly in allocating resources, and that centralised structures will inevitably be corrupted by powerful private interests. Harvey makes the point that here that 'market exchange' becomes an 'ethic in itself, capable of substituting for all previously held ethical beliefs, and that the project of neoliberalism is thus to extend this principle to all spheres of social life' (2003:2–3). Essential to the success of neoliberalism has been the contemporaneous emergence of networked forms of information and communications technologies. It is no coincidence that these forms of technology have become pervasive features of life during the entrenchment of neoliberalism. A decentralised form of socio-economic organization that relies upon market exchanges requires 'technologies of information creation and capacities to accumulate, store, transfer, analyse, and use massive databases to guide the decisions in the global marketplace. . . . These technologies have compressed the rising density of market transactions in both space and time. They have produced a particularly intensive burst of . . . space-time compression' (pp. 4–5).

At the same time, these technologies, and the possibilities that they offer, have begun to have a profound effect upon the territorial organization of the international system, and have played a role in altering the relative balance between territory, scale, place, and networks (Jessop, Brenner, and Jones 2008). The splintering and commodification of national space inherent in the ideals and practices of neoliberalism has created a set of new spatial forms that jump scales and tie various fragments of global space together in novel ways. This has the effect of changing the very nature of the state, leading not to its demise, but to a change in the nature of relational state space.

What kind of spaces does a neoliberal SMP produce? The proliferation and increasing salience of a variety of decentralised and networked forms of social organization has been widely noted. Castells (2004) uses the concept of the 'network society' to capture the ways in which technological change shapes and is shaped by the movement from hierarchical to networked forms of organization in every aspect of society:

> A network society is a society whose social structure is made of networks powered by microelectronics-based information and communications technologies. By social structure, I understand the organizational arrangements of humans in relations of production, consumption, reproduction, experience and power expressed in meaningful communication coded by culture. A network is a set of interconnected nodes . . . a network has no center, just nodes. Nodes may be of varying relevance to the network. Nodes increase their importance to the network by absorbing more relevant information, and processing it more efficiently. The relative importance of a node does not stem from its specific features but from its ability to contribute to the network's goals. (p. 3)

Castells takes seriously the position outlined earlier on the social shaping of technology. For him, the rise of the network society is a result of historical contingency, the convergence of innovation, accident, the confluence of events at a particular historical conjuncture, and their interaction within a particular historical context and institutional framework. Castells identifies the interaction of three strands as crucial in shaping the network paradigm. The first is the ongoing set of technological innovations emerging from the microelectronics revolution and the digitalisation of information. It provides a historically unprecedented capacity to process and communicate information in terms of volume, complexity, and speed. The second driver that the new technological paradigm interacted with is seen to be the culture of personal freedom, openness, and individuality that grew out of the Western countercultures of the 1960s, particularly the cultures of U.S. university campuses. These cultural trends, in their stress on individual expression and entrepreneurialism, and in their desire to rescue technology from the grip of corporations, shaped the new technologies' emphasis upon resisting hierarchy and centralisation—resulting in the personal computer. The third strand, the crisis-led global economic restructuring of the 1970s, linked up with the first two in a historically contingent fashion. The result was that the new global configuration of capital was both enabled by, and went on to shape, the emerging technological paradigm. Digital technologies enabled capitalism to deterritorialise and reterritorialise at new scales that overcame the limits of the statist paradigm and the bounds of the territorial state system. In their wake, they called forth the functional requirement of decentralised command and control, a strategic function that networked global cities have emerged to provide. These developments herald a shift in the nature of the state, but it is also clear that, in both the space given to countercultures, and in the interplay between economic restructuring and digital technologies, the state has played an important shaping role in the constitution of this paradigm.

The final interlinked area I cover here is the shift in the relation between states, markets, and global governance that these developments signify. The rescaling dynamics unleashed by neoliberal ideas, and the creation of a material infrastructure for transnational networks, has made possible new forms of governance, increasing the reach of nonstate actors. Global cities may be read as liminal entities, both as a material structure, yet possessing the capacity to be global governance actors in their own right. I pointed out earlier their centrality to command and control functions in the global economy, which signals their crucial role in facilitating the functioning of global markets. Indeed, emerging regimes of global governance and markets tend to be reliant on each other: Global governance has seemed to draw its rationale from a market-based philosophy, while markets increasingly require new forms of transnational governance to sustain themselves. This, again, rests upon the strength of the neoliberal state, which remains large and strong, despite the minimalist figure it cuts in neoliberal thought (Gamble 1994).

The noted preference for horizontal and networked forms of governance, rather than the failed hierarchical and centralised statist models of the past, has given rise in the contemporary period to a variety of hybrid forms of governance participants: private actors, policy networks, public-private partnerships, issue-led coalitions. New technologies are absolutely key to the possibility of transnational linkages enduring over time and space as social ties. It has been noted that, in the emphasis upon bottom-up dynamics, self-organization, learning, adaptation and socialisation, the spontaneous generation and natural equilibrium markets, and the role of rational individuals pursuing interests unfettered in civil society, such forms of governance draw on a very long Western liberal tradition (Hurrell 2007:96). But it is in the possibilities offered by technologically enhanced networks (in tandem with the active encouragement of the neoliberal state), that nonstate actors may find governance solutions to global problems. The role played by the neoliberal state, it is suggested, may amount to a process of disaggregation of the state itself, where sovereignty morphs into something more contingent and contractual, as the state's different institutional arms seek to partner with private actors and facilitate solutions to governance issues. The principle being embraced here is that this combination of market, disaggregated state, private authority, and epistemic communities can find efficient solutions to pressing governance issues, such as financial regulation and climate change, in ways that a statist paradigm has not been able to. It is the taking of this path that has augmented the governance capacity of contemporary cities.

In many ways, cities are the ideal mechanisms for such forms of governance. It has been argued that cities and markets are intrinsically connected. The urban critic and theorist Jane Jacobs (1984) famously argued that the special qualities of cities emerge from the density of population that they alone achieve and are essential for economic growth and development. Urban density leads to its own particular problems, but also, Jacobs argued, generates the creativity and innovation that arise in response to those problems. Emerging from the interaction of the uniquely heterogeneous and diverse mixtures of people found in cities, Jacobs perceived the generative force behind all trade, wealth, and economic development: Innovation was a normal result of agglomeration economies of city life. Jacob's ideas have been revived in recent neo-Marshallian debates about the crucial role of geography and location in economic modelling (Krugman 1995; Glaeser 2011) and in the influential literature on 'creative cities' (Florida 2002).

Jacobs (1969) had begun her career in the 1960s, that decade of urban social unrest and crisis, combatting what she saw as the decline and decay of the great U.S. cities. Jacobs (1972) reacted against the modernist utopian planning regimes that had begun to change the face of cities in the United States and Europe, arguing that the separation of commercial and residential districts would kill the spark of economic life so central to the nature of the city. She wanted to protect the freedom, unplanned spontaneity, and the cultural diversity that gave cities their creative dynamism, supporting the market against centralised planning. These battles highlight the inherent and recurring tension between the state and the city. In essence, one of Jacobs's key political points was that it was the city, and not national governments, that drove macroeconomic development, and to think otherwise was to court the danger of destroying economic growth altogether. City life, for Jacobs, was the spark of all major economic development: Without it, there could be only stagnation and decline. The city and its region are thus seen as the only entity with the generative power to build wealth consistently and promote growth spontaneously from within its own resources. In the present period, these kinds of ideas can be supplemented with the emerging global governance models that cities and city networks are engaging in, where learning, adaptation, information sharing, and best practice models are being applied to crisis areas in global governance, such as climate change.

GLOBAL GOVERNANCE AND GLOBAL ORDER

The debate on global cities has now been going on for a number of decades, but there is still a lack of clarity on the nature of city agency. The discussion has often been about the special nature of a certain class of cities, their functional status within the global economy, or their ontological standing. But there is often a latent expectation within these arguments that cities will begin to translate their growing status into tangible political activity. Until very recently, we have not seen this political dimension, but several recent developments indicate that political muscle may be following economic clout. First, the growing visibility and importance of the city mayor (think Bloomberg in New York, or Johnson in London) may be seen as a manifestation of these developments, as is the tendency of some cities to develop their own 'foreign policy' initiatives. But it is the recent formation of a number of city alliances or city networks, crystallising around particular political issues, which may be indicative of a form of multiscalar networked political agency that is genuinely new and important. As networked actors, city alliances are developing the ambition and, perhaps, the capabilities to have a real impact on global governance outcomes.

There are a number of instances of this trend that get more extensive treatment in the other chapters of this volume (and so refrain from discussing them extensively here). Mayors for Peace, with over 5,000 city members in 153 states, comprises a cooperative network of cities that strive to place the abolition of nuclear weapons on the international agenda, as well as issues surrounding poverty and refugees, local conflicts, and environmental change. Metropolis, or The World Association of Major Metropolises, has been around since 1985 and has over 100 members, offering a forum for sharing knowledge and best practices that promote urban sustainability. The World Organisation of United Cities and Local Governments represents a recent attempt to boost the political representation of local government in the international arena, in particular with the United Nations' agencies that deal with urban issues, such as UNESCO, UN-HABITAT and the World Bank. But perhaps the most interesting example is the C40 Climate Leadership Group, which now includes a 58-city membership drawn from around the globe and engages in strategic partnerships with a number of private actors, such as the Clinton Foundation's Climate Change Initiative and other private interests, such as multinational engineering corporations. The C40 group seeks to take a leadership role in tackling climate change, but in ways that realize that cities already have the potential resources to contribute to positive governance outcomes on the global stage. These efforts take the shape of collective action, joint coordination, and common strategy, including best practice models and sharing technical know-how in areas such as transportation, energy and waste infrastructures, and retrofitting projects. These initiatives represent a two-pronged approach to governance: engaging with national and international forums, but also developing a parallel, self-organizing track that bypasses traditional hierarchical channels.

A unifying factor in these projects is that cities and their populations are key players in globalisation. For example, they generate many of its problems, contributing disproportionately to emissions, but can also be a creative resource to generate solutions to such problems: It is increasingly recognised now that new ways of city living must be at the heart of any sustainable solution to climate change. Cities may well act as important 'norm-entrepreneurs' in setting global agendas. However, it is important not to take these forays into global governance too far in any arguments about the relative decline of the state. The autonomy and capabilities of cities do not replace or challenge the agency of states; they are both enabled and constrained by the power of states and the state-system. So far, none of these initiatives have had particularly impressive global governance outcomes: The Mayors for Peace's campaign has made no dent in the nuclear warhead stocks that states hold—security remains the preserve of the state. It is too early, of course, to judge the initiatives on climate governance, but some clear boundaries are visible here too. The C40 network's goals and activities remain well within the discursive space of the neoliberal discourse, framing their solutions in the language and philosophy of markets, offering technocratic agendas, and partnering with private foundations, business interests, and multinational corporations. The emerging strategies remain relatively cost free but ultimately seem to be destined to lack the necessary punch to deal with market externalities. At the same time, cities within these networks remain in competition with each other and often seek solutions to looming resource and climate crises by pursuing individual networked infrastructure security strategies. The all-encompassing neoliberal discourse remains a significant obstacle to developing truly systemic and relational solutions to what are systemic and relational crises (Hodson and Marvin 2010).

It is vital that when we look at these emergent political practices we do not lose sight of the role that state strategy has played in empowering cities in this way. The possibility of global urban networks has been tightly bound up with a neoliberal project to decentre political authority and rescale the national polity. In this sense, we might see the very conditions of possibility of networks of global governance as the outcome of the application of state power. And these conditions must be traced back to the creation and maintenance of a system of global order that instantiates liberal principles, whether we consider that to be a type of neo-Gramscian hegemony underpinned by the projection of U.S. values onto the international stage (Cox 1981), or a looser form of nonterritorial hegemony based not simply on one state but on a wider international society of liberal states that promote a dominant liberal discourse (Agnew and Corbridge 1994; see also Hardt and Negri 2000).

When we consider the question of global order, however, the decentralised and devolving model that has empowered cities is not without challengers in the contemporary period. In particular, the rise of forms of authoritarian or state capitalism present a number of challenges to the rescaled market state, as a variety of other state forms have tapped into the expanding global market via such vehicles as state-owned enterprises and sovereign wealth funds (Bremmer 2010). Such variants of the state-market relationship are increasingly a feature of global order. It will be important to study how the cities of states that adopt state-capitalism are linking to the network of global cities emerging from the neoliberal SMP and how this feeds into new transnational forms of inclusion and exclusion that result from a networked paradigm. Although much more analysis needs to be carried out here, these alternative SMPs may well be showing us that the ideological battles that the liberal market paradigm emerged to resolve may be far from over, if the ongoing financial crisis had not already revealed that truth.

Finally, I consider the implications of the compact between the neoliberal or market state and the global city. For, despite using reconstituted urban forms in their rescaling strategies, there remains the possibility that such moves contain emergent and unexpected logics. For one of the key drivers behind the form of the global city, the continuing tension between logics of capital accumulation and logics of territoriality, mediated via the creation of this new transnational space, continues to shape international affairs. As the state reshapes and reforms its territory, it places great stress on those supports that have given it its modern form. In particular, the principle of modern territorial sovereignty, from which international order derives much of its logic, becomes increasingly problematic. The modern concept of sovereignty has typically produced sharply demarcated boundaries, clear insides and outsides. But, as Rob Walker has argued, modern sovereignty is not just a historically particular production of space—it is also a historically particular solution to a set of *abstract* philosophical and political problems. This solution emerged in response to the crises that wracked 17th-century Europe, but these problems (the balancing of universal and particular, the demarcation of self and other, the production of spatial and temporal structures) also beset *all* historical societies, and any unravelling of sovereignty will demand that these problems be solved in new ways. Thus, the creation of new spatial forms, including global cities and their networks, are but symptoms of 'the increasingly puzzling character of the problem of sovereignty' (Walker 2010:53). As the neoliberal state moves to unravel the previous spatial mode, privatising, parcelising, and commodifying its formerly homogenous national space, the most valued fragments are reconnected at the transnational scale, and new fractures and fault lines appear within the structures of modern international order. These developments bring into doubt the integrity of the modern spatial settlement and suggest an uncertain future in which this settlement must now be systematically renegotiated at every scale. The future of cities will be a central feature of this renegotiation in the 21st century: the urban age.

CONCLUSION

In this chapter, I have argued that the meaning and significance of global cities derives not simply, or even primarily, from their standing within the global economy, but from the prior political and ideological struggles that have underpinned the creation of such a global economy and replaced some of the failed statist paradigms of the 20th century. In this sense, the global city form, including transterritorial network and node structures, transnational regional agglomerations, and a reliance on bottom-up logics of self-organization, are the outcome of the application of state power. Decentralisation and spatial reconfiguration is a policy choice, and here that choice is linked to a particular set of political philosophies. It is a project that tends to see markets as self-generating, natural formations, but this is to mask the role of the state (and state-system) in their very conditions of possibility.

The continued success of the neoliberal political project is by no means guaranteed, as rival forms of state capitalism, and the continued instability of capitalist markets, show us. But undoubtedly global cities are playing key governance roles in the global economy, in managing capital flows and generating economic dynamism while, as we have seen, developing some potential to contribute to climate change governance. All of this is limited thus far, however, by the horizons of the tightly scripted hegemonic discourse of neoliberalism. Behind this lies the power of the state and the evolving global order that states have created among themselves: even if that order is now being problematised by the very rescaling processes that leading neoliberal states have unleashed. Will global cities, as places, be the locus of new forms of cultural identity and new understandings of sovereignty beyond the national? Time will tell here, but they are good candidates for such profound changes, which may truly push beyond the contemporary configuration of global order. The political theory of the global city is the largely unexplored terrain of a research programme that has the potential to be at the cutting edge of international theory.

NOTES

1. For Castells (2004:36) the space of flows

    refers to the technological and organizational possibility of practicing simultaneity without contiguity. The space of the network society is made up of the articulation between three elements: the places where activities are located, the material communication networks linking these activities, and the content and geometry of the flows of information that perform the activities in terms of function and meaning.

    For Castells, the space of flows becomes dominant over physical spaces, which do not, of course, disappear, but now receive their meaning from their function as nodal points within specific networks.
2. In addition to Brenner (2004), another thinker central to this movement is Stuart Elden (2004, 2009), who has been instrumental in translating some of Lefebvre's later work on the state into English (see Lefebvre 2009).

2 The Global City
From Strategic Site to Global Actor

Kristin Ljungkvist

URBAN POLITICS IN A GLOBAL AGE

Global Cities[1] have become actors in world politics. For more than 350 years, cities—as organizing entities of political, economic, and social life—have been embedded within and subordinated to the modern nation-state. During this period, local governments in cities have had nothing, or at least very little, directly to do with the conduct of international relations and foreign affairs. Under the principles of the political order often referred to as the Westphalian international system, foreign policy and security affairs have generally been monopolised by and considered a core function of the state. This appears to be changing in the 21st century, as local governments of cities are taking on new roles, claiming international political authority, and becoming engaged in world politics.

What passes as *urban* policies today is increasingly suffused with issues that every so often touch upon '*high* politics'. In relation to events such as 9/11, the SARS crisis, Hurricane Katrina and Hurricane Sandy, and the London and Madrid bombings, or in relation to climate change, academic scholars and political practitioners alike have emphasised the increasing importance of cities and their local authorities in the management of various global risks and security challenges.

In the light of traditional claims of state sovereignty, independent foreign and security policies on the part of cities should be deemed impossible, and in the light of the continuous fiscal constraint that most local governments operate under, it is certainly puzzling that they find such 'mission creep' to be in their city's interest at all. And yet, we are seeing many local city governments around the world that are breaking the institutional chains of municipal politics and are becoming global actors in issues ranging from nuclear proliferation, human rights, climate change, mitigation, and counterterrorism. Considering that contemporary urban politics engage with a wide array of issues that International Relations (IR) and security studies scholars understand as part of the 'new' and broadened security agenda of the globalised post–Cold War world, and that the urban engagements on those issues do not end at the jurisdictional boundaries of the city but reach well beyond, and that local governments of large metropolitan areas around the world are taking new roles and tasks upon themselves and are increasingly becoming engaged in world politics and global governance, I argue that the time has come to reexamine the narrow economistic understanding of the Global City. In this chapter, I suggest that the possibility for local city governments to become strategic global political actors is in part due to the increasingly prominent place of cities within contemporary globalisation and security imaginaries.

ARE CITIES REALLY INTERNATIONAL ACTORS?

Since the late 1980s, the study of cities and globalisation has become its own well-established social scientific discourse, and theories of Global Cities, sometimes also referred to as World Cities, have become established as a major framework for research on contemporary cities, globalisation, and the changing spatial organization of the world. The key contribution of this literature has been to illuminate the role of cities in international political economy and on the functions that they fulfil as spatial command posts for globalised capitalism. Flows of capital, labour, goods, and raw materials, in combination with the opening of national economies and deregulation, privatisation, and supranational entities such as free trade blocks and global digitalised markets, together articulate the new global economic context that becomes localised and materialises in global city regions (Sassen 1991; Knox and Taylor 1995; Brenner 1998; Scott 2001; Swyngedouw 2004a; Smith 2005). However, in recent years, we have seen an increasing awareness of and discussions about the *active* presence of cities and their local governments in the realm of world politics, international affairs, and global governance. But what empirical evidence do we really have that shows that local governments are in fact *acting* internationally? What examples of an active presence beyond the already well-accounted-for role and function in the globalised economy can we see of Global Cities and their local governments in the realm of international affairs and global governance? I focus in particular on three aspects of an active political presence of cities and their local governments in world affairs. The first has to do with cities as objects and agents of international norms and regulations; the second with cities developing a foreign policy of their own; and the third with cities and security policies and global risks. Before going into these questions specifically, I briefly comment on a general global trend that arguably is also of importance in relation to the general phenomenon of cities' claims to international political authority—namely, urbanisation.

WELCOME TO THE URBAN FUTURE

It has been said and written many times, in the media and in popular science, in various forms of powerful and intriguing slogans that 'for the first time in the history of human kind, more than half of the world's population live in urban areas',[2] that 'the human species has become an urban species';[3] that 'we have entered the Urban Millennium'.[4] According to the United Nations (UN), one of the most powerful trends of contemporary globalisation processes is urbanisation. Urbanisation is by no means a new phenomenon but has been a defining feature of human societal development for more than 10,000 years. However, the speed of the ongoing demographic shift is described as being without precedent in human history. In an announcement at the fourth World Urban Forum, held in Nanjing, China, in 2008, Anna Tibaijuka, the then Excecutive Director of UN-HABITAT, was qouted stating that:

> The 100 years from 1950 to 2050 will be remembered for the greatest social, cultural, economic and environmental transformation in history—the urbanization of humanity. With half of us now occupying urban space, the future of the human species is tied to the city. (UN-HABITAT 2008b:2)

According to the UN, in 1900, about 10% of the total world population lived in cities. In 2007, more than half of the world's people had become city dwellers. Every week, approximately 3 million people move into cities worldwide, and the trend of urbanization is escalating. The United Nations forecasts that by 2050, 70% of all people will live in cities (UN-HABITAT 2009). According to numbers provided by the World Bank, two billion new urban residents are expected worldwide in the next 20 years (World Bank 2009:3).

The production of often staggering statistics and numbers has become a central feature in the discourse of the 'Urban Millennium'. For example, today, the mayor of a mega-city such as Mexico City governs more people than 75% of the world's state leaders (humansecurity-cities.org 2007:9). According to David Satterthwaite (2007:1) it took humanity roughly 10,000 years to go from 0 to 1 billion urban dwellers (ca. 8,000 BC–1960), while it is expected to take only 15 years to go from 3 to 4 billion (2002–2017). And according to UN-HABITAT (2011):

> The number of cities in the world with populations greater than 1 million increased from 75 in 1950 to 447 in 2011; while during the same period, the average size of the world's 100 largest cities increased from 2.0 to 7.6 million. By 2020, it is projected that there will be 527 cities with a population of more than 1 million, while the average size of the world's 100 largest cities will have reached 8.5 million. (p. 2)

According to Neil Brenner and Christian Schmid (2012:13), the current hyperurbanising world can no longer be understood through the traditional urban/rural distinction. Extensively urbanised interdependencies are consolidated within and between extremely large and rapidly expanding mega-metropolitan regions, or what they refer to as 'urban galaxies', that often span multiple national boundaries. In today's world, the urban represents an increasing worldwide condition in which political-economic relations are enmeshed:

> This situation of *planetary urbanisation* means, paradoxically, that even spaces that lie well beyond the traditional city cores and suburban peripheries—from transoceanic shipping lanes, transcontinental highway and railway networks, and worldwide communications infrastructures to alpine and coastal tourist enclaves, 'nature' parks, offshore financial centres, agro-industrial catchment zones and erstwhile 'natural' spaces such as the world's oceans, deserts, jungles, mountain ranges, tundra, and atmosphere—have become integral parts of the worldwide urban fabric. (Brenner and Schmid 2012:13)

In 2001, United Nations Centre for Human Settlements published the first of its series of biannual reports on urban conditions and the world's cities, and according to Kofi Annan, who was Secretary-General at the time,

> [The report] represents a milestone in the efforts of the United Nations to build and disseminate knowledge for policy-makers and the general public: for the first time, the city, rather than the country, is used as the basic unit of analysis. (United Nations Centre for Human Settlements 2001:2)

Annan also declared that sustainable urban development is one of the most pressing challenges facing the human community in the 21st century and he argued that cities will be the arenas where some of the world's biggest social, economic, environmental and political challenges will be addressed, and where solutions will be found. According to Annan:

> 'As globalization proceeds, more cities will find themselves managing problems and opportunities that used to be the exclusive domain of national governments'. (United Nations Centre for Human Settlements 2001:2)

In relation to these developments, British-Canadian journalist Doug Saunders (2011) argues in his book *Arrival City: How the Largest Migration in History Is Reshaping Our World*:

> What will be remembered about the twenty-first century, more than anything else except perhaps the effects of a changing climate, is the great, and final, shift of human populations out of rural, agricultural life and into cities. We will end this century as a wholly urban species. (p. 1)

Saunders provides an optimistic narrative of how, at this 'final century of global urbanization', cities are the force of lasting progress which, if managed properly, can provide answers to poverty, overpopulation, and sustainable economic developments. Equally excited is Jeb Brugmann (2009) who, in his book *Welcome to the Urban Revolution: How Cities Are Changing the World*, welcomes us to the 'urban revolution' and argues that current demographic shifts into cities are as significant for humanity and social change as was the Industrial Revolution, and that the solutions for many of the major global problems of our time, such as poverty, marginalisation, conflict, and environmental degradation, lie in the clever design and governance of cities (Brugmann 2009:xx).

Harvard Professor Edward Glaeser (2011) similarly applies an expressive language and an optimistic narrative as he argues in his book *Triumph of the City* that the city as a human habitat has triumphed over all other forms of human habitats. Just like Saunders, he declares humanity to have become an 'urban species' and argues that cites are 'our species' greatest invention' (2011:6). According to Glaeser, cities of the West are wealthier, healthier, greener, and more alluring than ever, and cities in the world's poorer places provide the clearest way from poverty to prosperity (2011:1).

Cities are indeed rightfully magnets for those seeking a better life because, according to the UN, cities and towns offer the hope of greater employment, higher wages, and a remedy to poverty. UN data from all countries show that as the share of urban population increases, so does gross domestic product and per capita income. Urban-based economic activities are more productive than rural-based ones, and urban life offers the prospect of a greater general economic welfare (UN-HABITAT 2007:9). But according to the UN, massive urbanisation trends should be understood within a context of both opportunity and risk. The ongoing increase of urban populations is most dramatic in the poorest and least urbanised continents, Asia and Africa. Although much of the urban expansion is occurring in a context of rapid economic growth, it is a highly inequitable process and many local governments lack the capacity to provide basic services and security to all their urban dwellers. Growing numbers of urban residents live in poverty, lacking basic infrastructure and services such as water and sanitation, under unsafe conditions, and without tenure security. The rapid urbanisation means that each year more and more people are living in informal and impoverished slums and shantytowns, and the year 2007 also saw the number of slum dwellers pass the 1 billion mark (UN-HABITAT 2007:9).

Mike Davis's (2006) bestseller *Planet of Slums* is equally as dramatic in tone as Saunders, Glaeser, and Brugmann, but provides a gloomy counternarrative. Although Davis in a similar fashion refers to the current demographic shifts into urban areas as an 'epochal transition' constituting a 'watershed in human history, comparable to the Neolithic or Industrial Revolution' (2006:1), contemporary urbanisation is, according to Davis, not driven by the supply of jobs in the cities. Instead, Davis argues that current urbanisation trends are driven by a neoliberal world order causing reproduction of poverty (2006:16). The World Bank and the International Monetary Fund

(IMF), Davis argues, have been the driving force, and Structural Adjustment Programmes—mechanisms of conditionality imposed on borrowers or debtors negotiating repayment—have been the means. He argues:

> The global forces "pushing" people from the countryside—mechanization of agriculture in Java and India, food imports in Mexico, Haiti and Kenya, civil war and droughts throughout Africa, and everywhere the consolidation of small holdings into large ones and the competition of industrial-scale agribusiness—seem to sustain urbanization even when the "pull" of the city is drastically weakened by debt and economic depression. As a result, rapid urban growth in the context of structural adjustment, currency devaluation, and state retrenchment has been an inevitable recipe for the mass production of slums. (Davis 2006:16–17)

Slum growth has also become one of the central concerns of UN-HABITAT, and the organization shares Davis's concerns regarding the highly inequitable aspects of urbanisation and what UN-HABITAT refers to as the 'Divided City', where extreme wealth and extreme poverty exist side by side in urban areas all over the world. This is also reflected in the UN's Millennium Development Goals in which the 7th goal has as its 11th target to have improved the lives of at least 100 million slum dwellers by 2020. But the challenges facing urban areas are not seen as restricted to the developing world. Even in well-resourced cities, local leaders struggle with unmet housing and transportation needs, crime and violence, environmental degradation, and disaster vulnerabilities (UN-HABITAT 2009). However, while Davis and many others have painted a bleak picture of the future of cities, UN-HABITAT sees, just like Saunders, Glaeser, and Brugmann, the city as key to finding solutions to many of the global challenges facing the world.

Since the 1990s, and especially since the turn of the millennium, the idea of a rising importance of cities and urban regions in world affairs has become an increasingly established part of contemporary globalisation discourses. In 2010, I visited the World Bank in Washington, DC, to conduct interviews, and one of the World Bank's leading urban specialists told me in an interview:

> The interest for cities is now enormous. The increase of urban populations is probably one factor. The fact that more than 50% of the world population now lives in cities has probably been important for our mindset. But most importantly, cities are starting to get their act together and are starting to make their voices heard internationally. (interview with World Bank official, December 2, 2010, in Washington, DC)

The idea that this World Bank civil servant is giving voice to is that the escalating trend of urbanisation has led to an increasing general interest in cities and that cities and urban regions are of increasing relevance for our global future and in world affairs. This in turn is empowering cities and their local governments in global politics. But in what ways are cities 'making their voices heard internationally'? What examples of an active presence of cities and their local governments can we see in the realm of international affairs and in global governance?

CITIES AS OBJECTS AND AGENTS OF INTERNATIONAL NORMS AND REGULATIONS

Over the past three decades, cities and their local governments have increasingly become the objects of international and transnational regulations (Blank 2006). Various international bodies such as UN agencies and the European Union (EU) attempt to regulate, on the one hand, the course of urban developments and, on the other, the relations between local and central governments. By targeting cities and local governments as objects of regulation, issues such as physical planning, economic structure, housing schemes, and poverty reduction are made the business of international and global institutions and not only that of local and national governments, and institutional links can be established directly between local and international levels (Blank 2006:899).

A central idea and rationale for the international regulatory attempts in relation to cities and urban issues has been to promote an agenda of *decentralisation*[5] and *subsidiarity*.[6] There is a prominent paradigm relating decentralisation to democratisation and 'good governance', and the idea that democratisation is dependent on decentralisation has had far-reaching leverage internationally. Since the late 1990s, the concept of good governance has become the main international mantra for development in developing countries. Although the term *good governance* has come to mean different things,[7] *decentralisation* is a common central trait. International agencies like the World Bank and the IMF are, for example, boosting decentralisation in developing and transitional countries as they have adopted decentralisation as part of their philosophy for a worldwide reform agenda to strengthen democracy and good governance (Kumar Sharma 2005:11).

During the 1980s, an economic perspective with ideas about privatisation and deregulation dominated as the World Bank and the IMF sponsored structural adjustment programmes for public sector reforms in developing countries. But in 1997, the World Development Report[8] instead emphasised the importance of strong and effective institutions at all levels, rather than of rolling back the state. Ever since, the World Bank has put a great deal of emphasis on the local development in cities, and in 2009 it launched its new urban strategy: Systems of Cities: Harnessing Urbanization for Growth and Poverty Alleviation. According to the World Bank,[9] the basic rationale for the new strategy should be considered to be no less than a paradigm shift in the way the World Bank and its donor partners think about how to address the opportunities and challenges of rapid urbanisation.

Decentralisation is also a dominant theme and agenda for UN-HABITAT, as it has evolved into an international body that promotes the empowerment, autonomy, and independency of local governments worldwide. The Habitat Agenda (ch IV, pt. D, § 2) calls for decentralisation through increased local autonomy and participation in decision making, resource mobilisation and use, and the strengthening of local cooperation directly with the UN and other international networks. This plea for decentralisation builds, according to Yishai Blank (2006), on an idea of the local government as the one 'closest to the people' and as a 'schoolhouse for democracy', and Blank suggests that a global localist ideology in which international bodies are becoming heavily involved and invested in the transformation of state-local relations and in the empowerment of local authorities has taken form. By the empowerment of local authorities, and by treating local governments as 'partners', international organizations can make use of local governments as vessels through which various international policies are advanced (Blank 2006:902–903).

Also the EU has to some extent been promoting a localist ideology through the principle of subsidiarity, which is a general guiding principle in EU law. The subsidiarity principle is intended to ensure that decisions are always taken as close as possible to the citizens and that constant checks are made as to whether action at community level is justified in the light of the possibilities available at national, regional, or local level. The Lisbon Treaty states that subsidiarity is one of its fundamental principles.[10]

In contemporary academic globalisation discourses, decentralisation is often seen both as a function of globalisation, rendering traditional government setups dysfunctional, and as a necessary ingredient in processes of democratisation and as a part of 'good governance' (see, for example, Dillinger 1994; Jun and Wright 1996; United Nations Centre for Human Settlements 2001 Kumar Sharma 2005). Decentralisation is seen as reinforcing local levels of governance. While significant powers and functions along with fiscal responsibility to carry out theses powers and functions are being transferred to local levels of government, they are subsequently being strengthened vis-à-vis the nation state (Dillinger 1994; Jun and Wright 1996; Kumar Sharma 2005).

There is also a well-established idea that local authorities and cities are becoming empowered internationally due to the global spread of ideas. Because people, ideas, practices, and values float freely around the globe, 'global thinking' has inspired policymakers and public administrations at the local level and influenced local institutional reform. Because of this, local politicians and administrators have become more aware and prepared to take innovative action independently of their national governments (see, for example, Jun and Wright 1996; Tsukamoto and Vogel 2007). Thus, at the same time as local governments have increasingly assumed roles within the global legal order and become actual 'legal creatures' capable of meaningful participation in processes of global governance and of international and transnational regulations, they have also increasingly become more autonomous bearers and pursuers of international norms and rights such as human and civil rights, environmental issues, or disarmament. Local leaders and local authorities sometimes decide to take an active stance on a particular global issue. According to one of the lead urban specialists at the World Bank:

> If you want to change the world, you need to change a handful of gate keeping global cities. These cities define culture and social norms. Take for example the issue of gay marriage. The issue was debated on a national level for a long time, but it was the Mayor of San Francisco who ordered the county clerks to start issuing marriage certificates. That started the real change.[11] (interview, December 2, 2010)

There are various ways in which cities engage in the diffusion of international norms. Social movement scholars have, for example, argued that cities have become the strategic *locale* for national and international protests and that urban space has become a symbolic and material site for representation in the global-local struggles of social movements (see, for example, Köhler and Wissen 2003; Rabrenovic 2009; Harvey 2012). Antiglobalisation demonstrations in Seattle and Genoa or anti-Iraq war demonstrations in Berlin in recent years exemplify the urban 'gravity' of the actions of these types of 'glocalised' social movements. More recently, we have seen the Arab Spring spreading from city to city in North Africa and the Middle East and the Occupy movement spreading in Western cities. Through international mobilisation, social activists forge transnational ties and articulate common transnational agendas to address issues such as democratic change, social injustices, and immigration and labour rights, and the epicentres of such mobilisations are typically city centres. Sidney Tarrow (2005:59–76) argues that local activists have as a strategy tried to cognitively connect local issues to global symbols, and that they therefore have taken part in producing a new 'global thinking' on local levels. Other scholars have argued in similar ways that transnational social movements are playing an important part in the widespread shifts in values and culture that are fostering a new urban political culture featuring more diversity, citizen activism, and a more attentive, and potentially stronger, local leadership (Clarke 2000; Borraz and John 2004).

A FOREIGN POLICY OF CITIES?

As indicated earlier, cities can play a role in international norm diffusion when their local leaders and local authorities decide to take a stance on a particular global issue. Human and civil rights along with environmental and climate change issues are probably the global issues most often pursued internationally by local governments. But this does not only involve local leaders making symbolic statements in favour or against a particular issue. What is even more noteworthy is that cities are in fact pursuing what appear to be their own independent foreign policies.

An often mentioned example is a U.S. case from the 1990s, where 20 local and state governments adopted international human rights laws targeting Burma (despite the fact that the U.S. federal government had not done so), and economic sanctions were imposed by these subnational governments on companies that traded with Burma. This particular case eventually reached the U.S. Supreme Court and was declared unconstitutional. Despite this, there have been many more similar examples where local governments in the United States have taken a stance and adopted and enforced laws in compliance with international human rights. Yishai Blank (2006:917–918) describes several such examples with respect to, for example, Northern Ireland, apartheid in South Africa, Indonesia, Nigeria, and Cuba. Blank also states that local governments in the United States are adopting laws in compliance with international human rights norms to preserve the environment and protect various minority groups such as migrant workers.

The concept of *paradiplomacy* (or sometimes referred to as city diplomacy, substate diplomacy, or multilayered diplomacy) appeared in the 1980s when scholars of comparative politics and international relations in North America took an interest in these puzzling international activities of federal and local constituencies (see, for example, Duchacek 1984). The concept of paradiplomacy generally refers to the international relations and diplomatic activities conducted by subnational, regional, or local governments, with the purpose of promoting their own interests. Today, paradiplomacy and the international activities of subnational governments is the object of study among a small number of scholars of comparative politics, foreign policy analysis, and international relations (see, for example, Aldecoa and Keating 1999; Lecours 2002; van der Pluijm 2007; Criekemans 2010).[12]

Paradiplomacy scholars have generally argued that the primary impetus for local transnational interactions has been the pursuit of economic interest through, for example, collaborations with foreign business enterprises, export promotion, and attraction of foreign investments (Kline 1996:332ff). Since the late 1990s, however, paradiplomacy scholars have also argued that there is an increasing involvement of local and regional governments in the international arena on broader political issues (Aldecoa and Keating 1999:1–14).

An increasing number of social science scholars have also noted that cities and local governments all over the world are engaging in foreign affairs as they jointly develop and institutionalise transnational, international, and global policy programmes and networks. The scope and range of these transnational policies and strategies go well beyond traditional town-twinning activities. Current transnational exchanges between cities have evolved into new forms of cooperation in world city networks and various transnational organizations of local governments such as the United Cities and Local Governments, a global association of municipalities engaged in various global issues ranging from urban management of water resources to gender equality and peace building; ICLEI—Local Governments for Sustainability (ICLEI), a global association of local governments committed to sustainable development; C40 Cities, the world's largest cities committed to jointly tackling climate change; the M4 meetings in which the mayors of Berlin, Moscow, London, and Paris come together to discuss the common challenges such as terrorism, organized crime, and climate change; Eurocities, a network of 130 European cities; Mercocities Network comprising 160 cities in the Mercosur region; and the aforementioned Mayors for Peace, a coalition of local governments against nuclear weapons.

Many cities and local governments around the world have also chosen to establish a specialised department or unit for international affairs within their administrations—their very own ministries for foreign affairs. According to one of the lead urban specialists at the World Bank:

> 25 years ago, no city had a department for international affairs. Today, every city with more than 1 million people has one. And the person heading the international department is usually high up in the local governmental hierarchy, often working closely with the Mayor. So in 25 years we have gone from nothing to international affairs becoming as important for the city as the city planners are. (interview with World Bank official, December 2, 2010, in Washington, DC)

The new internationally and transnationally oriented departments within local governmental bureaucracies are often responsible for coordinating the international/transnational engagements in which the city is involved (often in cooperation with transnational city-organizations and networks), developing international strategies, marketing the city internationally, and keeping tabs on global developments and events of special interest to the city (Aldecoa and Keating 1999). Some academic scholars have even argued that transnational city networks and 'city diplomacy' are representing nascent structures of authority in world politics (see, for example, Aldecoa and Keating 1999; Lachapelle and Paquin 2005; van der Pluijm 2007).

URBAN SECURITY POLITICS?

In a rapidly urbanising world, many of the world's major security challenges and risks are increasingly understood as tied to urban life—be it of a technological nature involving infrastructure breakdowns (see, for example, UN-HABITAT 2007; Graham 2010b); biological, involving viruses and infectious disease (see, for example, Sclar, Garau, and Carolini 2005; Kjellstrom et al. 2007; Keil and Ali 2007; Fischer and Katz 2011); social, involving organized crime and violence (see, for example, Brennan-Galvin 2002; humansecurity-cities.org 2007; UN-HABITAT 2007); or ecological, involving climate change and resource shortages (see, for example, Lambright, Chjangnon, and Harvey 1996; Collier 1997; DeAngelo and Harvey 1998; Betsill and Bulkeley 2004; Bouteligier 2013; Bulkeley 2013).

The 2007 UN-HABITAT Global Report *Enhancing Urban Safety and Security* argues that cities are inherently 'risk prone' due to the concentrated nature of settlements and the interdependent nature of the human and infrastructure systems. In the report, it is argued that urban settlements are increasingly becoming 'hot spots' for disaster risk. Other scholars have argued that the density of cities tends to intensify phenomena such as civil unrest, environmental degradation, natural disasters, diseases, and poverty, and because many large cities concentrate economic wealth they therefore have the potential to spread negative consequences of disasters and crises across the global economy (see, for example, van den Berg et al. 2006; Coaffee, Wood, and Rogers 2009; Graham 2010b).

In an edited volume from 2010 called *Disrupted Cities*, Stephen Graham and an international team of scholars discuss the complex processes and politics surrounding infrastructure disruptions and failures and show how the everyday life of the world's population is increasingly dependent on a global urban infrastructural system. Energy networks, water systems, food and waste distribution systems, shipping, trade, finance, highways, air traffic, train and road complexes, flows of commuters, migrants, tourists and refugees, materials and commodities, electronic communications systems— all rely on a vast and unimaginably complex circuit of infrastructures within which cities invariably act as the dominant hubs of networks, the predominant centres of demand, and the dominant centre for generating waste and pollution of all forms. Graham and his colleagues argue that as the world becomes increasingly urbanised, the political, social, economic, and environmental importance of cities and urban infrastructures can only continue to grow (Graham 2010b:1–2).

It is probably only with some difficulty that one can speak of urban security studies as an academic field of its own. However, having said that, we have during the last decade seen an increasing number of interlocking fields of research focusing on urban security dimensions such as terrorism, critical infrastructure failure, climate change, and transnational organized crime. In a special issue of *Security Dialogue* on urban security from 2009, editors Rita Abrahamsen and Michael C. Williams (2009) argue that the following:

> For security studies and international relations, urbanization raises important issues and substantial analytical challenges. For these disciplines, which have traditionally been focused at the level of interstate relations and whose intellectual roots are firmly in clear distinctions between politics 'inside' and 'outside' the state, between crime and war,

and between the police and the military, the city is an awkward object of analysis. (p. 364)

Nonetheless, they argue, cities have become key sites for contemporary international security practices. Abrahamsen and Williams argue that in an age when security is as much about monitoring and directing flows of capital, people, and information as it is about defending borders with conventional military forces, cities are increasingly seen as key sites for security policies and interventions, giving rise to new policing technologies of risk, surveillance, and profiling (Abrahamsen and Williams 2009:364). In a similar fashion, Jon Coaffee and David Murikami Wood (2006) have argued that security as a contemporary concept, practice, and commodity has been rescaled and reterritorialised as it has become more civic, urban, domestic, and even personal.

What has so far been typical for most academic writings on contemporary securitisation and militarisation of urban space and on urban security is that the city is conceptualised as *site* rather than as *actor*. The city and urban space is most often approached as a space and context in which contemporary (globalised) international security discourses and practices typically unfold. However, in the U.S. context there are quite a few scholars who have highlighted the localised responses to new security challenges and argued that cities and municipalities are playing an increasingly important *active* role in homeland security politics and in the provision of security (see, for example, Eisinger 2004; Gerber et al. 2005; Clarke and Chenoweth 2006; Chenoweth and Clarke 2010). Similarly in the European context, Coaffee and Murikami Wood (2006) have studied counterterrorism, particularly in the United Kingdom, and showed how a new protective and regulatory system has emerged through a rhetoric of 'resilience' in which security responsibilities have been dispersed to all levels of governments, including local ones. Jon Coaffee and colleagues (2009) argue that local authorities are not simply implementing *national* policies but are also pursuing security policies autonomously. According to Coaffee et al. (2009:6), we are seeing a trend in which urban authorities in collaboration with police and the private security industry are focusing on building 'defensive urban landscapes' and are 'designing out terrorism', or 'designing in counterterrorism'.

In a comprehensive report from 2007,[13] dealing with human security aspects of urbanisation and contemporary urban life, the Canadian Consortium on Human Security (CCHS) argues that cities have an important role to play in improving global security and have the best chances of providing it. The CCHS (humansecurity-cities.org 2007) points out that the city historically was the first form of organized political unit capable of protecting people from outside threats:

They were the first sites of a conscious social bargain through which some individual freedoms were exchanged for a set of common rights and responsibilities maintained by civic authorities. Most security issues were local issues. Walls protected the city from external attack from local and regional enemies, and the city itself provided public security for people within its walls. These were among the first forms of collective public security—cities that protected people within a defined urban space. Today's cities protect people not with walls but with effective public security forces capable of maintaining the rule of law. (p. 23)

The CCHS argues that cities today yet again are the logical entry points for policy interventions that seek to enhance public security and build peace. It argues that cities feature unique characteristics that have the potential to make them resilient to conflict; that effective, inclusive, and responsive governance at the local level can play a key role in preventing and mitigating violent conflict; that the proximity of local leaders to the community allow them to be more responsive to the needs of their constituents, while also engaging civil society actors to empower people and build trust; and that well-managed cities can take advantage of the built environment and population density to promote resilience. According to the CCHS, municipal governments can—if only they have sufficient resources, effective leadership, and a degree of autonomy—take advantage of their local institutions to promote public safety and security (humansecurity-cities.org 2007:23).

In what follows, I show more specifically how some of the contemporary global security challenges and risks are understood as specifically tied to cities and urban life, and how cities and their local authorities have directly been engaging in such global issues.

CITIES AND COUNTERTERRORISM

According to Hank Savitch (2008:3–7), approximately 3 out of every 4 incidents labelled as a terror attack and 4 out of every 5 of its subsequent casualties, occur in cities. In the last four decades, cities have been subject to more than 12,000 incidents deemed as terrorism, causing over 73,000 casualties. Savitch argues that the complexity of cities makes them ideal to hide terrorist plots, and after the events of 9/11 in 2001, it became evident that al-Qaida and other terrorist networks have operated with impunity in a number of European, South Asian, and Middle Eastern cities (Savitch 2008). As cities are centres of power, they are also magnets for media attention. Densely populated urban space facilitates extensive loss of lives, and damage to buildings with strong symbolic meaning generates high levels of anxiety for large populations. The various and complex functioning of the city can be undermined and disrupted not only by the attack itself and its immediate aftermath, but also by the insertion of a continuous existential insecurity (Molotch and McClain 2003).

The urban 'gravity' of terrorism as phenomenon and the increasing use of cities for maximum impact of terrorist attacks has made public security and protection a central issue on many local political agendas (Clarke and Chenoweth 2006; Savitch 2008). Erica Chenoweth and Susan Clarke (2010; Clarke and Chenoweth 2006) have argued that while urban security is a core national security issue in the United States, it is at the same time a local responsibility because it is cities and counties that control and finance the police, fire, public health, and emergency services most needed in the face of terrorist attacks. Local governments in the United States therefore play an increasingly critical role in homeland security politics (see, for example, Eisinger 2004; Gerber et al. 2005; Clarke and Chenoweth 2006; Chenoweth and Clarke 2010).

This has, according to many critical urban scholars, meant that fear is reshaping the geography and politics of urban space, and that concerns for security have led to increasing surveillance and expanded legal and physical measures scattering and fortifying public space, which are ultimately resulting in a militarisation of urban space (see, for example, Marcuse 2006; Graham 2010a). This is perhaps most clearly illustrated by the 'War on Terrorism', which has had highly localised and especially urban domestic fronts, while being fought on a global scale. According to Stephen Graham (2010a), cities and metropolitan regions have become the new battleground of warfare in the 21st century, and he argues that Western militaries and security forces now perceive all urban terrain as a potential conflict zone inhabited by potential enemies. Savitch (2008:253) has, in a similar fashion, argued that cities today represent the trenches in the 'war' against terrorism.

Traditionally, one of the most basic tenets of military theory, dating back to Sun Tzu in the 4th century BC, is that cities should be avoided in warfare (Warren 2002:615). Urban war zones have been understood as posing serious challenges to military tactics, communications, and weaponry, and have been associated with low performance and high cost. However, since the end of the Cold War, there has been an evolving revision of the traditional military urban doctrine, and today, Western security forces assume that their military presence in cities, for humanitarian reasons, in peacekeeping, and for homeland security, is unavoidable (see, for example, Morrison Taw and Hoffman 1994; Desch 2001; Warren 2002). The perceived need for a new urban military doctrine resulted in the Military Operations in Urbanized Terrain (MOUT) doctrine, which has primarily been formulated in the United States after the end of the Cold War. MOUT was initially developed on the basis of the assumption that military operations were to be carried out in cities outside the developed world. However, the doctrine has also provided a template for police operations, and police forces are increasingly using military strategies to respond to large political mobilisations of citizens. This has been the case in police operations in Barcelona, Brussels, Gothenburg, Los Angeles, New York, Quebec, Washington, DC, and Seattle, where several MOUT tactics were used to deny people engaged in political mobilisation access to specific areas in the city (Warren 2002:615–616).

According to Stephen Graham (2010a:xviii), military tactics and technologies developed for urban war zones in for example Gaza and Baghdad are increasingly being used in security operations at international sports events and political summits in Western cities. According to Graham, the police forces in London, Toronto, Paris, and New York have started to use the same nonlethal weapons as the Israeli army is using in Gaza; and the construction of security zones around strategic financial cores and government districts in London and New York are directly imported techniques used in overseas military bases and green zones.

In the United States, a national survey conducted one year after the 9/11 attacks found that already in 2002, 26% of the local law enforcement agencies in metropolitan areas across the United States had developed specialised terrorism units and integrated counterterrorism functions in their departments (Davis et al. 2004). We have also seen examples where local police forces around the United States build their own independent information and intelligence networks and intelligence operations through, for example, developing exchange programmes, sending their officers to work with other police forces overseas, and creating liaisons with foreign agents. According to the report "Miffed at Washington, Police Develop Own Antiterror Plans" in the *Wall Street Journal* (Block 2005), police in cities such as Los Angeles; Washington, D.C.; Miami; Las Vegas; Seattle; and Houston are all sending their officers to work overseas with foreign police agencies as well as accepting liaisons from foreign forces.

CITIES AND CLIMATE CHANGE MITIGATION

Global warming manifests itself in many different ways in the biosphere, but two of the most commonly discussed are the progressive rise of the sea level and the increased intensity and frequency of extreme weather events leading to natural disasters (Bigio 2003:91). UN-HABITAT reported in 2007 that there has been a 50% rise in extreme weather events associated with climate change from the 1950s to the 1990s, and that coastal zones are the areas most exposed. According to the UN, 21 of the 33 cities in the world with 8 million inhabitants or more are located on coasts vulnerable to both hydro-meteorological hazards and sea level rise. If sea levels rise by just 1 meter, cities such as New York, Tokyo, Cairo, Rio de Janeiro, Manila, Mumbai, and Dhaka will be under considerable threat (UN-HABITAT 2007:vi). Other urban consequences of climate change include increased intensity of heat waves, where the urban heat island effect might induce extreme temperatures, seriously affecting human health; increases in intense rainfall events, which escalate the risk of inland flooding and landslides; retreat of mountain glaciers, with impacts on water availability and quality in urban regions; and increased risk of drought and water shortage in already dry regions; and, because of changes in temperature and hydrological cycles, shortening of maintenance and replacement cycles for key infrastructure, for example, energy production and transport, as well as decreased operational capacity, leading to blackouts or service interruptions (Corfee-Morlot et al. 2009:16–17).

Since the mid1990s, and especially in the new millennium, it has become widely recognised that local levels of governments in general and cities in particular are crucial for the implementation of international agreements and national policies on climate change (Lambright et al. 1996; Collier 1997; DeAngelo and Harvey 1998; Betsill and Bulkeley 2004). According to UN-HABITAT, cities and urban areas consume about 75% of the world's energy and produce up to 80% of its greenhouse gas emissions.[14] This means that, although cities have often been described as being at the centre of the problem, climate change scholars are increasingly arguing that they are also central to the solution (see, for example, Bulkeley and Betsill 2003; Dodman 2009; Rosenzweig et al. 2011a; Hoornweg et al. 2011). With their potential influence on the daily life of their citizens, local governments are described as more efficient than their national counterparts in controlling greenhouse gas emissions. For example, urban authorities and local governments have the ability to address and implement climate change mitigation programmes effectively because of the type of responsibilities they hold in relation to land use planning, waste management, public transportation, energy consumption, and enforcement of industrial regulations (Bulkeley and Betsill 2003:48; Dodman 2009:198). Many urban authorities have also set far more ambitious targets for emissions reductions than their national governments. For example, London has set the goal for a 60% reduction from 1990 to 2025, New York City for a 30% reduction from 2005 to 2030, and Tokyo for a 25% reduction from 2000 to 2020 (Corfee-Morlot et al. 2009:29). During the last decade, scholars of global environmental governance have begun to notice that local governments are increasingly surpassing their national governments when it comes to climate change, and we have seen a growing number of transnational city networks and local governmental initiatives. Transnational city coalitions, sometimes referred to as transnational municipal networks, are arguably even becoming important global climate regulatory players that seek to influence both the nature of the debate concerning climate protection and actions focused on this objective (Stewart 2008; Urpelainen 2009; Kern and Bulkeley 2009).

Cities and regions are also working together in transnational networks to strengthen their greenhouse gas reduction efforts, and there are now a dozen or more international networks for local initiatives on climate change and sustainability. For example, through the U.S. Mayors' Climate Protection Agreement, more than 1,000 mayors in U.S. cities have agreed to meet or beat Kyoto Protocol targets even though the U.S. government never ratified the Protocol. Another example is ICLEI, committed to reducing their CO_2 emissions to 20% below 1990 levels, including more than 1,000 local governments and their associations, representing more than 300 million people

(Corfee-Morlot et al. 2009). The C40 Cities Climate Leadership Group is a network of Global Cities and other large metropolitan areas around the world jointly committed to tackle climate change. The C40 was created in 2005 by former Mayor of London Ken Livingstone, and in 2006 a partnership was forged with the Cities Program of President Clinton's Climate Initiative to reduce carbon emissions and increase energy efficiency in large cities across the world.

CITIES AND TRANSNATIONAL ORGANIZED CRIME

Another of the contemporary global 'risks' described as having increasingly urbanised facets is transnational organized crime. Because globalisation is commonly associated with increasing cross-border flows, it is not surprising that globalisation is also seen as having enhanced the capacity of individuals to organize themselves to conduct crimes across borders, something which, according to Toni Makkai (2006), is occurring on a scale never seen before. Organized crime and trafficking is a growing global concern, and because it undermines public security in cities around the world, it is also an urban and local concern. According to Ellen Brennan-Galvin (2002:125), criminal organizations have been capitalising on the increased cross-border flows of people, goods, and money, and have expanded their territorial reach, positioned themselves in new markets, and expanded their range in illicit activities such as trafficking in humans and small arms and in wide-scale money laundering. In that process, they have also managed to increase their wealth and power relative to many national and city governments. As a result, virtually every major city, especially in the developing world, has seen an increase in international criminal activity. Much of the organized armed violence that takes place on city streets is perpetrated by groups that are linked to transnational criminal organizations. Also, the CCHS argues that rapid urbanisation is facilitating organized gangs and transnational criminal networks, which are taking advantage of failed public security within sprawling urban spaces. In some cases, more deaths are being caused by armed violence in cities within countries formally at peace than within countries experiencing civil war (humansecurity-cities.org 2007:17).

The CCHS argues that the globalisation and liberalisation of international markets have allowed trafficking of various forms to flourish. According to the CCHS, international human trafficking is enabled by large criminal networks with operations in major cities throughout the world. Cities such as Bangkok, Lagos, and Medellin serve as major transit points or end destinations for the many hundreds of thousands of women and children who are sold into the sex trade each year (humansecurity-cities.org 2007:45). Trafficking in drugs and weapons are often closely intertwined and mutually reinforcing, and crime associated with drug trafficking tends to have a significant positive correlation with homicide rates in cities, as the drug trade is usually accompanied with violent disputes over market shares among different criminal networks. Organized criminal groups, linked to global networks, also tend to tap into other local profitable activities such as gambling, prostitution, and extortion rackets, which often involve corruption of local government officials (Brennan-Galvin 2002; humansecurity-cities.org 2007).

The transnational dimensions of the illegal gun trade are, according to the CCHS, well documented and have clear linkages to urban armed violence. For example, many of Brazil's guns are smuggled illegally from Paraguay, and many of West Africa's guns are imported through Warri, a port town in southern Nigeria. The high rates of firearm violence in South African cities today are assessed to be the result of the influx of guns from the civil war in Mozambique. Many guns being smuggled illegally across the border into South Africa are the result of the limited success of disarmament efforts following Angola's conflict (humansecurity-cities.org 2007:97). There are also demonstrated linkages between arms and drug trafficking and terrorism, with profits from illicit trade being used to support terrorist networks. The proliferation of weapons such as small arms, machine guns, rocket-propelled grenades, and plastic explosives, in growing slums and shantytowns in cities in the developing world, facilitates terrorism as well as the growth of insurgencies and civil war (Morrison Taw and Hoffman 1994:5).

As crime has become increasingly internationalised, its financial aspects have become tied up with the global financial service industry, with the loci being in the large cities of the world. Well-financed and technologically adept criminal networks move large amounts of money through the financial institutions of the major cities in both the developed and developing world (Brennan-Galvin 2002).

CITIES AND GLOBAL PUBLIC HEALTH

Yet another example of what has been described as an urbanised global risk has to do with global public health. According to the World Health Organization (WHO), urbanisation is a major public health challenge for the 21st century. As urban populations are rapidly increasing, basic infrastructure is insufficient, and social and economic inequities in urban areas result in significant health inequalities (World Health Organization 2008:5). The global health challenge of the 21st century is, according to Sclar et al. (2005:902–903), in many respects reminiscent of that faced in the 19th century, when the first wave of urban industrialisation imposed similar health threats in the growing cities of Europe and the United States.

As mentioned previously, about one third of the world's urban residents dwell in slums and places characterised by insecurity of tenure, poor housing conditions, deficient access to safe drinking water and sanitation, and severe overcrowding, factors which all have a direct effect on physical and psychological health. Public health scholars have pointed out that the pace of urbanisation often exceeds the development pace of basic health services and infrastructure, something which can involve severe effects on people's health (see, for example, Sclar et al. 2005; Kjellstrom et al. 2007; Fischer and Katz 2011). For example, the lack of sanitation and waste removal creates breeding grounds for infectious diseases and exposures to microbiological hazards, and although communicable diseases are a major problem in urban populations in general, it becomes particularly hazardous for slum populations.

According to Sclar et al. (2005:901), almost half of the urban population in Africa, Asia, and Latin America is suffering from diseases because of lack of access to improved water and sanitation. Poor water management also creates conditions for parasites and insect vectors. Exposures to outdoor air pollution, indoor air pollution from burning solid fuels, unsafe drinking water, and toxic metals and chemicals in urban areas may underlie 25% of the global disease burden (Sclar et al. 2005; Kjellstrom et al. 2007; Fischer and Katz 2011). High rates of HIV/AIDS and tuberculosis are also an increasingly distressing factor of urban life, especially in developing countries. Incomplete or inadequate treatments also create conditions for increasing drug-resistance (Sclar et al. 2005; Fischer and Katz 2011). The prevalence of chronic diseases such as coronary artery disease, stroke, diabetes, and some cancers are also climbing in urban populations, again especially in developing countries. Unhealthy foods, sugared drinks, physically nondemanding work, and many hours spent every day sitting in buses or cars in traffic congestion leads to increasingly sedentary and unhealthy lifestyles (Fischer and Katz 2011).

According to Julie Fischer and Rebecca Katz (2011), the major cities of the world have, as they are crossroads for the movement of people, animals, and goods, also become crossroads for the health risks such movements carry. As demonstrated by the 2009 H1N1 influenza outbreak and the spread of SARS in 2003, the international movement of millions of travellers allows emerging infections to spread rapidly between air hubs (Fisher and Katz 2011). Sites of outbreaks like these are typically the city centres. But according to Roger Keil and Harris Ali (2007), cities have not only played a major role as sites of disease outbreaks, but also are also increasingly taking part in new forms of global health governance and are taking on responsibilities ranging from flu preparedness to surveillance. New York, Toronto, Rotterdam, Beijing, and Boston, among others, have all built their own biosafety laboratories, which means they do not need to rely on sending disease samples to national labs and thus do not have to wait for a response (Sample 20012). Thus, just like in the case of climate change, while cities have been described as being at the centre of the problem, that they are also seen as central to the solution (Keil and Ali 2007; Fischer and Katz 2011). The basic argument also looks the same: Urban areas and their local government have the potential to improve health via their various service provisions and cultural and aesthetic attributes (see, for example, World Health Organization

2008). Fischer and Katz (2011) argue that urbanisation actually improves the odds of ensuring better public health by, for instance, increasing access to safe drinking water and adequate sanitation. Urban water and sanitation systems can reach many more people, more cost effectively than small-scale water improvement projects in scattered rural villages. Increasing urbanisation and decentralisation of government functions means that local and municipal leaders are becoming increasingly responsible for public health challenges and effectively managed basic public services. A higher concentration of health and social services on the local level can ameliorate many of the hazards associated with population density (Fischer and Katz 2011).

A RENAISSANCE OF THE CITY-STATE?

It seems clear that we by now can assume that the empirical phenomena, where urban issues and cities are becoming understood as increasingly central and relevant in global politics, and where local governments of cities have begun to take part autonomously in global governance, foreign affairs, and security policies, is not random. Cities in general and Global Cities in particular are increasingly becoming actors in world politics. They are no longer merely strategic *sites* within the globalised economy; local governments of Global Cities have developed *actorness* on the international arena and in global governance. Given that cities—as organizing entities of political, economic, and social life—for more than 350 years have been embedded within and subordinated to the modern nation-state, and during this period have had nothing, or at least very little, directly to do with the conduct of international relations and foreign affairs, this represents a rather substantial change. And in the light of traditional claims of state sovereignty, independent foreign and security policies on the part of cities is certainly a puzzling phenomenon. So how can we interpret and understand this change?

Urban scholars have often argued that cities are the nucleus of change, a place where revolutions begin, new life styles form, technology develops, and where new ways of organizing work, economy, and politics are being born. Cities and towns have played a central role economically, politically, and culturally in all human societies and precede nation states by some 5,000 years. They concentrate control, power, knowledge, and information, and they represent crossroads where different ideas, visions, and beliefs are confronted with each other. During certain historical periods, cities or leagues of cities have even been the main entity and base for organizing political life. Urban empires such as Ur and Uruk in Mesopotamia 6,000 years ago, the ancient city-states of Athens and Sparta, the merchant cities such as Venice and Dubrovnik, and the Hanseatic League towns of medieval Europe are examples of such cities. The primacy of the city lasted roughly until the Enlightenment and, subsequently, cities played an important role in state-building processes. Some cities formally supported the establishments of principles such as territorial sovereignty upon which nation-states were founded and several cities were signatories to the Peace of Westphalia in 1648 (Mumford 1961; Törnqvist 1993; Short 1996). According to Edward Gleaser:

> Cities, the dense agglomerations that dot the world, have been engines of innovations since Plato and Socrates bickered in an Athenian market-place. The streets of Florence gave us the Renaissance, and the streets of Birmingham gave us the Industrial Revolution. The great prosperity of contemporary London and Bangalore and Tokyo comes from their ability to produce new thinking. Wandering these cities—whether down cobblestone sidewalks or grid-cutting cross streets, around roundabouts or under freeways—is to study nothing less than human progress. (2011:1)

From a historical perspective, the current rising importance of cities is arguably not something qualitatively new. But how can we explain or understand the current and somewhat paradoxical importance of the *local* and *urban* in the contemporary global and globalising age? Why now? U.S. philosopher Susanne Langer has argued the following:

> When we speak of fashions in thought, we are treating philosophy lightly. There is disparagement in the phrases, "a fashionable problem," "a fashionable term." Yet it is the most natural and appropriate thing in the world for a new problem or a new terminology to have a vogue that crowds out everything else for a little while. A word that everyone snaps up, or a question that has everybody excited, probably carries a generative idea—the germ of a complete reorientation in metaphysics, or at least the "Open Sesame" of some new positive science. The sudden vogue of such a key-idea is due to the fact that all sensitive and active minds turn at once to exploiting it; we try it in every connection, for every purpose, experiment with possible stretches of its strict meaning, with generalizations and derivatives. (Langer 1942:18)

Contemporary ideas about an 'urban world' and escalating urbanisation trends can certainly be considered a 'fashionable problem' and the 'Global City' a 'fashionable term'. But let us for a moment follow Langer's advice by not treating these ideas lightly but instead seriously consider their ideational impact in terms of a 'complete reorientation'. The demographic shifts currently taking place are described as having monumental importance to humanity, and as shifting important global political balances. The idea of an increasing importance of cities in the global era is not an isolated narrow academic idea, nor is it something that local governments in cities themselves have come up with—it is instead part of broad and general knowledge configurations about the contemporary state of the world. It is also something that is increasingly becoming part of cities and their local governments' *self-understanding* and sense of *self-worth* in the world. The 'Global City' concept, which started out as a social scientific category referring to a specific category of cities in the globalised economy, is now in wide lay use in society and has entered both the general globalisation discourse and urban policies and practices. Local governments in large cities all over the world are striving to obtain or sustain a status as a Global City. To be a Global City is to be of particular importance and influence globally.

Susanne Langer was, in particular, interested in the continuous process of meaning-making through the power of seeing one thing in terms of another. In the wake of ideas about an increasingly urbanising world, we have seen how 'global challenges', the 'urban millennium', and the rise of 'Global Cities' are increasingly seen in terms of each other. As humanity has become an 'urban species', many of our times' most pressing global challenges are also understood as tied to urban life. As global challenges are made into *urban* issues, local governments in cities also get the possibility to claim political authority on those issues, because how we talk about and frame a problem will also affect *what* we think ought to be done about it, and *who* we think should do something about it. The way in which a political problem is defined and represented is critical for understanding political agenda settings, because once a problem representation becomes established, it also conditions who gets to deal with it as well as the possibilities for how policies can be pursued on the issue.

As the global processes of urbanisation unfold, so the story goes, cities and their local governments around the world increasingly have to manage problems and opportunities that used to be the exclusive domain of national governments. A common red thread through the discourse is that even though the city is often seen as part of the various problematiques and challenges of globalisation, they are also understood as central to their remedies, and decentralisation is therefore required. The city is seen as the solution, both in terms of seizing the opportunities stemming from globalisation and in terms of dealing with its challenges. The idea is that as local governments are the 'closest' to the people and have the prospect to influence the daily life of their citizens, they are also potentially more efficient than their national counterparts in managing anything from the delivery of public services, controlling greenhouse gas emissions, providing basic safety and security, and promoting social trust and equity. In addition, local governments can do it all in an inclusive, democratic, and transparent way. If only they have sufficient resources, effective leadership, and a degree of autonomy—cities and their local governments are the main key to a successful future of humanity. Ideas about the urbanisation of global challenges have become a reality in social scientific discourses as well as in governance practices and public policies.

I would like to suggest that shared ideas about Global Cities and the urbanisation of global challenges has therefore significantly affected political dynamics and played a constitutive role in the structuration of global political and economic outcomes. As humanity has become an 'urban species', the city is understood as having regained its historical importance and relevance as a political entity and organizer of human communities—especially so the Global City. The Global City is the central site of global flows and global transformations and is therefore not just any city; it is a city of particular importance globally. Contemporary 'Global City-hood' in the post–Cold War era therefore entails a lot more than what the traditional economistic understanding has assumed as being narrowly focused on competing for and attracting mobile global capital, collecting revenue, and delivering public services. Rather, contemporary Global City-hood comes with a whole set of cultural understandings about what the Global City and its local government is supposed to look like, what is in its 'interest', and what constitutes legitimate policies and actions to be pursued locally as well as globally, not least so in relation to security.

The increasingly prominent place of cities in general, and Global Cities in particular, within contemporary globalisation and security discourses provides local governments with a 'condition of possibility' to become independent agents in foreign affairs and global governance, with what is now increasingly perceived as a legitimate international political agency. When the Global City officials determine their city's interest and construct policies in its name, they do so out of a historically specific contextual framework and knowledge configuration—and this is what constitutes the conditions of possibility. Through these knowledge configurations about the contemporary state of the urbanising world, which are providing these conditions of possibility, we can make sense of this given social phenomenon—cities as independent actors in world politics—in our particular spatio-temporal context.

NOTES

1. This chapter focuses primarily on the specific category of cities referred to as *Global Cities*, but most of its arguments are applicable to contemporary urban politics in large cities and metropolitan areas in fairly affluent societies more generally.
2. Reported, for example, by the United Nations Population Fund in 2007. See www.unfpa.org/swp/2007/english/introduction.html (accessed September 2, 2012).
3. Reported, for example, by National Geographic News on March 13, 2008. See http://news.nationalgeographic.com/news/2008/03/080313-cities.html (accessed September 2, 2012).
4. See, for example, the article "Welcome to the Urban Millennium" in the *UN Chronicle*, March–May 2001.
5. Decentralisation can take many different forms, such as fiscal transfers, delegation of public service delivery, or increased local political representation, administrative authority, and accountability.
6. The principle of subsidiarity originates from Catholic theology and generally means that central governments should act only when local levels of government are unable or fail to do so (Vischer 2001).

7. The World Bank, for example, has been associated with a mainly administrative and managerialist interpretation of good governance, while other United Nations agencies such as the United Nations Development Programme (UNDP) and UN-HABITAT have emphasised democratic practice; human and civil rights, and participation of civil society.

8. See http://wdronline.worldbank.org/worldbank/a/c.html/world_development_report_1997/abstract/WB.0-1952-1114-6.abstract (accessed September 5, 2012).

9. See www-wds.worldbank.org/external/default/WDSContentServer/WDSP/IB/2009/11/27/000333037_20091127004734/Rendered/PDF/518600WP0Urban10Box342051B01PUBLIC1.pdf (accessed December 12, 2013).

10. See http://en.euabc.com/word/879 (accessed November 11, 2012).

11. While surely being an internationally discussed issue, there is admittedly no explicit international norm with regards to same-sex marriage. However, the example given by the World Bank urban specialist still points to a particular type of phenomena. In the U.S. context, cities and local governments have been among the first to grant same-sex partners the same rights as heterosexual couples, and this serves as an exemplification of how cities sometimes take an activist stand against national standards of antidiscrimination issues and incorporate internationally influenced standards of human and civil rights. And what appears to have started in San Francisco has also spread internationally as nation after nation has started to grant same-sex couples the right to get married.

12. It should be noted here that this research tradition has its roots mainly in comparative federalism. As this discourse has had its primary focus on internal political balances of federal political systems within which substates can develop their paradiplomatic activities, the local governments of cities have not been as common as a unit of analysis.

13. The report is called *Human Security for an Urban Century: Local Challenges, Global Perspectives* and is here referenced as humansecurity-cities.org (2007). It can be found online at www.eukn.org/E_library/Security_Crime_Prevention/Security_Crime_Prevention/Human_security_for_an_urban_century_local_challenges_global_perspectives (accessed September 5, 2012).

14. See www.un.org/News/Press/docs/2007/gaef3190.doc.htm (accessed September 6, 2012).

3 A Networked Urban World

Empowering Cities to Tackle Environmental Challenges

Sofie Bouteligier

Since Agenda 21—the international agenda for sustainable development resulting from the Rio Summit in 1992 (United Nations 1992)—cities have been engaged in a positive way in order to stimulate environmental sustainability (Mega 2010:17) and transnational municipal networks (TMNs) that address related challenges have boomed (Borja and Castells 1997:203–232).[1] Today, a large variety in TMNs for global environmental governance exist: Some are large (International Council for Local Environmental Initiatives—Local Governments for Sustainability, or ICLEI) and others small (Mega-Cities Project), they can have a broad scope (Metropolis) or focus on a specific issue (Energie-cités) and they can appeal to smaller (Sustainable Cities and Towns Campaign) or larger (C40 Cities Climate Leadership group) cities (Bouteligier 2009). In these networks, cities learn from each other through the exchange of information, knowledge, and expertise. In most cases, external actors, from both the private and the public sectors, are involved in these networks, making them hybrid arrangements (Spaargaren et al. 2006:7). This involvement mainly happens in a pragmatic way, leaping at opportunities, which exemplifies volatile network boundaries. However, this does not rule out repeated collaboration. The inclusion of external actors aims mainly at increasing cities' capacity to act, because external actors can help technically (e.g., provide expertise, make available instruments, assist in setting up programs) or financially (e.g., invest in programs or ensure easier access to financing mechanisms). Multilateral institutions like the United Nations Environment Programme (UNEP), the United Nations Educational, Scientific and Cultural Organization (UNESCO), United Nations Human Settlements Programme (UN-HABITAT), the Food and Agriculture Organization (FAO), and the World Bank, have a remarkable record of cooperation with such TMNs. Although all these projects are independent, they share the same strategy, and therefore together arguably form a basis for a global agenda (Brugmann 2007:335), especially because cities from all continents are now participating in TMNs that enable them to move from innovative ideas to concrete implementation.

Several scholars have already assessed this phenomenon, showing how TMNs are part of the global (environmental) governance architecture

(Betsill and Bulkeley 2004; Bulkeley 2006; Keiner and Kim 2007; Toly 2008; Kern and Bulkeley 2009). Looking at one such network (C40 Cities Climate Leadership Group), this chapter reveals how a networked urban world gives cities the capacity to tackle environmental challenges, position themselves as leaders for sustainable futures in their country and region, and become vital actors in global governance. It also demonstrates that it is not only cities traditionally conceptualized as world or global cities that are empowered by TMNs. This indicates that we need to move beyond an approach that puts economic globalization at the center of any evaluation and ranking of world and global cities.

The chapter is structured as follows. The first section briefly introduces the evolution of the role of cities in the international arena and provides a conceptual lens to look at the role of cities and TMNs in processes of global (environmental) governance. Then, the network studied is described, pointing out a particular mechanism that cities employ to resolve urban challenges. This is followed by an analytical section that shows how trans-national municipal networks empower cities and indicates what this means for cities' emerging power position in the world. The chapter closes with a reflection on whether cultural, political, social, environmental, and ideo-logical processes linked to global governance "pass through" economic pro-cesses if they are to have any bearing in global governance results.

CITIES IN THE INTERNATIONAL ENVIRONMENTAL ARENA

Along with the rise of an international environmental agenda, thinking about sustainable urban development incrementally gained ground in the last decades. Discussions on the role of cities at the United Nations Confer-ence on the Human Environment in Stockholm in 1972 resulted in the first Habitat conference in Vancouver in 1976, which had a very broad agenda and was the first milestone in the human settlements agenda (Elander and Lidskog 2000:41; Barton 2006:33; UN-HABITAT 2006:154). The 1987 Brundtland report dedicated a chapter to the urban challenge and made explicit the causal link between urbanization and global environmental problems (Brand and Thomas 2005:37; UN-HABITAT 2006:156). It also expressed the view that city governments needed enhanced political, institu-tional, and financial capacity in order to be able to contribute to sustainable development (World Commission on Environment and Development 1987, Chapter 9).

In the decades to come, this statement would be repeated multiple times. (Local) Agenda 21 (LA21)—the resulting document of the 1992 Rio Summit—was a breakthrough in terms of engaging cities in a positive way to stimulate environmental sustainability (Mega 2010:17). Although no attention had been paid to human settlements in the preparatory meetings, Agenda 21 contained a special chapter on the topic (Elander and Lidskog 2000: 41). After the Rio Summit, the United Nations (UN) General Assembly decided to organize a second Habitat conference in Istanbul in 1996. Just like LA21, Habitat II—which had a very broad agenda whereby the environment was somewhat downplayed (Elander and Lidskog 2000:41)—encouraged cities and localities to play a role in the international arena, because local developments were increasingly thought to be relevant for the global level (UN-HABITAT 2006:156). By 1996, more than 1,800 local governments were involved in LA21 initiatives (Elander and Lidskog 2000:41). Other initiatives in the 1990s—like the European Union (EU) green paper on the urban environment in 1990 and the Aalborg Conference on European Sustainable Cities and Towns in 1994—further stimulated the debate about cities and the environment, and international meetings like Urban 21 in Berlin in 2000 and the 2002 Johannesburg Summit made clear that the environment had become a natural part of the urban development agenda (Brand and Thomas 2005:35). The run-up to the Johannesburg Summit stimulated publications on sustainable urbanization. It was, for example, the start of the biannual *State of the World's Cities Report*, published by UN-HABITAT (Holden et al. 2008:308). Sustainable urbanization had become "a new multidimensional concept that covered not only the impact of cities on the urban environment, but also their potential to manage the urban environment in a way that benefits urban residents both socially and economically" (UN-HABITAT 2006:156). 2002 also saw the creation of the World Urban Forum, a biannual global forum on cities hosted by UN-HABITAT (Holden et al. 2008:311). Also when introducing the Millennium Development Goals (MDGs), the crucial role of cities to reach them was played out (Mega 2010:185). These developments stimulated a paradigm shift away from pointing out the negative aspects of urbanization towards a message that stresses that cities are key to our future and that they can be places of experiments, demonstration, leadership, and innovation (Holden et al. 2008:314; Hodson and Marvin 2009:196; Mega 2010:16, 23).

Furthermore, ever more cities started giving a central place to the environmental agenda (Brand 2007:616) because they are in the frontlines of pressing problems (Sassen 2010) and because they hope to distinguish themselves from other cities by having a green image—which is invaluable in an increasingly competitive environment (Brand and Thomas 2005:xi). The increasing recognition of cities as actors in the international arena has coincided with a changed attitude of multilateral institutions towards sustainable urban development. Whereas these institutions focused on rural areas in the 1950s and 1960s (De Ponte 2002:206), accelerated urbanization at the end of the 1960s forced them to look more at urban areas, with a particular attention for big cities. During that time, the World Bank became the guiding institution for formulating urban strategies (De Ponte 2002:206–207). The 1980s introduced direct assistance to cities, thus bypassing central governments (De Ponte 2002:209) and increasing municipal and metropolitan capacity (Cohen

2001:37). In the 1990s, awareness in multilateral institutions of the role of (global) cities in development grew (United Nations Development Programme [UNDP] 2000; Wai-chung Yeung and Olds 2001:12–13), which was translated into the creation of numerous city programs, not only in UN-HABITAT (Taylor 2000), but also in several other multilateral institutions. For example, the Sustainable Cities Programme (United Nations Centre for Human Settlements 1991) emerged out of the cooperation between UN-HABITAT and UNEP and built partnerships at the local level with national and city governments, UNDP, the World Bank, and the International Labour Organization. The program also facilitated collaboration with several other major global networks and programs, like ICLEI and the WHO Healthy Cities program (de Leeuw 2001; Gebre-Egziabher 2004:71). UNESCO's Man and Biosphere Program (Alfsen-Norodom 2004) is another example. The World Bank increased its direct involvement in urban environmental management through the creation of programs with the support of UN agencies, bilateral development agencies, national governments of OECD countries, municipal governments, private companies, and civil society (Bigio and Dahiya 2004:6–7). Another development is that multilateral institutions started to value city networks (UNDP 2000), which has led to numerous collaborative arrangements, through which multilateral institutions want to increase cities' capacity to tackle global challenges. For the World Bank, for example, city networks like Cities Alliance and UCLG (United Cities and Local Governments) have a "preinvestment role" (World Bank 2009:24). Furthermore, the Executive Director of UN-HABITAT has already attended several city network meetings, like the C40 Climate Summit in Seoul in May 2009, thus recognizing the value and contribution of such gatherings.

The importance of cities and their networks in today's network society (Castells 2000a; 2000b; 2004) is widely discussed in world and global cities literature (e.g., Friedmann 1986; Castells 2000a; Sassen 2001; Taylor 2004). It conceptualizes cities as strategic sites—nodes—from which actors act and where globalization processes materialize (Sassen 1994:xiv). Originally, this literature focused on the role of cities and city networks for the global economy and named those cities that concentrated knowledge, services, and infrastructure world cities and global cities. Cities were approached in nonterritorial terms, as nodes in networks that receive their meaning from network interactions (Amin 2002:391). More recently, the literature has broadened its scope and also discusses the function of urban areas in processes of political and cultural globalization (e.g., Amin 2002; Presas 2004; Taylor 2005; Ergazakis, Metaxiotis, and Psarras 2006; Murray 2006; Nicholls 2008; Calder and de Freytas 2009; Lai 2009) because several actors and institutions—not only economic ones—have global activities, thus constituting global networks (Sassen 2002:2). The urban nodes in these networks are connected through flows, which results in the emergence of transnational urban networks. This literature adds insights to the debate on the contribution of cities to global environmental governance, which has known a new upsurge in the last two decades. As epicenters of production and consumption, cities' pivotal role in questions of environmental sustainability (UN-HABITAT 2008) and global environmental governance has been recognized (Borja and Castells 1997:254). In the environmental realm, it is especially TMNs—more than transnational urban networks as discussed in world and global cities literature—that have received attention (Betsill and Bulkeley 2004; Sassen 2005; Wall and van de Knaap 2006; Keiner and Kim 2007; Toly 2008; Kern and Bulkeley 2009), because combined efforts of local authorities enhance the chance that what happens at the local level will be significant for the global level.

Dynamics and processes described in literature on the network society and global cities also explains the boom in TMNs. First, apart from the stimulating role of Agenda 21, the revolution in communication and information technologies and globalization processes has facilitated the emergence of such networks since the 1990s. Second, not only local but also global environmental challenges now force cities to find new ways of governing, because these places greatly experience the costs of global environmental problems such as the consequences of climate change for coastal cities (Sassen 2009:7). This requires coordinated action at a global level and in a broader framework, which has led to the creation of relations between cities worldwide (Borja and Castells 1997:203). The following section presents the TMN this chapter focuses on. By describing its origin, structure, and functioning, the section provides the necessary information to then move on to an analysis of how a networked urban world gives cities the capacity to tackle environmental challenges, position themselves as leaders for sustainable futures in their country and region, and become vital actors in global governance.

C40

In 2005, then mayor of London, Ken Livingstone, brought together a number of large cities and smaller exemplar cities[2] in the World Cities Leadership Climate Change Summit (Mayor of London 2005). The initiative evolved into the C40 Cities Climate Leadership Group (C40). The communiqué that was signed and released at the end of the London Summit urged cities to cooperate and commit to reducing greenhouse gas emissions and adapt to climate change. Furthermore, the communiqué asked for the recognition of cities' actions at the international level and for the negotiation of a post-2012 climate agreement with massive global emissions reductions. Today, C40 has 40 participating cities, which have committed themselves to action and 18 affiliated cities, of which a large number functions as exemplar cities, and one observer city.[3] Cities from all continents are members, but no cities from the Middle East participate and the involvement of African cities is limited to 4 (C40 2010a). The geographical distribution is as follows:

Participating cities: Africa (4), Asia-Pacific (14), Europe (9), North America (Canada, United States, and Mexico) (7), and South America (6). Affiliate cities: Africa (0), Asia-Pacific (3), Europe (8), North America (5), and South America (2). London hosts the C40 Secretariat, the Steering Committee consists of Berlin, Hong Kong, Jakarta, Johannesburg, London, Los Angeles, New York City, São Paolo, Seoul, and Tokyo. The current Chair is Mayor Bloomberg of New York City.[4]

The 2007 New York City Summit communiqué and the 2009 Seoul Summit declaration reflected the same aims: Be a catalyst for action, show that cities take up their responsibility in the tackling of climate change, and urge national governments to "engage, empower, and resource" cities (C40 2007, 2009, 2010b). In order to reach its goals, workshops, conferences, and summits are held on a regular basis. These meetings facilitate the exchange of best practices, policies, and ideas. Since its inception, C40 has looked for the creation of partnerships with external actors in order to guarantee the implementation of projects and policies. In 2006, it signed an agreement with the Clinton Climate Initiative (CCI), which acts as its primary executive arm and with which it merged in 2011. CCI has set up city programs to lower energy use and emissions in the area of building retrofits, outdoor lighting, waste management, and transportation. Several CCI city programs can be realized because of the close cooperation between private companies (who provide services and products), financial institutions (who provide the loans), and the city governments. Furthermore, CCI created an emissions measurement toolset (Project 2°) in cooperation with Microsoft Corporation, Autodesk, and ICLEI (CCI 2010). In 2009, C40 together with Ecos, the World Bank, the Swiss Government (SECO), and the Canton of Basel City established the Carbon Finance Capacity Building Program (CFCB) that assists cities in the Global South to develop concrete projects, which reduce greenhouse gas emissions and generate carbon credits (CFCB 2010). Also in 2009, ARUP, C40, and CCI launched a partnership with ARUP—a multinational firm of engineers, urban planners and designers—for organizing UrbanLife workshops in six C40 cities (Toronto, Melbourne, São Paolo, Ho Chi Minh City, Addis Ababa, and Warsaw) in order to address a particular challenge related to carbon reductions. These six cities can then function as leaders within C40 and other members can learn from the projects that resulted from the cooperation with ARUP and engage with ARUP to develop and implement similar projects in their own cities (C40 2010c). In 2011, C40 set up partnerships with the World Bank, ICLEI, and the Carbon Disclosure Project. C40 activities are coordinated through the C40 Secretariat. Other managing bodies are the C40 Chair and the Steering Committee (since 2007), which sets the agenda and discusses membership. Although it is not C40's major priority, the network has a political role as well. For this purpose, it presented communiqués at the CoP11 and Meeting of the Parties (MoP) 1 in Montreal (December 2005), the G8 Summit in Heiligendamm (June 2007) and the UN Climate Change Conference in Bali (December 2007) and took part in the Climate Summit for Mayors—organized parallel to CoP-15 in Copenhagen—to urge national governments for action, ask their recognition of the responsibility of cities, and announce actions major cities will undertake to tackle climate change (City of Copenhagen 2010).

Apart from generating and enhancing knowledge and expertise—through C40 events, the best practices database on the C40 website, and the collaborative arrangements with external partners—C40 activities also result in the implementation of concrete projects. Some external partners are involved in an ad hoc way, taking advantage of opportunities. Yet C40 very much relies on solid and long-term partnerships with the business sector and financial institutions, which allows for having tangible results coming from C40 initiatives, because these partnerships set out clear targets. Because implementing climate policies is costly and often requires technical expertise, access to resources and partners also needed to be accomplished in case C40 wanted to be a real catalyst for action. The partnership with CCI enables this. CCI provides technical, project, and purchasing assistance, financial advice, network access, and analytical and measurement tools (C40 2010e). ARUP offers assistance with program development and strategic and technical advice throughout the process (C40 2010c). The partnership with the World Bank, SECO, and the City of Basel within the framework of the CFCB program gives C40 cities from the Global South advice, gives access to partners, and builds cities' capacity (C40 2010d). Furthermore, many of these initiatives aim at projects in all C40 cities, thus enabling all member cities to make progress. In this sense, C40 is not only an information clearinghouse or information warehouse, but also a catalyst for concrete action.

EMPOWERING CITIES

Studying C40 revealed that TMNs give power to cities in two ways. First, within these networks, subtle power relations emerge, giving some cities relative power in the sense that they shape the direction of the network and its activities (Bouteligier 2013). Second, the inclusion in TMNs empowers cities, because they get access to information, knowledge, and partners that are invaluable for advancing urban environmental policies and implementing concrete projects. Involvement in such networks then empower cities by giving them the capacity to tackle environmental challenges, position themselves as leaders for sustainable futures in their country and region, and become vital actors in global governance. This section explains this latter form of empowerment in more detail.

Strengthening Cities' Capacity

The environmental problems cities are facing today are highly complex and require access to state-of-the-art knowledge, technology, and sufficient financial resources. TMNs provide cities with these necessary resources. First, through circulating information and knowledge and enabling access to partners invaluable for advancing urban environmental policies and implementing concrete projects (Bulkeley and Betsill 2005; Owens, Petts, and Bulkeley 2006; Bulkeley and Castán Broto 2012; Román 2010). According to Feather (2004:137), information is a valuable property and "there is real power to be derived from its possession and a loss of empowerment caused by its absence" (Feather 2004:xiii). Even for major cities like New York City and London, they would be very unlikely to have the same kind of access to information, knowledge, and partners without involvement in TMNs like C40. As said, C40 is an information clearinghouse or information warehouse that has gathered information on so-called best practices and has made this information available to its member cities through its events (summits, workshops, conferences), its websites, and online databases. Even though the identification and dissemination of best practices is not a neutral act—because it indicates what is desirable—and might create hegemonic understandings (Sánchez and Moura 2005:32; Bulkeley 2006:1029, 1035), which can lead to the emergence of dominant patterns of social practice and global subjection, as well as the pressure to implement specific solutions and behave in particular ways (Dolowitz and Marsh 1996:349; James 2006:278; Mawdsley 2009:249), it may also beneficially advance policies in multiple places (Holden et al. 2008:315; Vettoretto 2009). Even if the selection criteria are not clear, precise, or made explicit, and vagueness remains around who identified the practices as 'best', cities are still interested in having access to information on successful policies, even when it cannot be guaranteed that they are transferable to their own urban setting (Bulkeley 2006:1037). This is because best practices have the benefit that they can inspire and can generate support (from the administration or citizens) for initiatives at home.

C40 also creates access to partners that are invaluable for developing innovative policies and implementing concrete projects. Through C40, member cities have gained access to multinational companies (MNCs) (e.g., ARUP), foundations (e.g., Clinton Climate Foundation), financial institutions (e.g., Citibank), and multilateral organizations (e.g., the World Bank), which provide beneficial terms of cooperation, because they gain access to a network of partnering cities. C40 further explicitly urges national governments to "engage, empower, and resource" cities (C40 2007; C40 2009; C40 2010b), asking national governments to take up their responsibility by giving cities the necessary authority and instruments and by partnering with their cities in order to advance global environmental governance.

The City of Melbourne's 1200 Buildings Program would not have been possible without access to C40's partners and the information and knowledge that circulates in C40 (author's conversations with interviewees). It was launched in 2010 and aims at the retrofitting of commercial, nonresidential buildings in the municipality of Melbourne. The program encourages and supports building owners, managers, and facility managers to improve the energy and water efficiency of their buildings by providing information, tools, educational seminars, and events. An innovative finance mechanism has been developed to enable retrofitting projects. The 1200 Buildings program is a key component of the City's Zero Net Emissions strategy. If commercial buildings improve their energy efficiency by approximately 38%, 383,000 tons of greenhouse gas emissions (CO_2-equivalent) will be eliminated each year.

Through C40, Melbourne also got access to ARUP, which organized an UrbanLife workshop in the city in March 2010. The workshop aimed at showing how the City of Melbourne could become a 'smart city' in which state-of-the art technology helps to reach carbon emission reduction goals. ARUP provided its knowledge and experience with projects in other cities, so the City of Melbourne could learn, for example, about ways to organize public transport more efficiently and apps that stimulate citizens to use public transport more easily. Then ARUP and the City of Melbourne together worked on the envisioning of three possible projects for the City of Melbourne (ARUP 2010b). Without being part of C40, Melbourne would not have had access to ARUP's advice in the same way, which exemplifies how TMNs give access to partners and enable the development of projects.

Making Cities Leaders

Another way in which TMNs empower cities is that they offer cities a way to act as a group, which helps them to move forward quicker than other actors in their country or region. C40, for example, asked all member cities to develop Climate Change Action Plans. These plans incorporate a long-term vision for the city and set clear (and ambitious) targets with regard to the reduction of greenhouse gas emissions. Such plans were formulated also when national climate change action plans and emissions reduction targets were missing.

An experiment made possible through the collaboration with C40 and CCI is the closing of the 927-acre Bordo Poniente Landfill in Mexico City. This will significantly reduce the city's greenhouse gas emissions and will generate electricity for residents. It's estimated that using methane captured at the site could generate more than 250 GWh of electricity, or enough power to serve approximately 35,000 homes. Methane capture at Bordo Poniente could also reduce the city's GHG emissions by 25 million tons of CO_2equivalent over the next 25 years. Apart from being an innovative project for the city, it will also serve as an example for the rest of the country. In other words, Mexico City is taking the lead to develop a solution that will be applied in other cities in the rest of Mexico. Using waste as a resource is a win-win effort, which C40-CCI also wants to support in other cities around the world (C40 2011).

During the C40 London Workshop on Transport in December 2007, the bike hire scheme of front-runner Paris was discussed multiple times. Cities could learn about how such bike hire schemes work, what the advantages and costs are, what barriers need to be avoided, and so on. In the years after, multiple cities—C40 cities and others—initiated bike hire schemes, which exemplifies the power of sharing knowledge and practices in a TMN. Front-runner cities are then seen as leaders that have experimented and show the way to move forward.

Making Cities Vital Actors in Global Environmental Governance

By connecting initiatives worldwide, TMNs like C40 mean that these initiatives lead to political empowerment and increased leverage (Meyer 1997:1132; Keck and Sikkink 1998:14). At the same time, global flows and practices "are intimately connected to the intensification and reworking of dependency" (Sidaway 2007:333) and a disempowerment of particular places and actors (Stanley 2005:195–197).

During CoP-15 in Copenhagen, C40—in cooperation with the City of Copenhagen and ICLEI—organized the parallel Climate Summit for Mayors to show how cities were advancing climate change policy and were implementing concrete projects, thus taking the lead and being ahead of other state and nonstate actors (City of Copenhagen 2010). According to Toly (2008), TMNs can be conceptualized as collective agents of global projects, pooling global influence, and having the potential to be norm entrepreneurs in global environmental governance.

Although great expectations have emerged about cities' role in climate governance, cities often need others—like environmental consultancy, engineering or urban planning firms, and energy service corporations—for their expertise and experience with similar issues in other cities (McCann 2008; Hodson and Marvin 2010; Hogan et al. 2012). The results of these interactions range from MNCs advising on and assessing cities' climate policies such as ARUP in Ho Chi Minh City (ARUP 2010a) and Melbourne (ARUP 2012) to harmonizing urban transport such as Siemens in London (Siemens 2012:7) and developing applications that encourage behavioral change and a reduction of citizens' carbon footprint such as Cisco in Amsterdam (Cisco 2011:12). However, MNCs also increasingly see cities and their networks as vital partners. Especially TMNs like C40 are very appealing, as they give partnering MNCs access to a market of more than 40 large cities. Siemens has set up a Centre for Urban Sustainability,[5] AECOM created the Global Cities Institute,[6] IKEA's investment arm Landprop is developing a new neighborhood in London,[7] and IBM has set up a Smarter Cities Challenge.[8] The press releases announcing and illuminating these initiatives all talk about today's great urban challenges and about how MNCs can play a crucial role in creating more sustainable and livable cities, thus recognizing the importance of being involved in the developments in cities around the world.

CONCLUSION

This chapter focused on how cities deal with the growing environmental crisis and the challenges of climate change. In the form of TMNs, cities have set up networked forms of governance with the aim to learn from each other and attract partners that are invaluable for developing innovative policies and implementing concrete projects. As such, they hope to tackle environmental problems, position themselves as leaders for sustainable futures, and become vital actors in global governance. The chapter has shown that TMNs attribute power positions to cities—even to cities that are not global cities for the global economy. On the one hand, because some cities function as key nodes in these networks and thus gain relative power, and on the other hand, because through these networks cities gain the power to attract partners that help them to—as a collective of cities—take the lead in moving forward global environmental governance. Finally, the chapter indicates that processes linked to global environmental governance in part "pass through" economic processes, because neoliberal environmentalism is the dominant discourse (especially in C40) and because some global cities for the global economy are also important cities in TMNs that address environmental issues. At the same time, it is also clear that the significance of global(izing) cities is not only determined by economic processes, but also through environmental and political processes.

Yet inclusion in networks does not *necessarily* coincide with empowerment. Even if network accessibility is given, certain skills are required to fully exploit the opportunities and functionalities that networks offer (Keiner and Kim 2008). Different member cities make use of the opportunities TMNs offer in different ways. Some find themselves in more privileged positions because they take up particular roles in the networks that give them more access to information, knowledge, and partners. In the same sense, exclusion from a network does not automatically mean disempowerment. Those that are excluded are not subjected to the network's standards and can distance themselves from a particular approach.

NOTES

1. The findings presented in this chapter result from a PhD research project that started in October 2006 and has been finalized and publicly defended in October 2011. In this project, the author studied C40 and other city networks for global environmental governance on a wider variety of issues than the ones described in this chapter. The research also consisted of multiple direct observations of network meetings and interviews with 79 interviewees—see Bouteligier (2012).
2. Barcelona, Beijing, Berlin, Brussels, Chicago, Curitiba, Delhi, Florida, Kingston (Jamaica), London, Madrid, Melbourne, Mexico City, New York, Paris, Philadelphia, Rome, Saint Denis, San Francisco, São Paulo, Shanghai, Stockholm, Toronto, Victoria (Australia), Zurich (Mayor of London 2005).

3. Participating cities: Addis Ababa, Athens, Bangkok, Beijing, Berlin, Bogotá, Buenos Aires, Cairo, Caracas, Chicago, Delhi, Dhaka, Hanoi, Houston, Hong Kong, Istanbul, Jakarta, Johannesburg, Karachi, Lagos, Lima, London, Los Angeles, Madrid, Melbourne, Mexico City, Moscow, Mumbai, New York, Paris, Philadelphia, Rio de Janeiro, Rome, São Paolo, Seoul, Shanghai, Sydney, Tokyo, Toronto, Warsaw. Affiliated cities: Amsterdam, Austin, Barcelona, Basel, Changwon, Copenhagen, Curitiba, Heidelberg, Ho Chi Minh City, Milan, New Orleans, Portland, Rotterdam, San Francisco, Santiago de Chile, Seattle, Stockholm, Yokohama. Observing city: Singapore.
4. Previous Chairs were Mayor Livingstone of London (2005–2008) and Mayor Miller of Toronto (2008–2010).
5. See www.siemens.com/entry/cc/en/urbanization.htm.
6. See http://globalcities.aecom.com/.
7. See http://strandeast.com/.
8. See http://smartercitieschallenge.org/about.html.

4   An Urban Affair
How Mayors Shape Cities for World Politics

Michele Acuto

CHALLENGES AND CONSTRAINTS: A TIME FOR LEADERSHIP?

The anarchical nature of the international society has for long been blamed for many of the shortcomings in addressing common concerns. Scholars and policymakers alike, confronted with the "glacial" pace of international responses to global challenges, have often blamed, as former United Nations Secretary General Kofi Annan put it, "a frightening lack of leadership" and called on diplomats to "show courage" in the wake of "the greatest challenges of our time" (Harris 2008). It is then no surprise that much of the public debate on worldwide issues such as climate change, global financial crisis, and nontraditional security threats points to the need for front-runners and innovators to lead the way and to create the political momentum necessary to overcome the limits of international politics. Yet, as NASA senior scientist Cynthia Rosenzweig (2011b:70) recently highlighted, global research communities might have been focusing on the wrong kind of leaders: Rather than diplomats, swift and efficient global action might be better situated with mayors. City leaders have been promptly responding to this opportunity for more than a decade.

This "internationalization" of mayors is, however, not purely a bottom-up reaction. In the past few years, city leaders have in fact had to deal with a progressively challenging context characterized by mounting transnational concerns such as migration or climate change while facing unprecedented resource constraints in financial, commercial, and economic terms. Ade Kearns and Ronan Paddison, for instance, have aptly pointed out how local governments are nowadays faced with three interrelated challenges: First, "interurban competition has become fiercer" because of the heightened interconnectedness and pervasive territoriality of the global market; second, "homogenising" global pulls are "accompanied by simultaneous attempts to develop a city's local distinctive culture to attract business investment;" third, "cities have viewed national governments as less able to help them and less relevant to their fortunes" (Kearns and Paddison 2000:845).

The response to these governance shifts have been variegated. Yet it appears clear that city leaders are increasingly preoccupied with acquiring space for transnational action and cooperation as a strategy to cope with a changing political-economic environment. Seeking to breach the "great divide" that hides them from world politics, criticizing states and international organizations for their lack of effective action, and forging not only alliances but new constituencies of "urban" citizens, mayors raise key questions for global governance which have been widely ignored in international relations theory. Against this scholarly oversight, this chapter discusses how the influence of mayors in global governance has a catalytic role on world politics. Providing evidence of this agency, the chapter focuses on how it is framed by the discursive production of new "international" identities for the cities these leaders claim to represent across a series of global governance challenges.

MAYORS' CATALYTIC DIPLOMACY

Confronted with the shortcomings of international political processes, many scholars and diplomats have frequently turned to the nongovernmental organization (NGO) sphere in search of more practical action on global challenges. It is not uncommon to find today calls for global civil society engagement, public-private partnerships, and citizen diplomacy in almost all contexts of international relations. Yet this search for agency in the NGO sector might be missing some very crucial participants in world politics. What if much of the catalytic influence needed for crosscutting problems such as climate change or social polarization is instead to be found deep inside entities that academics and practitioners have sometimes too rapidly dismissed?

In search of evidence we might, for instance, turn to individuals like New York mayor Michael Bloomberg, who has in the past few years publicly criticised international process for producing "too much hot air" in opposition to the real everyday action of city leaders.[1] Chairman of the Climate Leadership Group, which gathers some of the most prominent cities worldwide in an attempt to offer urban solutions to global warming, Bloomberg has then recently reiterated this at an interview for BBC. Commenting on how at the "national, international, and state levels" there is "an awful lot of hot air" on climate change, he declared that "it is up to mayors" to solve environmental problems. This self-appointment to the center stage of global climate politics (if not world politics in general) is effectively building on a momentum for "urban solutions" steadily developed in the past decades. Since at least the mid-1970s, the United Nations (UN) have also sought to tackle urban issues steadily arising not solely in the environmental agenda, but also in terms of poverty, development, and security, by setting up a dedicated agency, United Nations Human Settlements Programme (UN-HABITAT), which has grown in size and breadth of activities ever since. For example, in 2000, UN-HABITAT established a UN Advisory Committee of Local Authorities to provide a direct channel between the UN and the representatives of city governments worldwide, and has been charged by the UN General Assembly with the task of implementing the Millennium Development Goals agenda (and in particular target 11 on slum dwellers) in urban areas. Similarly, the World Bank has also promoted a centralization of cities in international politics: Beginning with the 1991 Municipal Development Program, the Bank has been enlarging its urban development desk substantially after issuing a strategy document titled "Cities in Transition" in 2000, recently replaced by an updated and extended new policy alignment in 2009, which now underpins the organization's growing regard for the paradigmatic shift brought about by the present urbanization trends. Yet mayors have not just been appointed to the role of policy implementers: In the past two decades, city leaders have also joined in partnership with several other international actors. An example of this growing urban participation in the implementation of the broader climate agenda is the European Sustainable Cities and Towns Campaign, launched in 1994 by a joint initiative of the European Commission, the City of Aalborg, and ICLEI—Local Governments for Sustainability, with an initial commitment of 80 municipalities to initiate Local Agenda 21 processes in their authorities and bring forward the process at the urban level. Similarly, the European Commission has more and more explicitly targeted the "urban" as a realm of implementation of regional targets and common goals, as demonstrated by the recent issuing of a guide to the "Urban Dimension in EU Policies" that, first produced in 2007, has now been revised to a substantial set of city-targeted programs and initiatives.

However, mayors are also networking, not just being networked, in global governance. This is well represented by the World Association of the Major Metropolises (or Metropolis), which was created in 1985 and is formed by 129 active members from across the world coordinated by a Barcelona-based secretariat and operating as an international forum for exploring issues and concerns common to major cities and metropolitan regions. As such, mayors have often demonstrated a solid handling of the current diplomatic agenda and of the intricate policymaking pathways of world politics.

Nonetheless, city leaders are also very often well attuned not solely to the dominant dynamics of international relations, but also to some of the emerging themes that promise to lead the world political debate in the decades ahead. This is for instance evident in the Istanbul Water Consensus—an initiative by Istanbul's mayor Kadir Topba and ICLEI that now gathers more than 1,000 across more than 56 countries. Building on the previous Local Government Declaration on Water of 21 March 2006 (promoted by Mexico City), which expressed an awareness by local leaders concerning water and sanitation and called on national governments for a more effective sustainability partnerships, the Consensus is a declaration aimed not only at advocating urban solutions with central governments but also at undertaking a comprehensive assessment and inventory of water policies in view of potential policy exchange. As cases such as the Water Consensus or the Mexico City Pact point out, there is today a plethora of mayor-sponsored regimes that are not solely of a regulatory nature but are also, if not chiefly, aimed at pooling resources and policymaking capacity.

These "city diplomacy" processes have thus been pushing the emergence of an urban international agenda led by mayors of major metropolises such as New York, Seoul, or São Paulo, influential across all governance spheres.[2] This is of course not just limited to climate change or sustainability. Other cases of this proactivity can also be found in international political realms other than environmental policymaking. City leaders have in fact undertaken several security and peacebuilding efforts. For example, in 2004 Sister Cities International has, with the help of funding from the U.S. Department of State, promoted an "International Partners for Peace" initiative to strengthen relationships between five U.S. and Iraqi communities. Through public-private partnerships, the project is aims at fostering cooperation on humanitarian aid programs and knowledge exchanges, trainings, and reciprocal learning, and involving major U.S. metropolises such as Dallas, Tucson, or Philadelphia. City leaders have in this sense developed a policy reach that is nowadays active at all levels of global governance from the most localised spheres of metropolitan and domestic affairs to globalized issues such as climate change or water security. This means that these leaders now catalyze and influence policy both domestically and internationally. For example, the Federation of Canadian Municipalities (FCM) has since 2005 been campaigning through its Standing Committee on Increasing Women's Participation in Municipal Government for greater gender equality in the public sector. Promoting initiatives like the recent "Getting to 30% Project" that aims at increasing the number of women in municipal government by roughly 100 every year for the next 15 years, FCM has undertaken a number of initiatives to encourage women who are considering running for municipal office and to promote greater sensibility for gender issues in politics.

Can we then compare the impact of mayors such as Bloomberg to that of state diplomats? The issue is certainly still open to debate. First, there is the problem of representation. In some cases, city leaders are elected by constituencies that group more than national citizens, representing urban residents more in general, but is far from the norm: Often times it is at best questionable whether many of the mayors widely proactive in international affairs are legitimately representative of their metropolises. Second, there is the limitation of West-centricity in city diplomacy. Many of the key municipal networks shaping global governance today, like Metropolis or the Climate Leadership Group, are dominated by European and U.S. global cities, but the trend is changing. Asian and Latin American metropolises, as well as some Middle Eastern and African cities in a minority of cases, are rapidly stepping up to central political positions in these networks. Lastly, and perhaps more fundamentally, there are the limits of funding. Many of the aforementioned city networks and mayoral initiatives tend to rely quite heavily on implementation partners and donors such as the European Union (EU), the World Bank, or the Organisation for Economic Co-operation and Development (OECD), thus raising more than a few concerns as to their independence and individual capacity—a challenge that, at the end of the day, is nothing but a well-established truism of the NGO world. Yet, at present, mayors remain particularly proactive catalysts that are unlikely to lose policymaking clout in an increasingly urbanized world. So, if on the question of city leadership in international affairs the jury is still out, facts from across most of the spectrum of global governance seem to indicate some growing diplomatic clout.

Yet this agency should not go unscrutinized. While mayors are progressively heralded as the "local hand" of climate action and while city leaders worldwide are taking decisive advocacy roles for "global" action on transnational challenges, scholars in international studies should seek to problematize the sources and politics of this ascent. What kind of leadership do mayors promote? How are these claims implemented? What are the political-economic structures that underpin these city networks? Certainly, as the variegated realms of city agency described above can testify, addressing these questions is not easy task. When we step beyond the simplistic rhetoric of urbanization that pervades the more superficial discussions on this internationalization, we are confronted with an extremely complex puzzle that cuts across several realms of global governance from the economy, to the environment, and security. While piecing together such a multiplex picture might be beyond the purview of this limited chapter, we can however start by asking ourselves: What kind of international actors are these cities? To provide a preliminary response to this issue, it might therefore be productive to start hereby unpacking the international identity presented by city leaders in this mounting variety of urban initiatives in global governance.

NEW INTERNATIONAL IDENTITIES

Many are the media and policy contexts in which cities have been depicted as inevitably crucial for the future of humanity. Urban issues have regularly featured, for instance, in the yearly "Cities Issue" of *Foreign Policy*, which has been reporting to the international audience on failures and successes of major metropolises since 2008. Likewise, as noted earlier, urban issues are now a constant of the vast majority of major UN and World Bank conferences dealing with population, climate, social equality, and economic development. Cities, and most of all large metropolises, have acquired a growing global importance vis-à-vis pressing challenges that have become commonspeak in most international processes. City leaders, whether in their mayoral position or in equivalent institutional hats, have a key stake in representing cities on the international stage. Yet the nature of this representation has thus far gone largely unproblematized.

As I argue here, the framing of cities and mayors as leaders in international affairs has, especially in the past two decades, been identified in terms of five main features that characterize the "new" identity of cities. Respectively, mayors have presented cities as central to global challenges, capable to address them, proactive in formulating responses while not waiting for others to call them up, and hybrid in the nature of their governance initiatives. Yet this has also been coupled with a framing that charts city leaders as "responsible" for devising an effective and transnational momentum to tackle the limits of the international system. Taken together, these characteristics set mayors and their increasingly pervasive agency in a particularly interesting light in the contemporary global political scenario.

Centrality

Since the early 2000s, and thanks to the growing city emphasis of key global actors like the UN, urban issues have entered prominently in the discussions of policymakers in international fora. While we are perhaps still relatively far from a complete urbanization of international politics, it is quite obvious that cities are being recurrently invoked alongside many of the central concerns for International Relations (IR). The EU has for long been one of the leading international actors in recognizing the potential of cities as agents of global governance. Fostering a variety of initiatives through the Union's Committee of Regions, which acts as the EU's assembly of regional and local representatives, the Union has promoted the participation of cities in regional and international governance since its early days. This has now interestingly spread to bilateral relations with the growing giants of 21st century international relations. While the Union has regularly held meetings with China and India for the past decade, these have been extending to a variety of subnational authorities that might play an essential role not only in strengthening and relaxing political relations between Europe and the Far East, but also in developing joint efforts with real-world applications of direct impact for the lives of millions of urban dwellers. The EU-China Mayors' Forum first held September 2012 was the first annual flagship event of a newly inaugurated "EU-China Urbanisation Partnership" that was in turn launched at the occasion of the 7th China-EU Summit to address urbanization challenges in China through cooperative EU-China efforts between stakeholders at national, regional, and local levels. As the Forum's presentation put it: "Given the array of challenges they face in adapting to the "urban century," China and Europe have a strong interest in working together to build better cities."[3]

The meeting included EU and Chinese mayors with a variety of delegations of city planners, local businesses, and NGOs, and has been devised to share experience in sustainable, integrated, and efficient urban solutions.

While it remains a purely consultative and peer-to-peer project, it none-theless holds important potential to promote paradiplomatic exchanges between local governments and urban stakeholders, involving for instance the Chinese Association of Mayors and the European Covenant of Mayors in a range of cross-sector activities and a multiplayer events open to all relevant actors. The meeting tackled challenges facing modern cities as they struggle to cope with increasingly mobile urbanites, increased traffic and problems of waste management. Likewise, it has ventilated a set of possible avenues for cooperation with the perspective of China and Europe joining forces to meet the demands of China's urban billion—with city leaders at the center of this initiative.

Mayors, not just international bodies like the EU, have been key drivers of this increasing centrality of the urban in international agendas. City lead-ers have in this sense widely promoted how cities stand today at the heart of many global challenges as both initiators of transnational problems as much as core stakeholders in tackling these. Environmental issues are of course at the heart of this discourse of centrality. Consider the following column pub-lished by Vancouver mayor Gregor Robertson in occasion of the February 2012 Vancouver Cities Summit:

> Failure is not an option, because it's in our cities that many of our big-gest opportunities and most potent challenges are playing out. Cities are the source of 70 to 80 per cent of greenhouse gas pollution today; dou-bling that would be disastrous. We must dramatically reduce our carbon footprint. Communities and local economies that can withstand our current levels of energy consumption and waste will find them far more damaging as cities scale up rapidly. Cities that deplete their resources and degrade their environments in a race to build the tallest or fastest or biggest will find their victories short-lived as global demand shifts toward efficiency and sustainability. It is this shift that offers real hope that we can still get it right. Because rapid urbanization holds tremen-dous promise alongside that risk. Done right, it creates jobs, con-serves resources and improves quality of life. We can build the cities we need to build for future generations, and create economic opportunity in today's climate of uncertainty.[4]

This discursive framing, common across the vast majority of fora in which mayors have presented their role in rising to global challenges, tends to high-light the inevitable role of the city as the locus for the future of humanity. "Failure is not an option" as Robertson puts it, because of the pervasiveness of urbanization on the world's population, and thus because of the tangible presence of the city as a more and more natural landscape for all sorts of realms of global governance.

Yet this framing is not necessarily negative. The city is in fact not gener-ally depicted as a Dickensian context that overwhelms dwellers and affects humanity like an uncontrollable amoeba. Rather, mayors have gone at great length to depict the centrality of cities in world affairs as a positive source for global action. The city is not simply the source of problems but also that unique milieu that "holds tremendous promise" alongside the pervasive risks of climate change, human security, or economic downturn. Certainly, much of this image of relatively positive centrality is portrayed by city leaders in order to speak with authority and hope, not merely as acknowledgment of faults, to the global audience they seek to engage.

Nonetheless, it is important to notice here how this discourse has been going hand-in-hand with a framing of cities, and especially of those major metropolises like London or São Paulo whose mayors we see quite constantly in international fora, as central in the global economy. As I note in several other features of the international identity depicted by mayors, a "green growth" logic that couples sustainability and human security with economic stability (when not development) is the dominant accent in the global discourses of most city leaders, regardless of political affiliations and party lines.

Capacity

City leaders have sought to assert this central positioning by demonstrating their aptitude for global governance. Mayors have in fact been presenting themselves as capable of carrying out diplomatic endeavors and establishing transnational networks while remaining strong of powers that emerge out of their very localised prerogatives such as planning, water and waste management, or transport policymaking. An obvious antecedent of this influence is the influence city leaders have long held on the internal politics of states. Yet mayoral capacity to shape domestic politics is not limited to "domestic" matters, and this is of course no novelty. The United States Conference of Mayors (USCM), a nonpartisan organization of mayors from 1,294 U.S. cities with populations of 30,000 or more, has been an active lobbying voice in Washington, D.C., for over 80 years since its establishment in 1932. The Conference has been lobbying in favor of metropolitan leaders and the Conference President, currently Los Angeles Mayor Antonio R. Villaraigosa, serves as the "national spokesman" for USCM mayors. During the Conference's annual meetings in June, standing committees recommend policy positions that collectively represent the views of the nation's mayors and are distributed to the President of the United States and Congress. In addition to the ongoing work of the Conference's standing committees, mayors are often also organized into "task forces" to act on issues that demand special attention such as homeland security, energy, hunger and homelessness, and brownfields. The Conference has long sought to impact questions of everyday concern for international practitioners and scholars. For instance, in June 2011 the USCM passed a resolution urging President Obama and Congress to speed up the ending of the wars in Afghanistan and Iraq. As

Villaraigosa stated in assuming the presidency of USCM: "It's time to bring our investments back home: We can't be building roads and bridges in Baghdad and Kandahar and not in Baltimore and Kansas City."[5]

However, city leaders are not just influential through their diplomatic and lobbying roles. They also have a "strategic governance capacity," which can be crucial in solving environmental and social problems (Healey 2002). In fact, mayors are tasked with the daily management of most of the "global" challenges international relations specialists are so accustomed to. Importantly for both the way IR theory has conceptualized world politics and for the way international bodies have conceptualized "global" responses to transnational challenges such as climate change, mayors have framed this capacity not solely in terms of international networking but also in terms of their deep reach into the everyday realities of their metropolises. This is an "everyday" dimension of international agency that is perhaps best epitomized by the C40. For instance, in occasion of a recent "Ministers and Mayors" roundtable cosponsored with the OECD, for instance, the Climate Leadership Group has kick-started two collaborations, the Green Growth Network and the Sustainable Infrastructure Finance Network, to serve as action-oriented working groups capable of showcasing the effectiveness of city leadership. As Bloomberg stated in this occasion:

> We're the level of government closest to the majority of the world's people. We're directly responsible for their well-being and their futures. So while nations talk, but too often drag their heels—cities act. And the launch of these two networks also demonstrates C40's belief that when cities act locally, we can also have an impact globally.[6]

Capacity to address global challenges is coupled with presenting these leaders' proximity to most transnational problems as embodied in the conurbations they govern. Once again, as with the "positive" centrality featured in the previous section, mayors evoke this close geographical relationship to certify how their understanding of these challenges is in direct relation to people—as opposed to the "hot air" of the discourses of high politics. City leaders depict this proximity not just as advantage but almost as an absolute domain of their intimate relationship with city dwellers. They portray themselves as the "level" that is "closest to the majority of the world's people" and in doing so they assert their grounded agency as both locally reflexive as much as globally relevant, if only because of their jurisdiction over more than half of the global population. In this sense, city leaders frame their capacity to tackle international issues as quintessentially "glocal."[7]

This conjunctly global-local identity is today sponsored by a number of city networks and is perhaps best embodied in the advocacy of the Glocal Forum. The Forum is a network of over 140 cities on five continents that partners with nearly 100 public and private sector actors, aiming to create "a more equitable balance between the global and the local through a new pattern of diplomacy—the diplomacy of cities."[8] Founded in 2001, the organization encourages global powers to have broader respect for local powers and cultural diversity in a process defined as glocalisation. This is the basis for city-to-city project activity in fields critical for sustainable development and peace. "Glocalisation" initiatives focus on socio-economic development, tourism, youth, sports, culture, media, and information technology through the involvement of civil societies. Innovative networking frameworks are created primarily through the organization's annual Glocalisation Conference and multicultural events, while a dedicated think tank is developing a set of policy recommendations that incorporate and forward the ideas of glocalisation. A similar "glocal" framing has been mobilized in an increasingly large set of venues, and not least the last UN Conference on Sustainable Development in Rio de Janeiro ("Rio+20"). In doing this, mayors present their identities as key bridges between the global processes concerned with Earth as a whole and localised dynamics emerging from the visceral realities of their own cities. Likewise, by speaking in a glocal tone that continuously refers the urban to the world and vice versa, they sketch the role of cities as essential gateways for global governance.

Capacity is not solely a matter of rhetoric. Mayors like those of the Climate Leadership Group have effectively expanded their local management capacities to encompass a plethora of activities aimed at tackling global challenges both through more effective urban policymaking and through transnational networking. The recognition given by actors such as the World Bank to this increasing influence is not casual. Most metropolitan mayors, both in the West, and in the Global South, can today display powers that allow them some substantial policymaking competence to tackle international issues. Yet recognizing this requires of international scholars a perspective beyond the traditional view of diplomacy. ARUP, another corporate consulting partner of the C40, has extensively documented this policy capacity in its June 2011 report titled Climate Action in Megacities.[9] While recognizing that "not all problems of global warming can be tackled at a city level," the report has detailed the wide reach of mayoral powers across at least nine sectors of activity: transport, existing buildings, waste management, water, energy supply, outdoor lighting, planning and urban land use, and food and even agriculture. Considered in terms of service ownership and operation, the capacity to shape public policy demonstrated by the leaders of the 36 C40 cities surveyed by ARUP is decisively substantial, documenting how these key metropolises have undertaken at least 4,734 "climate actions" to try and tackle the environmental challenges they are nowadays confronted with. As this emblematic study tells us, mayors generally have some extensive influence (even if this remains fundamentally hidden to the "internationalist" eye) in those tools of metropolitan management that are certainly not the bread and butter of IR theory.

Proactivity

Capacity to tackle global challenges, and a central positioning in these, are not left to the often loose ends of rhetoric. By appearing in a mounting variety of international fora, public events beyond their constituencies and, not least, academic venues, mayors have been signaling their cities' willingness to take global matters in their hands. This entrepreneurial approach has, as noted earlier, been framed against a view of states dragging their feet in international processes, with no end in sight. The former Mayor of Toronto David Miller articulated this message at the UNFCCC Copenhagen summit in December 2009: "While climate change demands global action, we have shown that we are not waiting for others to act."[10]

The problem of states "waiting" is a common rhetoric that, popularized by city diplomacy on climate change, has expanded to several realms of the internationalization of mayors. This framing is not simply accusatory. City leaders have pointed at the sluggish processes of international politics also, if not predominantly, to demonstrate their proactivity in responding to pressing needs. At the tune of "Cities: leading by doing" advertised by the World Bank, more and more one of the main sponsors of the internationalization of city leadership, the rhetoric that opposes stalling, inconclusive, or lethargic talks of the state-centric scenario to the action of cities worldwide has become a well-accepted mantra by most urban envoys to international fora.[11]

While reasserting centrality and capacity, this "proactivity" discourse aims at displacing the source of global initiative in favor of city leaders and their nongovernmental partners. Proactivity has been in many sectors inextricably entangled with the view that, to truly "go global" on matters such as sustainability or socio-cultural integration, cities need to seek partners across a variety of governance layers. As I illustrate in the following sections, this constitutes a cornerstone of another facet of the city's "international" identity in the 21st century—that of its hybrid (i.e., public-private) globalizing nature. Yet it is already important to highlight here how this entrepreneurial reach into the nongovernmental world, characterized by an exponential growth in global public-private partnerships for urban solutions and a substantial shift in the popularity of "city themes" amongst business actors, has been shaping quite significantly the most proactive cities in international affairs. The emergence of the Climate Leadership Group (C40) as one of the most popular city networks, for instance, has been inextricably intertwined with the progressive sprawl of institutionalized connections with the private sector. If, at its founding event promoted by London in 2005, the Group had been supported by mostly local U.K. corporations like BP and major domestic service providers like Thames Water, the growth of the Group in the following years has followed step-by-step its proactive engagement with major international and economic actors.[12] Hence the Group has expanded rapidly after the partnership with the Clinton Foundation in

2006, the growing commitment by Bloomberg Philanthropies since 2007, and the successful private procurement system set up by the Foundation's Climate Initiative and the C40 secretariat to attract major global investors like Honeywell. Similarly, the Glocal Forum is regularly sponsored by a number of corporations, including MTG, Tele2, Millicom, and Metro International SA. This is not an isolated story but rather an emerging feature of present-day city diplomacy.

However, this does not mean that central governments have been jettisoned from the picture altogether. This partnering view of urban action on global issues has also been extended to national governments, which have been progressively treated as both in need of local leadership and in need of strategic realignment not to hinder the most effective sources of transnational initiative. Take the last communiqué issued by the OECD Roundtable of Mayors and Ministers:

> There is no "one-size-fits-all" model for implementing urban sustainability. Strategies will differ across cities as they do across countries, according to urban forms, economic and institutional settings, resource endowments and particular environmental pressure points. Despite these differences, cities have great potential to share local solutions, to transfer practices across national and continental boundaries, and to work collaboratively to advance innovative new approaches for financing critical infrastructure. At the same time, national governments must recognize and embrace the critical role they can play in establishing the right framework to advance solutions that do not inadvertently limit or prevent local action.[13]

This discourse responds to global pressures with specificity. Cookie-cutter solutions and universalization are not the prerogative of cities. Against the "one-size-fits-all" model, city leaders emphasize the productivity of difference and the importance of leading by example against framing mandatory minimums. Transnational problems that city leaders seek to address are, as with their cities' centrality, quintessentially glocal matters: They differ in their localized manifestation, yet are similar in their geographical reach across states, continents and, of course, conurbations. Caught in the midst of the "transnational" pervasiveness of problems piercing sovereign bodies and of the "glocal" nature of much non- and sub-governmental action responding to these, national governments are, in most cases, portrayed as lacking the hands-on expertise of local authorities. This context has however been mostly characterized by rhetorical accusations with no clear target, aimed at signaling the limits of central government action while not necessarily alienating them altogether.

What is left to states, at least in the scenario that city leaders have been framing, is the inevitable partnership with those authorities that were once considered as the lowest administrative tier. National governments "must recognize" the centrality and capacity of cities and are required to reform, or at least realign, their prerogatives to the initiative of city leaders while embracing their responsibility to "establish the right framework" that would allow for effective multilayered action. However, in the discourse of most mayors and mayoral initiatives, the true leadership for global action remains with cities. As the OECD Roundtable communiqué continues:

> Cities can, and must, take a leading role in greening our economies and achieving urban sustainability. They pursue these goals, however, in the context of national and international policies. Coherence between national and local policies is vital: initiatives taken at different levels can at times be mutually reinforcing, but, if poorly co-ordinated, they can also undermine one another. The better the national framework, the easier it will be for cities to address their specific challenges in ways that enhance rather than undermine their competitiveness.[14]

The agency of cities and national governments becomes, in this view, "mutually reinforcing" only if based on those innovative terms championed by mayors and increasingly well-tested in the partnership between cities and the nongovernmental sector. Overall, initiatives like the OECD Roundtable contribute to reinforce a "leveling the playing field" approach between mayors and their national and international counterparts. They stand in favor of a proactive reconfiguring of global governance structures that starts not from the uncertain structure of the international system, but rather from the synergies that can be created deep "inside" and across states.

Hybridity

Whether in those cases aimed at setting up formal regimes for concerted action, or in those circumstances when city leaders are more concerned with "best practice" exchanges, the transnational role of mayors produces "hybrid" structures across the geography of global governance (Conca 2005). Hybridization is in this sense a function of several policy factors. First, following the broader trends of world politics, city networks are progressively reliant on public-private partnerships to deliver on implementation and project funding. This phenomenon promotes the integration of cities with the private sector and global markets both in the delivery of essential services as well as in the production of transnational paradiplomatic initiatives. Conversely, corporations and major industries (as "delivery partners" for urban public policy) are allowed to expand deep into the governance of major cities worldwide. Then, transnational processes promoted by mayors tend to be inherently multiscalar, encompassing not only local governments, but also international organizations, localised and transnational NGOs, some central governments and various corporate actors, as in the case of the Cities Alliance or the Canadian Sustainable Cities Initiative.[15] Yet the hybridity of these connections also spans into the realm of political ideologies: Precisely because of this twin public-private and multiscalar nature, city networks tend to conglomerate a variety of approaches to world politics. This often favors the encounter of IR stances that are frequently presented in academia as contrasting: For example, within the Cities Alliance or the World Association of the Major Metropolises, quintessential neoliberal interests that are market oriented and business friendly (as represented by, among others, World Bank or major corporate actors like Knight Frank) meet with bottom-up claims more typically identifiable with postcolonial and cosmopolitan voices, such as those of the Shack/Slum Dwellers International (SDI) or Habitat for Humanity. The transnational agency of city leaders has the capacity to forge spaces that allow encounter and experimentation among more traditional international actors and novel forces emerging at a variety of societal levels. These processes of hybridization tend to promote the production of policymaking structures across multiple spheres of governance. City leaders have thus been functioning as policy implementers and governance facilitators of broader agendas. For example, the Cities Alliance is the result of a coalition of governments, NGOs (such as SDI), municipalities, and international organizations (World Bank, EU, Asia Development Bank, and UNEP), which supported its activities with more than 70 million dollars in pledges. The Alliance mainly acts as a trust fund that provides grants for city development strategies, slum upgrading, and sustainable financial strategies to attract international capitals (Pieterse 2008).

In a context of transnational challenges, lacking national leadership and marked resource constraints, the necessity to attract international capital and private support to implement innovative governance approaches is paramount. As such, even the more progressive mayors have generally been reframing the importance of acting vis-à-vis urban challenges with a consideration of socio-economic realities. This is well represented, for instance, in a popular interview by Doreen Massey with then mayor of London Ken Livingstone in 2007, when the leader of the Greater London Authority argued as follows:

> But big business is now a strong ally on a whole range of fronts—climate change, improving skills in the workforce, investment in public transport and so on [. . .] This is not the world you create, it's the world you're in. (Massey 2007:25)

Indeed, most contemporary city leaders venturing into international affairs tend to argue in a similar direction. While not oblivious to the variety of critiques that have for long been addressed to "big business" and private actors in global governance, the understanding that the political-economic restraints for city diplomacy require compromise and entrepreneurship is largely shared by those many mayors concerned with the sustainability and international reach of their cities. Now this does not mean, as one could easily infer, that mayors are oblivious to the pervasive "business privilege" that characterizes most major cities (Thornley et al. 2005). Take the following statement by Boris Johnson at the 2010 World Economic Forum in Davos:

> I have consistently criticised the current orgy of excessive bonuses and how certain parts of the industry seem so oblivious of the dissatisfaction of wider society. This is why I am very pleased that these banks have stepped up and are now contributing to initiatives that will help young Londoners. I would encourage many more to follow suit. There never has been a better time for them, and big businesses, to show their altruistic, charitable side and increase their giving back to the capital, which in turn provides them with the best location to live in and work.[16]

As in several other cases, mayors have widely encouraged this "giving back" by framing their cities as much more than simple global economic hubs. The attention of city leaders from metropolises like London, Tokyo, or Singapore has progressively shifted to illustrating the strategic importance of livability in their cities and, conversely, the need for "big business" to appreciate the uniqueness of the localised conditions they can offer. Appreciation of the unequal socio-economic status quo in which mayors operate notwithstanding, city leaders have for the most part voiced their necessity to come to terms with such a system in order to maintain minimum levels of livability for their cities.

Perhaps even more than their sovereign limitations, resource scarcity and need for more extensive financing have been pushing cities towards transnational networking and capital pooling, which have allowed them to set up public-private hybridizations like those heralded in the Climate Leadership Group. This, as I have illustrated more at length elsewhere, implies a partly "schizophrenic" view of the identity of cities in international affairs (Acuto 2013). Wary of the impediments and dominance of a mostly neoliberal global governance cities shift the locus, rhetoric and object of global agency towards alternative (urban and transnational) scales in order to bypass such structural limitations. Yet, on the other hand, many metropolises exert networked influence and gain room for maneuver by perpetrating the centrality of systemic market logics. This demonstrates that city leaders, when framing the role of cities globally, are equally conscious of the possibilities that a neoliberal system allows for "individual" agency. While this trend is per se a possible cause of concern, we should nonetheless not forget how mayors have also been reminding the international community at large that they stand as responsible agents for the "citizens" they govern—another theme of wide resonance in contemporary IR.

Responsibility

If one was to end this narrative on the troublesome marriage between local government and global business, as several accounts have recently done, the story of the discursive framing of cities by their own leaders would very likely be unjust to the important political reach that mayors have been presenting to international audiences. Responsibility towards "their" citizens, as multicultural and often relatively mobile constituencies, is in fact not a lesser piece of this emerging language. Many mayors have, once again across all sides of the political spectrum and the geographical atlas, put much emphasis on their duties towards their cities, and on the responsible nature of the internationalization of their "local" agency. This rhetoric, of course, also emanates from the need to restate the political prerogatives of mayors on millions of urban dwellers against the general indifference to city leaders in international political fora. As Bloomberg has reiterated at a roundtable in occasion of Rio+20: "We have the responsibilities, but not the say. Exclusion of local government in these processes [Rio+20] is a major gap in the negotiations."[17] Mayors demand space for discussion, recognition and legitimacy. In turn, they offer testimony of their capacity to act despite the oversight of diplomats. As the Hiroshima Appeal issued in 2005 by Mayors for Peace reasserted:

> Threats to civilians are not limited to nuclear weapons. In this world, an incredibly large number of people are exposed in their daily lives to such threats as hunger, poverty, infectious diseases, discrimination, violence, conflicts and environmental destruction. Though national leaders worldwide are well aware of these challenges, their attention is focused on pursuing national and economic interests rather than on implementing effective measures to deal with these challenges. It is always citizens who are the victims of wars, violence and environmental destruction. We mayors are responsible for the protection of the human rights and security of our citizens.[18]

Mayors, amid the limited action of diplomats, are those left responsible for the well-being of city dwellers. As the discursive framing that most city leaders deploy testifies, this situation is embraced by many City Halls worldwide, demonstrating not only a "passive" but also a proactive embracing of this responsible role. While obviously targeted at gaining further political legitimacy and room for action in relation to global governance, this rhetoric also signals a relative understanding of responsibility as "duty of care" that is very much in tune with contemporary IR discussions (Arbour 2008). Additionally, this "we mayors" rhetoric sustains the production of collective, or at least coordinated, transnational action by city leaders. If this cross-boundary identification with equal (or similar) layers of government had mostly been expressed in terms of "paradiplomacy" in the 1980s and 1990s, the current wave of city internationalization promises more complex engagements with the global role of mayors.[19] Different from the early city-to-city processes that, perhaps best represented by Sister Cities International and the long-lived practice of "city twinning," sustained the initial interaction of mayors with the international system, today's generation of city diplomats aim at pooling resources with peers to attract nongovernmental, national, and international attentions. Responsibility, and thus direct influence, certainly also plays a key role in drawing actors such as major energy service companies (the so-called ESCOs) or development actors like the Asian Development Bank, to City Hall rather than towards central governments. Framing the importance of city leadership in terms of responsibility, in fact, also highlights once again how mayoral proximity to city dwellers is associated with legitimacy. Seen from this angle of legitimacy, as former mayor of Bogotá Enrique Peñalosa (2008) puts it, "the citizens' perception of how much their dignity and well-being is a priority to their state" becomes crucial.

This discussion has, of course, the potential to spiral into direct accusation of the illegitimacy of international action versus the direct responsibility of city leaders. If mayors, who represent by virtue of their elected status more than half of the global population, are excluded from global negotiation, is it then fair to say that these latter are not properly representative of people's interests? Has the pursuit of "national and economic interests" rather than the implementation of "effective measures" aimed at "citizens" derailed global action from its real-world and everyday origins? Are mayors the "true" representatives of the John and Jane Smiths of the world? The dangers of this line of thought has, to date, been aptly avoided by mayors worldwide. To begin with, city leaders are not free from some of these critiques. In the cases of London and New York, for instance, there is a well-established lineage of critiques from both media and scholarship against the privileged role that mayors have carved for big business as a friendly ally to City Hall interests. This consideration does not stop at the major metropolises of the West, but spans most global cities, and, recently, has also been directed at city networks like the C40, Cities Alliance, or ICLEI, who have been partnering with major economic actors like the World Bank. Moreover, a fight over direct political responsibility between city leaders and national governments would yield to near-unsolvable deadlocks that neither mayors nor state diplomats would want. As noted earlier, beyond the surface critique on the lack of effective action, mayors are often in search for national partnership as a key facilitator (or at least a removable barrier) for their internationalization. Besides, the differentiation in governmental and administrative prerogatives, and the vast variety of constitutional settings that separate most "internationalized" mayors today, also acts as a disincentive for this line of critique.

Rather, responsibility is invoked by city leaders as a legitimization of action. This notion of responsibility, while not exclusively grounded in the rhetoric of Western mayors, has much to do with a traditional Western liberal philosophy that sees responsibility as premised on the concept of agency, possibly attributing to these "responsible" actors much more freedom for action than actually available.[20] This seems, in most cases, to be the reaction of city leaders to the assumed structural constraints imposed on both cities and more generally global action by the inelastic frameworks of the international system. Take Rio de Janeiro mayor Eduardo Paes's intervention at the Rio+20 roundtable shortly after Bloomberg's aforementioned quote: "As a mayor, I don't want to be in a framework like the UN. It takes too long. We need to get things done. We just need to act."

Mayors have a responsibility to find creative and innovative ways of governing. This duty to their constituencies is discursively embedded in the daily reality of City Hall and in the figure of the mayor in his or her proximity to urban citizens. This "ground-up" view has been recently voiced, for instance, by former Washington, DC, mayor Tony Williams at the 2012 New Cities Summit in Paris: "As a mayor, you have to come up with real solutions in deconstructing the reality and trying to come up with classical ways of governing."[21]

The role of the mayor as necessarily embedded in a governance context that demands not just management of routine problems but also continual innovation in the governmental responses to multiplex problems such as crime, waste, pollution, or social polarization, has been a long-standing rhetoric deployed by city leaders across the globe. This framing signals a sensibility to local problems as necessarily linked to an expertise in disentangling governance structures and economic relations in a pragmatic, hands-on way.

I ♥ CITIES

The expression "I ♥ New York" is not just a globally recognizable brand of the Big Apple: Often the rebus that was devised in the 1970s to promote tourism in the sprawling U.S. metropolis has melted in its government's city diplomacy and has echoed in the words of its mayor. Borrowed from a similar publicity logo for a Montreal radio campaign, affixed to New York by its State Commissioner for Commerce Bill Doyle, and fast transferred onto the skyline of Manhattan in the imaginaries of global audiences, the story of "I ♥ New York" is in many senses much similar to the discursive trends I sought to unpack earlier. The campaign, conceived by native son and graphic designer Milton Glaeser, was built to seduce people to a city that had lost the headlines of the international media and had been decaying in the mundanity of everyday municipal management. Explicitly, "I ♥ New York" appealed to the seduction of a unique place. Originally conceived as a brief three-month experiment, the logo remains to date impressed in the minds of millions globally, has its own special place in the city's Museum of Modern Art, has been a gateway to the pop revolution that redefined the American and Western cultures, and has contributed to reinstate the Big Apple as a global center of attraction.

The story of the "heart" campaign is not dissimilar to what city leaders are now doing when presenting their metropolises to the wider world of international affairs. "I ♥" could be easily be followed these days by the likes of London, Sydney, Singapore, Rio, and so forth. Countless are the cases where we can easily read the same tentative seduction in the words of mayors not just towards tourists and visitors, but also policymakers and diplomats. By presenting themselves (and their cities) as central, capable, proactive, hybrid, and responsible, urban leaders have sought to establish a new "feeling," a renewed attachment, a meaningful relationship, between global politics and the city. The discursive framing of this global appeal is solidly embedded in international economic dynamics. As with the heart rebus, it requires people to step back and reinterpret their usual international alphabet in the perhaps more mundane language of City Hall. Maybe like "I ♥ New York," it is destined to be less than a transient vogue and more of a milestone of a new era of world politics. For IR, in its scholarly and practical applications, the mayoral attempt to inspire a global affair with the city can develop a renewed appreciation of these "everyday" leaders and their emerging impact on the governance of transnational challenges. Yet, as with the simplified façade of the heart campaign, the claims of mayors should not be taken at face value. Rather, while appreciating the socio-political importance of this narrative, we should now seek to analyze the discourses, investigate the practical applications, and test the revolutionary limits of the "I ♥" tactics that city leaders are seducing us with.

NOTES

1. Mayor Bloomberg, "Too Much 'Hot Air' on Climate Change," *BBC News*, 27 May 2011, available at www.bbc.co.uk/news/world-us-canada-13582351.
2. I rely here on the analysis spearheaded by van der Pluijm (2007).
3. The Forum concluded with a preliminary agreement on a partnership (or 'Charter') sustainable urban development. Available at www.euchinamayorsforum.eu/home.html. See also Acuto (2012).
4. Gregor Robertson, "Global Cities: Vancouver Can Lead the Way," *The Vancouver Sun,* 31 January 2012, available at www.vancouvercitiessummit.org/news.
5. Michael Cooper, "Mayors Call for a Quicker End to Wars So Money Can Be Used for Needs at Home," *New York Times*, 20 June 2011, available at www.nytimes.com/2011/06/21/us/21mayors.html?_r=1.
6. New York City mayoral press release PR-087–12, 8 March 2012, "Mayor Bloomberg Launches New C40 Global Networks," available at www.nyc.gov.
7. In the academic sphere, the expression 'glocal' is alternatively attributed to Erik Swyngedouw (1997) or Roland Robertson (1994).
8. As described on the Forum's goal statement at http://glocalforum.flyer.it/.
9. ARUP and C40, *Climate Action in Megacities*, launched as part of the C40 summit in São Paulo, Brazil, 1 June 2011, available at www.arup.com/Publications/Climate_Action_in_Megacities.aspx.
10. City of Copenhagen press release, "Mayors Close the Copenhagen Climate Summit," 16 December 2009, available at www.kk.dk/Nyheder/2009/December/ClimateSummitClosingEvent.aspx.

11. Dan Hoornweg, "Cities Act as Talks Go On," *World Bank Blog*, 20 June 2012, as posted in http://blogs.worldbank.org/sustainablecities/cities-act-as-talks-go-on.

12. On the early funding of the Climate Leadership Group see www.london.gov.uk/media/press_releases_mayoral/mayor-brings-together-major-cities-take-lead-climate-change.

13. Chairs Communiqué of the 4th Meeting of the OECD Roundtable for Mayors and Ministers, Chicago, 8 March 2012, p. 1, available at www.oecd.org/urban/roundtable/49893305.pdf.

14. Chairs Communiqué of the 4th Meeting of the OECD Roundtable for Mayors and Ministers, Chicago, 8 March 2012, p. 1, available at www.oecd.org/urban/roundtable/49893305.pdf.

15. See, respectively, http://citiesalliance.org and http://sustainablecities.net/.

16. See www.london.gov.uk/mayor-davos-january-2010.

17. Reported in Tara DePorte, "NYC's Mayor Bloomberg Points His Finger at National Governments for Lack of Action," *Human Impact Institute Blog*, 20 June 2012, available at http://blog.humanimpactsinstitute.org/2012/06/nyc.

18. "Hiroshima Appeal" declaration, issued on the 6th General Conference of Mayors for Peace Commemorating the 60th Anniversary of the Atomic Bombings, 6 August 2005, available at www.mayorsforpeace.org/english/activities/meeting/6th/hiroshima_appeal_en.pdf.

19. The idea of "paradiplomacy" as shorthand for "parallel diplomacy" underpins processes of internationalisation of subnational authorities that run collaterally to, but not necessarily in agreement with, traditional state diplomacy. This is, for instance, the case of the early days of the internationalisation of the U.S. Conference of Mayors or the initial municipal efforts towards city-led peacebuilding in the Middle East. On paradiploamcy see Aldecoa and Keating (1999).

20. For a discussion of this limit in the Western liberal view of responsibility see Ainley (2012).

21. "Governing the Metropolis" roundtable, New Cities Summit, Paris, 14 May 2012. Full transcript and video of the talk is available at www.newcities foundation.org/index.php/events/new-cities-summit/new-cities-summit-2012/.

5 Globalization, Governance, and Renaturing the Industrial City
Chicago, IL, and Seattle, WA

Nik Janos and Corina McKendry

Global economic and environmental crises are colliding in the major cities of the global North, with important implications for social justice and environmental sustainability. On the one hand, deindustrialization and globalization have exacerbated inequality and forced city leaders to find new ways to compete for the mobile capital and skilled labor of the postindustrial economy, pressures that have been heightened by the onset of global recession. On the other, cities are increasingly expected to take leadership roles in addressing climate change and other global environmental problems. In the confluence of these two pressures, cities have become prime sites of the production of new social and environmental spaces.

The production of these new socio-ecological spaces can be seen particularly clearly in the renaturing of the increasingly peripheral industrial areas of globalizing cities. As industry loses its importance as a prime driver of the urban economy, city leaders are striving to find new ways to create value and promote capital accumulation in industrial and formerly industrial sites. One way this is being done is by cleaning up and renaturing heavily impacted industrial spaces through the rehabilitation of wetlands, the construction of natural amenities (hiking trails, environmental centers, etc.), and the creation of wildlife habitat. Though the reimagining of industrial urban spaces as places of nature may have real environmental benefits, we argue that the renaturing of the city needs to be understood as part of a broader reconfiguration of the capital-city relationship in the globalized economy. Furthermore, though the renaturing of the industrial city has the potential to reconcile long-standing tensions between nature, justice, and capital, it may also serve to further exacerbate unequal social and ecological development in the global city.

CITIES, NATURE, AND ENVIRONMENTAL JUSTICE

Since at least the industrial revolution, the relationship between cities and nature has been shaped by cities' relationships to the global economy. Until quite recently, the pollution, disease, and grime that defined industrial cities established them in the public imagination as the antithesis of nature, and for at least a century, urban planning was focused on separating people from the environmental ills of the industrial city (i.e., Howard [1902] 1965). The public health movement in the late 1800s and the environmental movement and improved regulation on pollution in the middle of the 20th century alleviated many of the most egregious environmental problems of the industrial city. However, the idea that nature is "out there" in the wilderness and that the city is inherently "unnatural" remained deeply embedded in the public mind, particularly in the preservationist strand of U.S. environmentalism (Cronon 1996)

In the past 15 years, this has begun to change. Many are pointing out that city dwellers in wealthy countries often have smaller ecological footprints than their rural and suburban counterparts (Owen 2004; Sanders 2010; Glaeser 2011), and political leaders from mayors' offices to the United Nations have argued that moves towards improved environmental sustainability by city governments is going to be an important part of efforts to mitigate climate change and other global environmental problems (United Nations Centre for Human Settlements 1998; City of Chicago 2008; City of Seattle 2011a; UN-HABITAT 2011). As the "greening" of cities has become increasingly ubiquitous, some even argue that proclaiming a commitment to sustainability has become a requisite of good urban governance (Gibbs, Jonas, and While 2002). Indeed, in a notable change from the post–World War II Keynesian decades of environmental regulation that focused on national governments, cities are now seen as key spaces of global environmental governance.

As cities work to reduce greenhouse gas emissions, enhance green spaces, and promote themselves as environmental leaders, interesting contradictions are emerging among the renaturing of urban spaces, deindustrialization, and environmental justice. Though the poor have long borne the brunt of industrial pollution (see Engels [1845] 2006), environmental justice advocates have highlighted the maldistribution of the dirty side of industrial society on poor communities, particularly poor communities of color, in the United States (Bullard, Mohai, Saha, and Wright 2007). As cities of the global North deindustrialize, interesting questions regarding the distribution of the environmental ills of industry emerge. Deindustrialization may remove many sources of industrial pollution,[1] creating an opportunity to soften some of the most egregious impacts of environmental injustice. However, whether the removal of some of these environmental "bads" addresses the broader issues of inequity that is at the heart of calls for environmental justice is by no means clear. While eliminating some sources of pollution, deindustrialization also causes job loss among working class communities, and the renaturing of formerly industrial areas often threatens gentrification and displacement of poorer residents (Checker 2011). Whether the production of new environmental spaces in postindustrial cities furthers inequity or moves global cities to a more "just sustainability" (Agyeman 2005) will depend on recognizing the extent to which city greening may exacerbate uneven environmental development in the postindustrial city. Yet the possibility of doing so is limited by the perceived need of city elites to renature postindustrial spaces in ways that help their city successfully compete in the global economy. Understanding this tension requires an analysis of how city environmentalism fits within the broader political economic transformation that cities have undergone in the era of neoliberal globalization and the ongoing transformation of environmental governance at the local scale.

URBAN GREENING AND GLOBAL ENVIRONMENTAL GOVERNANCE IN THE GLOBALIZED ECONOMY

The role of cities as important players in global environmental governance is intimately connected with their increasing importance as central sites for the establishment of the conditions necessary for capital accumulation. For urban areas in the United States, globalization was marked by two key changes. The first was the relocation of production away from former industrial centers, enabled by the elimination of capital controls and improvements in communication and transportation technology (Spencer et al. 1986; Harvey 1989). The second was national government abrogation of many of the Keynesian tools used to maintain high levels of consumption and employment in the post–World War II era, including significant resource transfers to urban areas (Judd and Ready 1986; Palmer and Sawhill 1986; Gaffkin and Warf 1993). In the face of these changes, city leaders had to find new ways to promote economic development and attract investment. This was a notable shift from the Keynesian era in which national states played the principal role in regulating the fickleness of global capital. Indeed, some argued that the growing importance of cities in the globalizing economy became so pronounced that they largely "replac[ed] states as the basic territorial infrastructure of capitalist development" (Brenner 1998:5).

Concurrently, cities gained increased responsibility for environmental governance. To speak of governance does not simply refer to government agencies, institutions, and actors. Instead, governance refers to the manner and practices by which state and nonstate actors organize the political economic and spatial makeup of the city by means of law, policy, provision of services, and economic development. In the context of the global economy, power has been rescaled in a process by which the national state has "rolled-back" Keynesian era responsibilities and then "rolled-out" (Peck and Tickell 2002) responsibilities to both city ("local") and global institutions and actors such as the World Trade Organization and the North American Free Trade Agreement (Uitermark 2002). We can see evidence of roll-out strategies with regards to environmental governance in the United States. For example, as will be seen in the following sections, Chicago and Seattle illustrate how the Superfund[2] law and the Environmental Protection Agency

(EPA) have given state and nonstate actors responsibility for environmental governance within the framework of a national law. Purcell (2008) argues that what was once a law designed to hold the primary polluters responsible has instead become a way for the national state to pass responsibility to local actors in new public-private partnerships. Environmental governance, therefore, operates through a myriad of scales, spaces, and places, from the supranational, national, and the urban.

Bulkeley and Betsill's work (2003, 2005) on environmental governance looks at horizontal scaling through interurban cooperation on global climate change as a form of multiscalar politics. Typically scaling is seen as ordering, most often as the process of forming scaled hierarchies (Swyngedouw 2004b). Although governance practices at "higher" scales, such as national or global, seem to exert more power in relationship to urban, regional, or local, this is not always the case, as can be seen in the way that cities take on increased governance responsibility (Brenner and Theodore 2002; Peck and Tickell 2002). The circulation of capital significantly shapes the formation of governance practices and structures, yet capital is not the only factor. Nature is increasingly becoming an organizing object of urban governance, though, as we explore in the following case studies, the governance of nature is both shaped by and impacts the circulation of capital in urban areas.

In order to compete for the investment capital and skilled labor of the global economy, city leaders began adopting a series of policies that came to be called urban entrepreneurialism, "in which traditional local boosterism [was] integrated with the use of local governmental powers to try to attract external sources of funding, new direct investments or new employment sources" (Harvey 1989:7). One of the main strategies of urban entrepreneurialism is the remaking of the built environment of the city in such a way as to promote wealth accumulation for property owners and to make the city appealing to investors, business tourists, and the skilled workers of the knowledge economy (Hubbard 1995; Weber 2002; Hackworth 2007).

More specifically, deindustrializing cities worked to reinvent their images and their economies through the creation of amenities aimed at securing the headquarters of global corporations, attracting middle class residents back to the inner cities, enticing conferences and business tourism, and generally "enhance[ing the city's] position in the spatial division of consumption" (Hackworth 2007:67). Efforts were untaken to rebuild and reimagine formerly industrial cities to make them relevant and appealing to the needs of the elite of the postindustrial economy (Peck and Tickell 1994; Rodríguez, Swyngedouw, and Moulaert 2003). Thus began the massive investment in large-scale entrepreneurial prestige projects such as stadiums, convention centers, and new or renovated theaters, museums, and concert halls. Cultural amenities were accompanied by luxury downtown condominiums in hopes of attracting well-to-do residents, particularly the "creative class" (Florida 2002; Storper and Venables 2004) to the transformed urban center.

The renaturing of the city soon became an important aspect of urban entrepreneurialism. Projects of "green urban entrepreneurialism" (McKendry 2011) include the construction of high-profile city center parks, such as Millennium Park in Chicago or the proposed Central Waterfront Plan in Seattle, the reclamation of waterfronts as sites of consumption and recreation, and tree planting and other efforts to increase the literal greenness of the city. Like renovated theaters and luxury condominiums, the physical greening of urban areas strives to appeal to the mobile skilled labor of the postindustrial economy by providing the lifestyle and amenities desired by this population. City leaders tended to defend such efforts by the economic benefits they would provide to the city more than for the environmental benefits of increased green space and natural amenities themselves (McKendry 2012).

Meanwhile, the federal government was pressing local decision makers to clean up and renature postindustrial spaces under the auspices of the Superfund law. The original mandate of Superfund came at the tail end of the "environmental Keynesian decade" (1970s), just weeks before Ronald Reagan became president (Purcell 2008:136). However, the governance process that emerged over the following decades followed the broader trend of the rescaling of environmental governance. Rather than the federal government taking over these toxic spaces, Superfund has created a matrix of responsibility, shared between government agencies (local, state, federal), responsible parties, and citizens at large. In turn, this allows cities to launch green urban entrepreneurial initiatives in these spaces, their environmental mandates being used to reimagine polluted industrial areas as sites of nature with the potential to promote capital accumulation. This has significant implications for the people living in such areas, including the risk of gentrification. However, the inclusion of local residents in this rescaling of environmental governance also opens the door for citizens to demand a say in the renaturing process. As such, in the confluence of the pressures of globalized capital and the rescaling national environmental regulation, the potential for participatory urban environmental governance has emerged. Whether such practices will create more just and sustainable socio-ecological relations in areas that have been scarred by industrialization is, however, by no means guaranteed.

CASE STUDIES: CHICAGO, IL, AND SEATTLE, WA

Chicago and Seattle are two major cities that have used urban greening to help weather the transition to the postindustrial economy, and have done so quite successfully. They have been particularly successful at using green urban entrepreneurialism and their commitment to urban sustainability more broadly as part of their postindustrial "branding" (Greenberg 2008; Pasotti 2009). Mayors of both cities have been very visible in their efforts to be leaders in urban sustainability, with Chicago's Richard M. Daly (mayor from 1989 to 2011) frequently proclaiming his goal of making Chicago the greenest city in the country and Seattle's Greg Nickels (mayor from 2002 to 2010) presided over the branding of the city as "metronatural," proclaiming October 20, 2006 "Metronatural Day."[3] With a long list of environmental accomplishments, both cities rank high on the myriad lists of the country's greenest cities (e.g., Alter 2008; Sanders 2010). In 2007, Chicago was called "the green star by which aspiring cities sail" (Schneider 2006). In 2011, Seattle was named greenest city in the United States by the city of Växjö, Sweden, on the basis of information from ICLEI—Local Governments for Sustainability (City of Seattle, 2011b). The success with which both cities have worked to transform themselves as cities of nature is closely connected to their successful engagement with the postindustrial knowledge economy. Seattle and Chicago both boast a strong presence of skilled, high-tech workers, business headquarters and executives, and a lifestyle that appeals to the highly coveted global creative class. Both cities have worked successfully to market their natural amenities as part of the desirable lifestyle opportunities provided by the city.

Despite their successes as leaders in urban environmental governance and renaturing of their urban cores, Seattle and Chicago also have areas that have been severely degraded by decades of heavy industry that have been less successfully transformed. In both cases, these areas include ecologically significant waterways, high concentrations of low-income residents, and ongoing, though greatly diminished, industrial activity. As such, leaders in both cities are trying to figure out how to transform these areas in a way that incorporates them into the city's broader economic development goals while wrestling with different demands for social and environmental justice and environmental protection. In Seattle, the Duwamish River Cleanup Coalition is working within the Superfund governance structure, but with its own agenda, to push for a participatory and inclusive renaturing of the Duwamish River Valley. In Chicago's Calumet region, rehabilitation of wetlands is being accompanied by entrepreneurial efforts to create spaces of consumption in renatured industrial areas. Yet these efforts sit uneasily with initiatives to attract more heavy industry to the region, and the classic tension between jobs and the environment complicates questions of socio-ecological justice.

Duwamish River Valley, Seattle

Arguably, the two most prominent environmental issues in Seattle are the plight of salmon and the pollution of the Duwamish River Valley. The Duwamish River Valley is the site of the largest and oldest concentration of manufacturing and industry in Seattle. Home to the Port of Seattle, a massive Boeing airline manufacturing plant, and a myriad of other industries, the lower Duwamish River is extremely polluted. The area is also home to some of Seattle's poorest and ethnically and racially diverse residents. The Duwamish River has a storied history—the home of Duwamish tribe, the tribe of Chief Seathl who the Euro-American founders of Seattle used as their inspiration for the name of the city—and the area is the most heavily transformed environment in all of Seattle. Over the past century and a half, the Duwamish River has been merged with the Cedar River and its once meandering section that flows into Elliot Bay was straightened to allow water vessels easy passage.

The creation of the Duwamish Waterway and the rerouting of the Cedar River into Lake Washington was one of the largest such socio-ecological transformation projects. The Duwamish Waterway project straightened the Duwamish/Green River as it approached its mouth at Elliot Bay. South Seattle and Harbor Island were created from the terraformed hills of Seattle. The Duwamish Waterway would provide the home for the Port of Seattle and the industrial center of the Puget Sound. This river system also included the Black River, the Cedar River, and the Green River, all historically containing heavy salmon runs. In the 20th century, horizontal expansion transformed the banks of the other rivers and the forests that surround Seattle into new suburbs and edge cities, home for middle-class residents and new capitalist enterprises such as Microsoft.

In 1999, Seattle, along with Portland, Oregon, became the first urban area to have a threatened species listing under the Endangered Species Act. National Oceanic and Atmospheric Administration, a subdepartment of the Department of Commerce, issued a threatened species listing for Chinook salmon in the Puget Sound, including the rivers that flow through Seattle. In rivers and watersheds up and down the West coast, salmon species were on the verge of extinction, and in some 40% of their historic spawning rivers they are extinct (Lichatowich 1999). Newspapers highlighted the numerous groups that would be affected by the listing: commercial timber companies, owners of small timber stands, farmers, dairy farmers, developers, and urban and suburban dwellers (Dobrovolny 1999:2). Urban development was now seen as a major contributor to the decline in Puget Sound salmon. The Duwamish and Green River system was listed as a site of concern.

In 2001, salmon and Superfund made their confluence in the Duwamish Valley. The heavy concentration of industry has polluted the water, soil, and sediment with polychlorinated biphenyls (PCBs), polyaromatic hydrocarbons, mercury, phthalates as well as the numerous sewer overflows that drain untreated sewage into the river (Purcell 2008). In response, the EPA declared a five-and-a-half-mile stretch of the river from the Harbor Island to the neighborhoods of South Park and Georgetown a Superfund site. Superfund regulation requires that the entities primarily responsible for causing the pollution must take responsibility to clean it up. In the Duwamish River Superfund site, the EPA and the Washington State Department of Ecology (typically called "Ecology") are the joint oversight agencies. The actual responsibility for cleanup has gone to a private-public entity called the

Lower Duwamish Waterway Group (LDWG), which was originally formed as a voluntary study group in 2000 and comprises four entities: The Boeing Company, the City of Seattle, King County, and the Port of Seattle. These four entities were identified under the law as the available and remaining "potentially responsible parties" (PRPs) (Purcell 2008).

Since 2001, the Superfund cleanup has progressed in stages. Stage one was the formal listing on the EPA National Priorities List (Superfund list) and in 2002 Ecology's Hazardous Sites Listing. After the LDWG was identified as the PRP, the next phase, which lasted most of the decade, was the conducting of a Remedial Investigation and Risk Assessment. This was essentially a multiyear set of studies to identify the "early action cleanup areas," those areas that present a threat to people and the environment before the whole Superfund area can be cleaned up as well as produce a Feasibility Study. The Final Draft Feasibility Study was presented to EPA, Ecology, and the public on October 15, 2010.

Ten years after the Superfund listing, the first project in the Duwamish River cleanup began in October 2011. The City of Seattle began work on decontaminating Slip 4, a 6.4-acre navigational area on the east bank of the waterway (McGinn 2011). Slip 4 is considered 1 of 5 Superfund "hot spots," which account for over half the chemical contamination of the river (McGinn 2011). The City purchased the land at Slip 4 in order to convert it from industrial use to habitat. Although the City is bearing responsibility for the cleanup of this site, it is working with its partners, King County, Port of Seattle, and Boeing (the PRPs) to prepare clean up on the other hot spots in preparation for the EPA-guided complete cleanup of the entire Duwamish River Superfund. In December 2011, the City released a report indicating that cleanup was ahead of schedule and under budget. The report states,

> The City has been and continues to work closely with EPA and the contractor to ensure there are no significant impacts on Tribal fishing or nearby communities and businesses. The City has also monitored water quality in the slip throughout construction, and the results are good. Construction activities have not affected water quality; no monitoring limits have been exceeded. (City of Seattle 2011c)

The success (or failure) of Slip 4 cleanup can be seen as a barometer of the Superfund cleanup. James Rasmussen, Duwamish River Cleanup Coalition Coordinator, said the decontamination of Slip 4 is "just the beginning of the river cleanup, but a very important step" (McGinn 2011). The EPA released the proposed cleanup plan in early 2013 and is moving into another round of public comments before cleanup begins.

Both the Threatened Species Listing in 1999 and the Superfund listing in 2001 made the Duwamish River Valley a space to reimagine the relationship between city, industry, and nature. Under the Threatened Species Listing and the Superfund law, nature became an organizing focus to re-regulate economic and social conditions in the Duwamish Valley. Long a playground for industry, hence the extreme contamination, the EPA mandate opened up a space for City leaders, industry leaders, as well as inhabitants to offer new ideas and plans for the socio-natural relationships in the Duwamish River. However, each set of actors has a different stake in the space and a different idea of what the Duwamish Valley should become.

The original impetus for the creation of the LDWG was to preempt the EPA Superfund listing in 2000 (Purcell 2008:139). Citing neoliberal ideas of "efficiency" and "cost-effectiveness," LDWG argued that operating without a Superfund listing in a new and nimble public-private partnership was the best way to proceed with the cleanup. At first, the EPA went along. But an agreement between the LDWG, Ecology, the EPA, and trustees, which included the National Oceanic and Atmospheric Administration, U.S. Fish and Wildlife Services, the Muckleshoot Tribe, and the Suquamish Tribe fell apart. As a result, the EPA declared the area a Superfund site in 2001.

In yet another neoliberalized governance practice (Purcell 2008), the EPA/Ecology had the LDWG sign an Administrative Order on Consent in December 2000 and then had the PRPs conduct an investigation and feasibility study for the Lower Duwamish Waterway (Lower Duwamish Waterway Group 2012). Those deemed responsible for the contamination were given responsibility to study its causes, consequences, and cleanup prospects. Despite that the original impetus for the Superfund cleanup came from the federal government, control over the investigation and cleanup shifted to the city and county and businesses (LDWG). The Port of Seattle and the Boeing Corporation were dragged into action and partnered with public agencies that shoulder much of the burden (see aforementioned Slip 4 cleanup example).

The City of Seattle has developed other reasons besides the EPA mandate to cleanup and renature the Duwamish Valley. Council member Richard Conlin has been one of the most outspoken proponents of the renaturing of the Duwamish River. He writes, "Cities thrive when they integrate the vitality of urban life with their natural surroundings. That's why so many of us live here and wouldn't trade our access to Puget Sound, the Olympics, and Mount Rainier for anything" (Conlin 2011). He argues that instead of each business creating an individual environmental plan, the City could "create an Eco-Industrial Park, where environmental responsibility is built into the fabric" (Conlin 2011). For Conlin, the Superfund and heavy pollution in the river create an immense opportunity to make the space the center of sustainability within Seattle. He proposes something dramatic:

> The Duwamish, although it has contaminated sediments, has a relatively clean water column supporting the aforementioned salmon runs and areas of ecological health. It also has two historic residential communities, South Park and Georgetown, a thriving Port that has a strong commitment to environmental stewardship, and many acres of industrial

land that could support many more jobs and sustainable industries. We must stay the course on the Superfund cleanup, and at the same time use it as a way to provide jobs, training, and careers for the people of the adjacent communities, and to develop an environmental infrastructure for new industries. Industries that are part of the 'climate economy', providing green jobs building wind machines, processing local food, recycling wastes by turning them into resources, and creating sustainable products. (Conlin 2011:para 4)

Conlin sees the Duwamish Valley as a space to resolve the tensions between industry, residents, and nature. Seattle Mayor McGinn shares the idea that greening the Duwamish River can resolve the tension and

begin to restore a part of Seattle that needs help to once again provide healthy habitat for fish, birds, and people. We're not just cleaning up contamination in this process, we are also creating new habitats for fish and other wildlife. (McGinn 2011)

Despite the economic changes in the Seattle metropolitan region since the 1970s, the Duwamish River remains an important economic asset to the city. Industry and commerce along the waterway provide 80,000 jobs, contributing 13.5 billion dollars to the economy (Haeck 2011). For City leaders, the renaturing of the Duwamish River represents the best way to protect the environment, protect industry, protect and create jobs, and add value to the city.

Soon after the EPA declared the Superfund site in 2001, residents, community members, and activists inserted themselves into the Superfund governance structure. Within the Superfund law, CERCLA includes language for community involvement, specifically the formation of Community Advisory Groups (Purcell 2008:140). In the Duwamish Valley, a group formed called the Duwamish River Cleanup Coalition (DRCC) and petitioned to be a Community Advisory Group. The EPA accepted. The DRCC, now with nonprofit status, is an inclusive coalition comprising environmental, resident, tribal, environmental justice, and small-business groups (DRCC 2012). The DRCC says that they work

to ensure that the Duwamish River Superfund cleanup not only restores environmental health and protects fishers and families who use the river, but also reflects the priorities, values and will of the people who live and work in the region. (DRCC 2012)

As an official CAG, the group receives funding from the EPA to hire a Technical Advisor to assist in reviewing all cleanup plans and reports. The DRCC has been able to use the small provision within the Superfund law to advocate for the needs of the inhabitants of the Duwamish Valley, those not included in the EPA/Ecology, or the LDWG plans.

For over a decade, the DRCC has worked to make sure the conversation of cleanup is focused on environmental justice, and the needs of salmon and the ecosystem as a whole. Because it is a "coalition of coalitions" (Purcell 2008:144) the DRCC has had to work hard balancing the demands and foci of its myriad of members (Purcell 2008:144). Their vision statement reads:

> It is the vision of DRCC/TAG that South Seattle residents will be able to crab in the river without risks to their family's health, that endangered salmon will be able recover without PCBs or other toxic body burdens, and that the banks of the Duwamish River will be a welcoming and risk-free place for our children and their children to wade, fish and play. (DRCC 2012)

Fostering community involvement and organizing a myriad of voices is one of the DRCC's main objectives. The group has worked inside the Superfund governance structure, rather than as an oppositional movement working on the outside. However, they have not let the EPA/Ecology or the LDWG define the vision of a renatured Duwamish River. In 2009, the DRCC published the *Duwamish Valley Vision Map and Report*. They describe the report as

> an ongoing, comprehensive, community-based future visioning project, which engaged people who live, work or visit the Duwamish Valley through workshops, mapping and interviews. The project compiled over 500 diverse community ideas, concerns, and visions into a comprehensive 'future map,' which includes transportation, housing, recreation, jobs, and habitat restoration. (DRCC 2012)

They designed the participatory visioning process to accomplish three things: "(1) define the existing conditions, (2) conduct a future visioning process, and (3) develop strategies for implementation" (DRCC 2009:16). The DRCC solicited input from a wide array people: residents, business owners, industrial workers, recreational users, youth (teens and children), low-income community members, homeless and transient populations, fishermen and subsistence harvesters, immigrants and non-English speakers, social and community service providers, and environmental stakeholders. A total of 260 people participated in Visioning Workshops. The DRCC also conducted one-on-one interviews with individuals who were not easily reached through the workshops (typically Spanish speakers). Through this participatory visioning process the DRCC was able to produce a vision map that represented design ideas with broad support as well as those more particular to certain sections of participants.

Going into the vision process, the DRCC was aware of the environmental justice and gentrification implications of a renatured and green Duwamish River. They state:

There are even unintended consequences of cleaning up our river that require us to consider how to manage these impacts as we move forward. Will a clean river make our community more attractive and lead to rising housing prices in our neighborhoods? Do we want condos on the shoreline? Will businesses move into or out of our community as a result of the cleanup? If so, where will we work in the future? And how can we prevent being pushed out of our community once we've improved our environment? (DRCC 2009:14)

The DRCC and the Visioning Project represent a desire by residents, small businesses, and concerned citizens to reimagine the Duwamish River as a space for human use and need, the needs of commerce, and the needs of the various plants and animals and ecological system more broadly.

Like the City, the DRCC sees the Duwamish Valley as a space to reconcile the tension between industry, inhabitants, and nature. Differently, they work from a bottom-up approach, however, an approach that delicately threads the line between confrontational politics and working within the Superfund governance structure. Their position at the table is evident in the fact that at the press conference for the launch of the Slip 4 cleanup the head of the DRCC joined Seattle Mayor McGinn and Dennis McLerran, EPA Region 10 Administrator at the podium. The long-term success of the DRCC to implement their comprehensive vision as an actual basis for the renaturing of the Duwamish River is unsure; it is an unfolding story. However, inhabitants and stakeholders of the Duwamish Valley have asserted their right to participate in the renaturing of the Duwamish Valley. Appropriating the tools of the Superfund law, groups like the DRCC have worked hard to produce a vision that meets the needs of the diverse human and nonhuman inhabitants of the Duwamish River Valley.

Calumet, Chicago: Nature and Work in the (Post)industrial City

Widely marketing itself as a world leader in urban greening, Chicago leaders' efforts to renature the city have been particularly successful in the downtown areas. In many ways, Chicago has indeed been transformed from a leading industrial city to a global, postindustrial center of business and consumption (Sassen 2004). Yet this transformation is still struggling to occur in the industrial region of the city and surrounding areas known as the Calumet. Stretching from the southeast side of Chicago around Lake Michigan and into northwestern Indiana, Calumet includes some of the most economically deprived and the most environmentally contaminated parts of the City of Chicago. Calumet has over one hundred acres of Superfund sites, including the 87-acre Lake Calumet Cluster Site, an EPA-designated national priority for cleanup (U.S. Environmental Protection Agency n.d.). Yet Calumet is also a crucial place for nature in the city, holding many acres of wetlands that have survived decades of industrial pollution and home to over a dozen endangered species. In Calumet can be seen the history of Chicago's economy, the role of the environment in the city's economic revitalization efforts, and the ambiguity of the creation of new socio-environmental spaces. Calumet raises important questions about the relationship between work, equity, and the renaturing of the city, and shows the ongoing tension between jobs and the environment, particularly to the extent that the loss of heavy industry—and the loss of jobs and the devastation of communities that accompanied deindustrialization—has itself enabled the improved environment in the area. Unlike Seattle's Duwamish Valley, the efforts to alleviate these tensions through participatory governance have been haphazard at best, and it remains unclear if a balance between people, nature, and the economy will be achieved.

From the opening of the region's first steel mill in 1875 until the last decades of the 20th century, Calumet was one of the country's primary steel-producing regions and a center of U.S. industry. The production of steel inspired other industries that relied on large amounts of heavy, expensive-to-transport steel to locate to the area, such as factories producing railway cars, agricultural machinery, and automobiles (Calumet is still home to a Ford manufacturing plant that was built in the 1920s). At the area's peak, many tens of thousands of people were employed in the factories of the region, and the plentiful jobs drew immigrants from all over the country and the world. Though labor uprisings and racial tensions deeply affected the area, the factory jobs paid well and local communities flourished (Field Museum 2009).

The prevalence of industry in the Calumet brought not only prosperity but also serious environmental contamination. Before the arrival of the steel mills, most of the Calumet consisted of small lakes, rivers, and wetlands, and the area was avoided as too difficult to build on or to navigate. Soon the benefits of the natural geography of the region—easy transportation through the area's waterways, access to the shipping routes of Lake Michigan, and bountiful water for industrial cooling and waste disposal—inspired industrialists to overcome these barriers. Over the course of the decades, factories were built, waterways were dredged, and slag from the steel mills and other pollution transformed much of the area into a toxic waste site (Hood 2010). Chicago was an industrial city, and the value of Calumet was as the city's industrial core. When industry left, however, so did Calumet's perceived value, and the region was left with high unemployment, social dislocation, and the lingering health impacts of the century of industrial pollution (Field Museum 2009).

As Mayor Daley began to actively incorporate urban renaturing into his economic development plans in the early 21st century, attention was slowly turned towards restoring value to the Calumet through the restoration of the natural environment. With unemployment well above Chicago's average, in 2000 the City announced plans to create a Calumet Open Space Reserve and a large environmental education center. Birds would be protected, and degraded wetlands would be restored. Hoping for the economic benefits of local ecotourism, bike lanes would be built to access the reserve from downtown (City of Chicago Department of Planning and Development 2005). Except for the environmental education center, which has been put on hold, most of these efforts were funded principally by the state and the federal government and pushed along by Superfund mandates. Over the past decade, progress has slowly been made on restoring many of the key natural areas of Calumet (Balde 2011; Garcia and Bryne 2011). As hikes and kayaking trips through the area proliferate, Calumet has become valued a site for the consumption of the natural environment.

The change in how Calumet is valued by local officials can be seen in City documents discussing the region. The 1986 Mayor's Task Force on Steel and Southeast Chicago report highlights the advantages of the Calumet area as

> competitively priced land suitable for manufacturing, easy access to key railroad and river transportation arteries, and the proximity of Lake Michigan. . . . several interstate highways . . . and the exceptional variety of manufacturers. . . . The region is also home to a highly skilled workforce that is expert in the trades and crafts required for complex manufacturing. (City of Chicago 1986:11)

Notably, the report bemoans that "the Port Authority's own development plans for Lake Calumet Harbor—once a mainstay of the local manufacturing economy—now emphasize the creation of recreation facilities such as a marina and golf course" (City of Chicago 1986:12). Twenty years later, the description of the area and of its recreational and consumption opportunities is very different, almost unrecognizable. The city's Calumet Open Space Reserve Plan offers a vision of the region wherein

> wandering through the Calumet Open Space Reserve will provide an opportunity different from many other habitat preserves. The journey between the large parcels will take the visitor through Chicago neighborhoods, across 19th century bridges and by state-of-the-art industry. The traveler will have the opportunity to stop at local restaurants, observe ocean-going vessels from around the world and remnants of Chicago's steel making heyday. A complex of bike trails, lanes and routes will be available for the explorers. (City of Chicago Department of Planning and Development 2005:24)

Using the consumption of nature as a driver for economic development is, of course, the crux of green urban entrepreneurialism. In the renaturing of Calumet, the goals of economic growth and attempts at participatory local governance are deeply intertwined. The 32-mile Calumet-Sag trail, for example, is one of the trails envisioned by the Open Space Reserve Plan that is currently underway. The trail, scheduled to open in 2014, will mostly go through lands owned by the Metropolitan Water Reclamation District. It is being funded by local nonprofits, businesses, and governments, and is relying on volunteer labor for much of its construction (Friends of the Calumet-Sag Trail n.d.). It will be easily accessible to over 185,000 people, including many poor and working class neighborhoods. Though also touting its heath and community-building benefits, in promotional materials the first justification used to defend the importance of the trail is its ability to "strengthen local economies" (Calumet-Sag Trail n.d.).

Throughout the region there are a wide variety of nonprofits that are providing environmental education and working with local residents, particularly schoolchildren, to encourage investment in the restoration and protection of the environment of the area. Support from the City has helped many of these groups expand their outreach programs and encourage people from the area to protect and appreciate the nature in their backyard (see http://fieldmuseum.org/explore/department/ecco/ CalumetIsMyBackyard). To the extent that residents have a say in how these projects are developed, a growing space for local environmental governance of the area can be seen.

This potential is limited, however, by skepticism among many low-income and working class residents towards the city's environmental agenda and its role in furthering gentrification. For many, there is little question that the City has focused its greening efforts on those parts of the city that are next in line for gentrification. As such, environmental improvements are often met with distrust as

> community leaders and residents are skeptical of why the City 'all of a sudden' decides to invest in street and sidewalk repairs, park improvements, and city buildings in [their] area. . . . Their communities have always needed and desired these improvements, but feel the City does not attend to them until the area is on the verge of gentrification. (Nyden, Edlynn, and Davis 2006:13)

In the neighborhoods such as those in the Calumet that were built on heavy industry, this distrust is deepened by decades of the City ignoring community concerns about the health impacts of environmental contamination in the area, particularly air pollution (Field Museum 2009).

As such, there are significant tensions within the renaturing of the Calumet. In some ways, it offers an example of how city, state, and national governments can work together with local community groups and environmentalists to heal some of the wounds that have been inflicted upon the natural world by industrial society. Then again, there is fear that if the area is too successfully transformed it will lead to gentrification and displacement of long-time residents. Adding to the ambivalence of the transformation, it is generally agreed that the renaturing of Calumet would have been inconceivable without the collapse of the region's industry (city sustainability staff member, personal communication, May 20, 2010). While generating an opportunity to reclaim wetlands, restore wildlife habitat, and create environmental recreation and learning centers, the collapse of industry in Calumet also devastated the working class communities of south Chicago, communities that are still suffering from high unemployment and its accompanying set of social problems. Though some attempts have been made by the city to create "green collar jobs" doing wetland restoration in the area, there is little evidence that these will be able to adequately make up for this loss.

Adding yet another set of social and environmental contradictions, even while it tries to create value through renaturing, the City is continuing efforts to reestablish industry in the Calumet. Harking back to the language of earlier decades, the City is again promoting the area's extensive availability of affordable industrial land and easy access to rail, water, and road transportation. Promises of tax exemptions and investment credits for industries that locate in the Calumet are also being offered (City of Chicago 2004). The results of these efforts have included new plans for a cement plant, expansion of a BP oil refinery, and a commercial composting center in the area. Each of these industries promises to create thousands of construction jobs and up to a few hundred permanent positions. Each has also promised that state-of-the-art pollution control technology will limit its impact on nearby neighborhoods (Lydersen 2011a, 2011b).

Despite reassurances from industry, community concern regarding increases in pollution has accompanied these proposals. Though some people are welcoming the jobs, hundreds of other people have turned up at hearings to express their concerns about the environmental burden these industries may put on communities already disproportionately exposed to environmental hazards (Salazar 2010; Lydersen 2011a, 2011c). Whether local resident concerns will influence the approval of these plans, and how concerns about increased environmental health burdens and impacts on the local environment will be balanced by other residents' and local political leaders' focus on job creation, remains to be seen.

Though many individuals and organizations are involved in different aspects of the greening of the Calumet, no clear, unified vision for the region has emerged. Though the City clearly sees the renaturing of the area as holding potential for furthering its green entrepreneurial agenda, the pressure to secure growth in the region has also led City leaders to continue to pursue more traditional smokestack-chasing activities. Local residents are likewise divided, some are welcoming a cleaner environment but concerned about gentrification. Others welcome the jobs the new industry will bring while others are fighting the new industries in the name of environmental justice. In the crux of these tensions, it seems unlikely that the future of the region will be one that balances the needs for community cohesion, economic growth, and environmental restoration.

CONCLUSION: NATURE, INDUSTRY, AND JUSTICE IN PERIPHERAL URBAN SPACES

The governance of urban areas has changed with the move towards globalization on one hand and the attempted renaturing of the city on the other. In embracing green urban entrepreneurialism, nature has been explicitly reincorporated into the urban fabric of postindustrial cities. As is typical with urban entrepreneurialism more broadly, however, most of these efforts have focused on the areas of elite consumption—improved parks, beautified downtowns, enhanced recreation opportunities. Yet the flip side of the postindustrial success of greening cities has been the transformation of urban spaces that have been severely damaged by decades of heavy industry. These spaces tend to be less conducive to elite consumption opportunities than downtown, have legacies of environmental contamination, and are home to working class and poor communities that have benefitted little from the emergence of the service economy. Because of their less privileged relationship to the global economy, these places have not been transformed as rapidly or as thoroughly as the areas of the city that are seen as most crucial to creating a postindustrial regime of accumulation.

No longer a primary source of accumulation through industrial activity, city leaders are working to find ways to create value in these spaces through the reintroduction of nature. Because the process of renaturing is less complete, more complicated, and more contentious than the greening of urban cores, these poor, industrial, and deindustrializing parts of the city offer particular insight into the way that nature is increasingly a part of the reconfiguration of capital-city relations in the global economy. Further, these spaces become areas where new urban environmental governance practices are rolled out. In both Chicago and Seattle, Superfund law is being used to push responsibility to new public-private partnerships. In the case of Seattle, though much less so in Chicago, inhabitants and nonstate stakeholders are using these new practices to assert their vision of renatured urban spaces. Lastly, both cases illustrate the social and environmental limitations of green entrepreneurialism and the new practices of urban environmental governance. Decision makers' goal of balancing jobs and economic concerns on one hand with the needs and desires of the poorest and most vulnerable inhabitants on the other, impacts the speed, and the attention given to environmental justice, with which these renaturing projects are implemented.

The attempted renaturing of the industrial areas of the city is complicated for a number of reasons. First, because these areas are unlikely to become centers of postindustrial consumption, the creation of natural amenities, though certainly being undertaken in these areas, is unlikely to create the same level of financial returns as green amenities in more central areas, making investment in them riskier; yet the need to find new ways to create value in these areas is even more pressing. Second, to the extent that industry remains in these areas, the long-standing tension between environmental and economic goals may emerge. Finally, because of the demographic realities of many of these areas, in these spaces questions of social and environmental justice, always prevalent in the neoliberalization of urban areas, are heightened. In particular, concerns emerge that the renaturing of these areas may, as has happened in the core areas of many postindustrial cities, lead to gentrification and displacement. Conversely, the potential that they hold is for the production of new socio-ecological spaces that can create value and promote capital accumulation while protecting local communities and healing some of the damage to nature caused by centuries of industrial misuse and neglect.

NOTES

1. Though they may be exported to countries with weaker environmental standards, an important issue that is beyond the scope of this chapter.
2. The formal name for Superfund is the Comprehensive Environmental Response, Compensation, and Liability Act of 1980 (CERCLA).
3. The City of Seattle defines *metronatural*—adj. as 1: having the characteristics of a world-class metropolis within wild, beautiful, natural surroundings 2: a blending of clear skies and expansive water with a fast paced city life—n. 3: one who respects the environment and lives a balanced lifestyle of urban and natural experiences 4: Seattle.

6 The International Activities of Canadian Cities

Are Canadian Cities Challenging the Gatekeeper Position of the Federal Executive in International Affairs?

Ian Madison and Emmanuel Brunet-Jailly

In November 1999, Mel Lastman, then mayor of Toronto, suggested that Toronto should become the eleventh province of Canada. Canadians were shocked! Yet the changing relationship between federal states and their subnational governments has been a central theme on the research agenda of political scientists for the past several years, who have primarily focused on how globalization processes transform the world economy, threaten state entities, limit sovereignty and empower, in many varied ways, 'World Cities' (Geddes 1949; Hall 1966; Cohen 1981; Sassen 1991; Taylor 2005). This debate is animated by two key themes. First, scholars have focused on the decline of the Westphalian order, which had inaugurated the modern European State system in 1648, arguing that the emergence of new social actors and polities both challenge and perforate the unique role of the nation state in the international system.[1] Second, scholars have explored the changing relationships between politics and market forces as a characteristic of new political orders: trans-border flows of goods, capital, information, and skilled workers create 'spaces of flows' that supersede 'spaces of places.' The bargaining capacity of cities is tested within traditional intergovernmental relations because of their increasingly visible activities in the international market place (Savitch and Kantour 2002); hence new questions such as '*whose city is it*' have emerged (Sassen 1996) underlining tensions and power struggles between 'spaces of flows' and 'spaces of places.'

The Westphalian state system suggests a hierarchy of political authority within which loyalty, identity, and functions of government develop into a territorial state that is an all-purpose organization; that is, all functional jurisdictions are grounded into the same territory. The Westphalian state system also suggests that central/federal executives are the legally enshrined authorities that enforce domination and control of all international and intergovernmental relations. In the Westphalian state system, the executive function (i.e., not legislative or judiciary) is the "statutory gatekeeper" of all international relations. Indeed, for instance, in the British and Canadian traditions because parliament is omnipotent it delegates by statutes specific functions to the executive (government). This, indeed, suggests that cities would have no legal ground to act internationally.

For the last decade, scholarly debates about the nature of the relationship among different levels of government (federal, state/provincial and local) and the rest of the world have hypothesized challenges to the sovereignty of the territorially demarcated nation-state characteristic of the Westphalian order. First, the Westphalian order has been called into question (Valaskakis 2000) because the dominant role of the state seems to be undermined by new subnational and international actors and polities that are challenging and perforating the unique role of central states in the international system (Duchacek, Latouche, and Stevenson 1988; Risse-Kappen 1995; Ferguson and Mansbach 1996; Smith, Chatfield, and Pagnucco 1997). Second, transborder flows of goods, capital, information, and skilled people, lead to a logic of "spaces of flows" that supersedes a logic of "spaces of places" (Castells 1996).

Doubts, however, have been raised regarding the extent to which those trends really do challenge sovereignty: First, economic globalization also happened at the turn of last century (Krasner 1999); Second, increased government activity and sovereign control parallels economic internationalization (Krasner 1978); Third, today's national political leaders have more choice and are the emerging winners (Krasner 1999), and; fourth, the growing transnational embeddedness of the economy does not destabilize the nation-states.

This foregoing debate, however, concentrates on external variables, which look at how broad changes permeate state systems. The questions raised by this scholarship are for instance: Are we the observers of a process of "debordering the world of states?" (Albert and Brock 1996). In other words, this debate has been ignoring the changes in the statutory allocations of executive functions that are at the core of the Westphalian state system: specifically, the gatekeeper functions organizing the domination and control of international and intergovernmental relations in classic Westphalian state systems.

However the legal grounding for such change is absent from the literature: For instance, the research carried out by the Globalization and World Cities Research Network (GaWC) at Loughborough University in the United Kingdom, which classifies cities as Alpha, Beta, and Gamma, focuses on cities' worldwide economic linkages in key service industries (accounting, finance, marketing, and law)—not their legal or constitutional capacity to act internationally. Similarly, a most comprehensive ranking, the *Global Cities Index* of the Chicago Council on Global Affairs administered by A.T. Kearney consulting and Foreign Affairs, which since 2008 ranks cities according to global influence, does not discuss the legal ground for cities international activities.

This research project, contrary to this literature, investigates the gatekeeper role of the executive, looking particularly at the statutory delegation of power, and specific dominant functions of the executive in domestic intergovernmental and international affairs in Canada. With Krasner (1999) this research hypothesizes that sovereignty is a two-dimensional concept, which links territory to government and makes the state, not the city, the only subject of the international system. It seeks to develop the argument that the critical analysis of the link between territory and the statutory executive function of central government best explains the changing nature of the relationship among federal states and between their subnational government levels. This is because new intergovernmental and international relations are the result of fundamental transformation of the formal statutory delegation of power of the executives of each level of governments and concurrent specific functional roles.

More specifically, the chapter reports on findings that address the following research question: Have evolving statutes in Canada weakened the federal gatekeeper position in favor of lower level governments; as a result of overlapping, cooperative, and increasingly segmented functional lines that affect domestic and international and intergovernmental relations, (Canadian) cities are more easily able to respond to globalization pressures to develop economically oriented international activities (Leitner and Sheppard 2002), to act internationally according to their specific needs (Mayer 1992; Peck and Tickell 1994) and specialization (Begg 1999), and therefore are able to channel social and economic, as well as core and intraregional claims (Keating 1995; Sassen 2001). In sum, are cities independently active internationally? To address those questions (1) the Canadian statutory functions of federal executives, (2) the statutory functions of subnational governments (Provinces); (3) the statutory protection of subnational governments rights and policy preferences in matters of domestic intergovernmental and international affairs are the focus of this research.

RESEARCH QUESTIONS

The key indicators in this study are ranked by order of importance with regard to the strength of the national gatekeeper position. The first indicator sets the general principles of foreign policy conduct and indicates explicitly the strength and breadth of the national executive's role.

The constitutional and legal rules of a state are a first area of research that helps us to evaluate the strength of the gatekeeper position of a federal national executive. These rules can be analyzed with respect to the following elements:

What is the overall rule regarding the overall responsibility of foreign policy?

Who has the right to make treaties?

Which level of government and which departments have been assigned the general competences to conduct foreign policy?

Does the constitution or other laws limit the foreign policy domain to national executives, or, are there rights specific to subnational governments, particularly cities?

Do the foreign competences of national governments cover all policy fields?

This first set of questions should be combined with the following second element—the legal norms that explicitly define the rights of subnational units to conduct foreign activities, so as to form a matrix that details the conduct of foreign affairs as it is explicitly defined, and what ambiguity and leeway exists in each specific political system. This allows us to evaluate the strength of the gatekeeper position of the national executive in relation to the autonomous foreign activities of subnational governments:

How important is the role of subnational actors, particularly cities, in the processes of preference building and implementation of international agreements?

Are there rights that codify the information and formal consultation roles of subnational governments, particularly cities, in international negotiations?

How much power do subnational governments, particularly cities, have in ratification processes?

The cooperative approach is a third dimension, which indicates how restricted the gatekeeper position in its conduct of foreign negotiation:

Do subnational government units, particularly cities, conduct their own foreign policy?

Is this an explicit or implicit right?

What is the scope of the autonomy of subnational foreign policy?

What means do national governments have to control subnational/cities' foreign activities?

The fourth dimension combines the elements that may least undermine the national gatekeeper position: These are the rights to get information during a negotiation process that might restrict the strategic use of the gatekeeper position, but are limited because there exist no direct contact between subnational and foreign actors. Similarly, when national executives consult with subnational actors before engaging negotiations with foreign actors, or when subnational actors mobilize in the lower chamber (senate) because they have a stake in the ratification process, the national gatekeeper position may be restricted because of the lack of direct relations between noncentral and international actors, but is not undermined. Such restrictions may actually serve national executives in their negotiations strategically. Game theorists, for instance, have shown that those negotiators who can bind themselves internally gain bargaining power in the external sphere (Aspinwall and Schneider 2001):

Are subnational actors included in national delegations (local public and elected officials)?

Do subnational governments, particularly cities, have a right to be included?

Are those rights codified?

Are there informal agreements that secure their direct participation?

Which roles do subnational members play in the national delegations?

This chapter addresses these four sets of questions in two distinct parts.

The first part of this chapter answers the two first sets of questions: What are the constitutional prerogatives of the Canadian federation regarding international relations, and, what rights do subnational governments have in international matters? In view of the evidence presented in the chapter, I argue that in the Canadian federation there has been no significant evolution of the "gatekeeper" position that would be a clear codified challenge to the international relations role of the federal executive because neither the constitution nor other specific legislation restricts international relations activities of lower government levels.

These findings are complemented by evidence of the varied international activities of the provincial capitals that participated in our surveys (see Appendix 1 and Appendix 2). This is presented in the second part of this chapter, in a section that answers the last two sets of questions: Do subnational governments conduct international relations, what federal control is there of those activities? And, to what extent and for what purpose are subnational governments included in national delegations? The data collected shows that Canadian cities have international activities. However, those activities are within the provincial statutory frameworks that define municipal policy realms. This is particularly interesting today because during the 1990s, most Canadian cities had been given natural person powers, and, the unbounded responsibility for spheres of policy (for instance in Ontario: public utilities, waste management, public highways, transportation system, culture, parks, recreation and heritage, drainage and flood control, parking, economic development services, structures, not covered by the Building Code Act; including fences and signs, and animals [Ministry of Municipal Affairs 2004]), thus, unrestricting the policy capacity of municipalities within those policy spheres. Furthermore, as shown in the last part of this chapter, there are very limited mechanisms of supervision, or either coordination or cooperation of municipal international activism, either at the federal or provincial levels of governments.

1. The Constitutional Prerogatives Regarding International Relations

1.1 What are the constitutional prerogatives of the Canadian federation regarding international relations, and, what rights do subnational governments, particularly cities,[2] have in international and intergovernmental matters?

Early discussion papers on the Constitutional form of the Canadian Federation may be traced to the Durham report of January 31, 1839 (Coupland 1945). Durham in his report lays the ground rules for the responsible government of a United British North America. His recommendations greatly influenced the formulations of the British North American Act of 1867 (BNA). At the time, the issue at stake was to develop an understanding of the reasons that had led the 13 American Colonies to secede from the British Empire; was it a complete rejection of British sovereignty or a problem of insufficiency of representative government? How should such similar requests in British North America be articulated with the imperatives of British rule?

Durham adopted the doctrine of 'diarchy': He suggested a division of the activities of government into colonial affairs and imperial affairs. He conceded a principle of responsible government to colonial institutions for the domestic life of the colony, and explained:

> If the colonists make bad laws and select improper persons to conduct their affairs, they will generally be the only, always the greatest, sufferers; and, like the people of other countries, they must bear the ills which they bring on themselves, until they choose to apply remedy. . . . The constitution of the form of government—the regulation of foreign relations and of trade with the mother country, the other British Colonies, and foreign nations—and the disposal of public lands are the only points on which the mother country requires control. (Coupland 1945:liii)

Two points of significance should be highlighted: First, responsible government is granted only for colonial affairs, and second, colonial government is exclusive of international relations of any kinds. International relations remain in the realm of interests of the British crown.

The later report of the Québec Conference of October 10, 1864, also works on similar views and enacts those ideas in the proposed division of powers between the federal government (general government) of the Federation of British North American provinces and provincial governments (Local Governments for each of the Canadas and the provinces of Nova Scotia, New Brunswick, and Prince Edward Island [PEI] . . . Newfoundland, the Northwest territory, British Columbia, and Vancouver).[3] It does not discuss international relations, which are to be assumed to be outside of the ambit of either levels of government, either federal or provincial, and it grants provincial legislatures (Local Legislatures) the power 'to make laws respecting the following subjects: municipal institutions.'[4] De facto, the Constitution Act of 1867 defined precisely the ambit of activities of Canadian provinces and also listed the activities of Federal government, leaving to government practice and tradition the practical definition of the federal realm as it evolved in time or because of political necessity. Section 132 of the BNA grants "all powers necessary or proper for performing obligations of Canada or any province thereof, as part of the British Empire and such foreign countries" to the federal government. And thus, in due time, as Canada progressively initiated more international relations, this ambiguity became a contentious issue between the provinces and the federal government. It was addressed in 1937 in a Lord Atkin decision that limits the absolute authority of the federal government in the sphere of international relations by constitutional interpretation, in other words, the federal government cannot encroach upon provincial jurisdiction (Leeson and Vanderelst 1973:1–11, 115–119).

When Constitutional discussions expanded during the late 1970s, and until the adoption of the Constitution Act of 1982, there were divergent positions regarding the formulation of the distribution of powers section of the constitution, while others also debated the necessity to include municipal governments. For instance, the Province of British Columbia's Constitutional Proposals specifically argue for a clearer formulation that would identify "a few central realms of subject matters such as international relations, economics, culture, education, health" and do not mention municipalities voluntarily (Province of British Columbia 1978:83–96). On the contrary, the recommendations of the Federation of Canadian Municipalities Task Force on the constitutional reform, established in January 1979, included four model articles recognizing that "municipal government constitutes a third level of government," that municipalities have "law-making autonomy, which should not be withdrawn or varied by the provincial governments except by the ordinary legal processes and procedures applicable to the amendment of provincial constitution," as well as "fiscal autonomy" and "institutional autonomy" (Federation of Canadian Municipalities [FCM] 1979). In the end, none of these propositions appear in the constitution because, as noted by then Attorney General of Saskatchewan Roy Romanow:

> There are good reasons for continuing provincial responsibility for municipal institutions. They have to do with the diversified nature of Canada. And the need for flexibility, to set up municipal structures that are tailored to the specific needs of each part of the country. (FCM 1979:48)

Hence, from a constitutional and a legalist perspective, the constitutional prerogatives of the Canadian federation regarding the respective roles of federal and subnational governments particularly, municipalities, in international relations are imprecise. However, what is clear is that originally Canadian cities were conceived as administrative units governed by justices of the peace, which very progressively incorporated during the 19th century to govern a small number of local policy issues, such as real estate matters. The Baldwin Act of 1849, which authorized and regulated such corporations, and Section 92 of the British North American Act (BNA) of 1867 clearly express those ideas. These conceptions are premised on very limited international activities.

Today, this interpretation of the Constitution Act, which does not recognize municipalities as an order of government but gives the legislative responsibility to provincial governments to establish the forms of municipalities and of other local governments and to allocate functions to local governments according to provincial needs, is still valid. Provincial legislations on the forms and functions of municipalities, however, vary from one province to another, and have also varied over time. The courts interpret those statuses narrowly. Clearly, in Canada the source of authority of a municipality is either their provincial municipal act or their municipal charter. Rarely do cities such as Calgary or Vancouver, however, have cities charters that grant them specific powers.

However, recent reforms to municipal acts in Alberta (1994), British Columbia (2000 and again 2003), Manitoba (2002), and Ontario (2002 and again 2003) have empowered municipalities by recognizing them as natural persons. Also, these new acts have given them full authority over "spheres" of jurisdiction. Most of these new provincial municipal acts differ from the original Baldwin Act, but none actually challenge the Constitution. What emerges from those reforms is that municipalities across Canada have undergone a profound transformation, particularly in Alberta, British Columbia, Québec, Nova Scotia, and Ontario, where they have gained legal power and autonomy and are also now more complex in their rights and responsibilities and more diverse in their size and functions. Those new institutional frameworks, and the amalgamations of numerous municipalities in Ontario and Québec, however, may now foster greater institutional and functional differentiation that has the potential to increase the capacity municipalities have to develop more international relations. For instance, Toronto developed its first ever policy framework regarding international relations after the amalgamation in 1999.

Hence, in Canada, the Constitution does not limit the foreign policy domain exclusively to national executive agencies. Foreign competencies of the central government cover only the fields that are not provincial responsibilities and concurrently in the policy realm of municipalities. Also, municipalities have seen their legal capacity, and the arenas in which to exercise those powers, expanded. However, does this mean that municipalities have a say in international agreements?

1.2 How important are municipalities, particularly cities in the process of preference building leading to international agreements? Are there rights that codify information and formal consultation roles of subnational governments? How much power do municipalities have in ratification processes?

Most provincial capitals declare having limited relations regarding their international activities with either provincial or federal government officials. Most provincial capitals express surprise at this question. Most declare few if any formal relations with federal or provincial governments regarding international relations. For instance, *Charlottetown, PEI,* answered that there were no formal or informal agreements to ensure the direct or indirect participation of the city of Charlottetown in international matters. City officials say that the city has no role in the process of preference building or implementation of international agreements, nor is it involved in any policy stage of the treaty process (including ratification and implementation). Charlottetown has no role in setting foreign policy. *Charlottetown, PEI,* expressed that the "federal government does not deal with the municipality directly with regards to international activities, nor does the provincial government."

Halifax, NS, on the contrary, stated that informal agreements ensured its participation in international matters, and that the city was given information regarding negotiations, and had in the past and was currently participating to international negotiations in an advisory function, including foreign policy issues. However, the city also noted that it was not formally associated to treaty negotiations and or treaty ratifications.

Iqaluit, NU, also explained that consultations on international matter were very rare events and always informal. City officials, however, noted regular consultations on environmental issues, particularly about effect of global warming on the city. Other issues include site contamination and clean-up requirements related to previously active military operation in its constituency.

Québec City, QC, confirmed similar limited relations with the provincial and federal governments on international matters. City officials, however, mentioned the important role of the Canadian Federation of Municipalities regarding the very participation of Canadian municipal staff to international missions for the development of cooperation with municipalities across the world. *Québec City* is currently involved in Burkina Faso for a project regarding the management of municipal human resources. Moreover, the city maintains close relations with the provincial ministries of immigration, international relations, and revenue. These are mostly informal relations regarding the international activities of the city but include funding relations for specific programs.

Toronto, ON, also recognizes functional relations with either provincial or federal government departments and ministries but acknowledges, as well, that there is no overview of the city international activities by the province. Its officials remarked that this may be difficult due to its noncentralized corporate organization. They point toward Québec City specifically as the opposite centralized model. There are no formal mechanisms to coordinate or consult on any specific issues with either superior levels of government. This, however, does not seem to compromise the coordination of specific activities. The intervention of the city in El Salvador in 2001, for instance, was in partnership with the provincial government. The city, however, notes that such similar partnerships never extend to their participation in any international treaty negotiations. Nor has the participation of the city ever been required. The city is consulted, however, on policy issues that pertain to city policies such as the management of human diversity, or human right issues, or economic development strategies, particularly, regarding hosting major international events. Memorandums of understanding are the legal basis for all its technical partnerships.

Regarding the Olympic games, *Vancouver, BC,* on the contrary benefits from clear and formal agreements. It has formal agreements with both the province of British Columbia and the federal government. Each agreement sets the terms of their mutual participation and obligation in the venture. A multiparty agreement sets the terms between each government placing responsibilities on each level of government but according to negotiated terms. Those terms place *Vancouver, BC,* in a leadership position for the Olympic bid and regarding the organization of the games. Particularly, the City deals directly with the International Olympic Committee and contracted directly with it to host the game. The city also signed information sharing and partnership agreements with Torino, Italy, for its experience in hosting similar games in the past. Vancouver officials, however, note that any other forms of participation to the preparation or signature of international treaties are extremely limited.

Similarly, *Winnipeg, MB,* does not feel limited in its international activities, nor are there any formal mechanisms that require participation of the city in provincial or federal international activities. City officials even note specifically that the provincial government has 'no involvement with the city' regarding international activities.

To sum up, regarding how Canadian municipalities relate to the federal government regarding international activities or relations, such as the implementation or ratification of international agreements, preference building, or the setting of foreign policy, the results indicate that it is a quite limited role. *Toronto, ON,* is sometimes consulted on the request of the province, as part of the province's formal consultation process with the federal government, on international matters that may have an impact on the city. *Québec City, QC,* appears to have a more prominent role, and is often either present, represented, or plays an advisory role in international agreements affecting the city, though this may be due to the city's shared role as capital of an internationally active province. Both *Vancouver, BC,* and *Edmonton,*

AB, indicate that any participatory roles involving international treaties or foreign affairs are either informal (Vancouver) or exist on an initiative-by-initiative basis (Edmonton). For *St John's, NL,* depending on the activity, the city may play an advisory role, though generally this is limited to areas involving information and support.

Also, the relationship between Canadian municipalities and provinces regarding international activities appears to be stronger than that between the federal government, though the nature of such relationships also varies to a large extent from city to city. The municipal involvement of *Vancouver, BC,* is limited to information sharing by the province to the Union of BC Municipalities, which in turn distributes information to its member municipalities. *Calgary, AB,* and *Edmonton, AB,* play larger roles, with Calgary participating with Alberta Immigration and Citizenship, as well as Immigration Canada, for international employment recruitment programs, while Edmonton reports being involved in discussions with provincial authorities leading to formal agreements stipulating roles, responsibilities, governance, and financial commitments. Both *Toronto, ON,* and *Montréal, QC,* as the largest cities in their respective provinces, are involved in provincial consultations regarding international matters that have potential impacts on their municipalities, with Montréal often actively collaborating with Québec's provincial international relations ministry and economic development industry in international activities. *Fredericton, NB,* sees its involvement with the provincial government limited more to ad hoc lobbying for particular outcomes on specific issues that relate to municipal interests. *Halifax, NS,* reports having no formal involvement with the province, but that it is working on increasing the municipal role regarding economic development, through trade missions and ways to increase the profile of the Halifax region for provincial business opportunities and investment attraction. *St John's, NL,* is often a participant in provincially led international trade events. Moreover, between St John's and its twin city of Waterford, Ireland, and the Newfoundland government's memorandum of understanding with the Irish government, there exists some intersection. Previously, for example, the city had a representative on the board of the Ireland Organisation of the provincial government. Indeed, *Whitehorse, YT, Victoria, BC,* and *Regina, SK,* report little to no involvement with their respective provincial governments in international activities.

Hence, despite clear functional differentiations, municipalities have no role in the determination of the terms of international agreements. Does this mean that they have no international activities?

2. The International Relations of Canadian Municipalities

2.1 Do subnational governments, particularly cities, conduct international relations? What federal control is there of those activities? To what extent and for what purpose are subnational governments included in national delegations?

The scope and extent of international activity pursued by provincial capitals and large urban municipalities vary depending on their size. One shared characteristic is the widespread presence of sister city (or twin city) relationships. The roots of these city-to-city networks, called town twinning in Europe, the sister city movement in North America, or the brother city movement in Asia, can be traced back to European municipal reform movements in the aftermath of the Second World War (Saunier 2001). Today, these relationships are based largely on cultural and social understandings of two cities or local government areas predominantly, though not exclusively, from different countries.[5] These formal twinning agreements are usually made by local officials, but occasionally they are also made by ad hoc citizen groups. The nature of sister city relationships varies considerably from one relationship to the next, ranging from preliminary declarations of intention and small-scale cultural exchanges to more formalized student exchange programs and economic partnerships. In Europe, the primary aim of such networks is to contribute to the development of European citizenship in the European Union as well as further European integration by developing joint projects on issues of common interest.[6] In the North American context, sister city relationships focus more on fostering cooperative linkages than building a shared identity. Begun in 1967, the U.S.-based Sister Cities International (SCI) now involves over 2,000 cities in 136 countries around the world.[7] The organization 'strives to build global cooperation at the municipal level, promote cultural understanding, and stimulate economic development.'[8] SCI provides assistance to prospective cities by finding compatible mates, offering technical advice, publishing a newsletter, and holding periodic conferences. In policy terms, this may involve exchanges in environmental technology, urban planning and public administration expertise, university exchanges and international student recruitment, and capacity building for localized conflict resolution.[9] Moreover, such linkages may help improve trade, business connections, investments, tourism activities, and personal contacts (Baycan-Levent, Akgün, and Kundak 2010). Generally SCI encourages agreements to be made with only one city in a given country, that places should be of comparable size and have the wherewithal to become compatible partners, implying shared economic, cultural, ideological, historical, or recreational concerns. However, relationships are also formed between widely dissimilar locations based on humanitarian reasons, facilitating technical or financial aid flows between cities (Zelinsky 1990).

For *Victoria, BC,* the sister city program is primarily aimed towards Asia. Broadly, it seek[s] to showcase Victoria as one of the world's most livable cities, as well as the strengths and opportunities in the local economy. From an economic development perspective, relations with Twin Cities and Friendship Cities endeavor to promote Greater Victoria's tourism, higher education, and technology sectors, leveraging the region's longstanding relationships with cities such as Suzhou, China, and Morioka, Japan.[10]

Sister city relationships in Canada range from small-scale exchanges from cities such as *Yellowknife, NT* (pop. 18,700), and *Iqaluit, NU* (pop. 6,184), and their respective sister cities of Yakutsk, Russia, and Sisimiut, Greenland, to more comprehensive agreements carried out by larger centers. *Toronto, ON,* maintains 9 agreements with international cities through its International Alliance Program (related to sister city programs), dividing them between 'partner cities,' which seek to enhance business links and investment, and 'friendship cities,' which have more ceremonial significance.[11] *Montréal, QC,* maintains 5 formalized sister city relationships, but is currently in various stages of establishing agreements with 17 others, by far the highest number of any Canadian city. *Québec City, QC,* manages sister city agreements with eight cities, ranging from St. Petersburg, Russia, to Ouagadougou, Burkina Faso, and maintains partnerships with 3 more. These agreements and partnerships involve activities ranging from basic informational exchanges to working groups and staff exchanges to teaming on issues such as municipal energy, water, and wastewater treatment or regulation. For example, Québec City is currently involved with Paris and Bordeaux (France), and Namur (Belgium) in exchange training programs for their staff, consisting of cultural exchanges focused on the French language, municipal museums, and schools, as well as policy issues such as water management and the practicalities of participatory democracy. Historical similarities are the main drivers behind the twinning efforts of *Halifax, NS.* The Regional Municipality chose to enter into a sister city agreement with Hakodate, Japan, because both cities share architecturally distinctive star-shaped citadels.[12] Campeche, Mexico, was chosen because like Halifax it is "a capital of a state" and is "a city of similar size to Halifax on or near the coast having rich historical tradition."[13] Norfolk, USA, Halifax's third Sister City, was chosen because like Halifax, its economy "depends heavily on the presence of the Armed Forces, and both cities are very proud of their military history."[14] *Vancouver, BC,* maintains one of the oldest twinning relationships in Canada with Odessa, Ukraine. The cities have been linked since 1944, a result of wartime assistance to the USSR (Zelinsky 1991:5).

Another shared characteristic among cities involved in the survey is the high level of cooperation and involvement with the FCM. The FCM is a civic advocacy group formed in 1937, adopting its current name in 1976. Though it has no formal power, it does have significant ability to influence debate and policy with regard to federal government departments and agencies. In 1987, the FCM established its international office as a major operation; indeed, roughly one third of the 120 permanent staff at the FCM work in the international office, and the office's budget has at times exceeded that of the rest of the organization's operational activities (Stevenson and Gilbert 2005:536). Moreover, the Canadian International Development Agency (CIDA) has on occasion had to depend on the FCM for the implementation of a part of its international cooperation programs related to urban or municipal issues (Stevenson and Gilbert 2005:545). The FCM's international focus revolves around the engagement of elected municipal officials and staff in international cooperation to share relevant knowledge, expertise, and experience with their counterparts overseas. This includes expertise in leadership, management, and administration; equitable delivery of services; diversity management; intergovernmental relations; and association management.[15] Canadian cities currently involved in FCM projects overseas are *Calgary, AB, Montréal, QC, Toronto, ON, Fredericton, NB,* and *St John's, NL.* This has included work to assist international cities following natural disasters (Calgary, Toronto, Montréal), as well as development projects throughout Asia (Fredericton) and Africa (St John's). A current example of FCM's international activities is the Haiti-Canada Municipal Cooperation Project, a cooperative venture between the FCM, the Canadian International Development Agency, and *l'Union des Municipalités du Québec,* which aims to provide strategic assistance for the reconstruction of Haitian municipalities following the devastating 2010 earthquake. Municipal members of the FCM will partner with Haitian counterparts to provide advice and training best practices in order to reestablish basic administrative capacity.[16] Similarly, thirteen Canadian municipalities, funded primarily by CIDA, are currently engaged in local democracy building and economic development initiatives with partner municipalities in Ukraine.[17]

Following these shared characteristics, many Canadian cities are also involved in other international associations. *Vancouver, BC,* has been a member of the International Association for Peace Messenger Cities, a United Nations initiative to "promote peace and understanding between nations," since 1988 and continues to serve on the Association's Executive Board.[18] *Toronto, ON,* is involved in a wide variety of international associations, such as the World Association of the Major Metropolises, the International Union of Local Authorities, and the ICLEI—Local Governments for Sustainability—all of which are concerned with the resolution of urban management issues. Environmental issues and water management are key concerns for Toronto's membership in international organizations such as the C40 Mayors for Climate Protection, the Great Lakes and St. Lawrence Cities Initiative, and the Mayor's Hemispheric Forum. Finally, cross-border business and investment links are the main focus of the city's involvement with the National League of Cities and its association with the U.S. Conference of Mayors. *Montréal, QC,* is also involved in a number of international city associations, such as the United Cities and Local Governments (dedicated to increasing the role of local government in global governance), the International Association of Francophone Mayors, Mayors for Peace (against nuclear weapons), the ICLEI, and is a *Villes de design de l'UNESCO.* Similarly, *Québec City, QC,* is a member of the International Association of Francophone Mayors, the International Association of Educating Cities, as well as member of the Organization of World Heritage Cities. *Halifax, NS, St John's, NL,* and *Calgary, AB,* are members of the World Energy Cities Partnership, dedicated to the exchange of energy industry knowledge and strategies.[19]

Much less apparent is the existence of institutionalized staff structures in Canadian cities dedicated to engaging in international activities. *Québec City, QC,* manages its international activities and 11 city partnerships through its International Relations Commission (CRI). Staffed by 11 personnel plus a commissioner, the CRI focuses on three main policy areas: immigration policies, institutional policies, and economic development policies. This includes promotion of the city as an attractive immigration hub through the offering of housing and language courses for newly arrived immigrants. *Toronto, ON,* organizes its international activities through the City Manager's Office-Strategic and Corporate Policy Division. The Division supports the Mayor in international activities and is responsible for the corporate international relations policy framework, which is currently under review. The Division also manages Toronto's international disaster relief policy and coordinates international technical partnerships, both of which are carried out in close cooperation with the FCM, the main coordinator of Canadian municipal response to international disasters. The Division, along with the city's memberships in its previously mentioned international organizations, also manages Toronto's participation in research projects and professional networks. *Montréal, QC,* divides its international activities between the *Bureau des affaires internationales institutionnelles,* with a staff of five professionals and one director, and the *Equipe de affaires économiques internationales,* staffed by two professionals. Other activities, such as Montréal's membership in international organizations of a specific nature, are dealt with by the relevant city department. For *Vancouver, BC,* institutional staff structures to deal with international activities appear to be created on an ad hoc basis rather than have lasting permanence. These have formed to manage the city's various international events, like the 2010 Winter Olympics, Expo 2010 Shanghai, and Expo 1986 Vancouver, as well as to manage the city's involvement in organizations such as the International Association of Peace Messenger Cities. No other Canadian cities in the survey had an institutionalized staff structure to deal with international activities.

All in all, most provincial capitals engage in international activities, for instance, *Charlottetown, PEI,* is involved in the Maritime Mayors and New England States Committee, and the Southeastern Massachusetts Atlantic Canada Association, and currently manages a twinning with Japanese cities. *Halifax, NS,* is also informally and formally engaged in international activities. It has initiated sister city and twinning agreements with Japanese cities, is active in consultative municipal groups, and participates in informal exchanges. *Iqaluit, NU,* mentioned two sister cities; Sisimiut, Greenland, and Labrador City, Newfoundland. *Vancouver, BC,* is another example of a city that is active internationally; perhaps the best example is its successful bid for the 2010 Olympic games. The city is also regularly invited to consult on its drug policies and drug enforcement. *Yellowknife, NT,* also reports a high level of international activities. Most of those activities focus on circumpolar relations. They are explained by city officials as being necessary due to its geographical position and to the importance of construction, mining, and industrial project in process in its constituency. The city reports being informally involved in negotiations regarding the status of indigenous people with Russia, as well as the negotiation of the Kimberly Agreement, an international protocol on diamond mining. It also consulted with federal officials regarding the impact of diamond mining on the economy of Northwestern Territories. The city is also active in the Association of Winter City Mayors and the Winter City Association that organizes circumpolar groupings and conferences.

Québec City, QC, is very active internationally. An International Affairs Commission manages its international activities. It is staffed with 11 persons and a Commissioner, previously a provincial civil servant lent to the city. The Commission advertises three main orientations: immigration policies, institutional policies, and economic development policies. Policies regarding immigration are designed and implemented with the full support and funding of the Provincial government. They aim to promote the city as an important immigration hub and offer services to new immigrants as well as promoting the positive impact of immigrants on the city and its region. For instance, they organize lodging or language courses for newly arrived immigrants. Also, since its amalgamation in 2002, Québec City's International Commissariat manages 42 pacts, friendship agreements, sister cities, and twining agreements. International cities such as Xi'an, China, Bordeaux, France, or Namur, Belgium, actively develop relations and partnerships with Québec City. These range from basic informational exchanges to working groups, staff exchanges to teaming on issues such as municipal energy, water, and wastewater treatment or policing. For instance, Québec City is currently involved with Paris and Bordeaux (France) and Namur (Belgium) in exchange training programs for their staffs, cultural exchanges regarding the French language, their municipal museums, or schools, but also water policies and the practicalities of participatory democracy. *Québec City* is also the host of the international secretariat of the Organization of the World Heritage Cities[20] and a member of the International Association of Francophone Mayors. Finally, the city also promotes and markets its enterprises internationally. In agreement with the provincial ministry of international relations, the city promotes internationally its usage of information communication technologies in municipal services. Also, it maintains close relations with South American and North American cities in Brazil, Mexico, and Chile on specific economic development issues.

Toronto, ON, is the most active and best organized city in Canada. Since the 1999 amalgamation, the city hall has established a policy framework to guide all its international activities (Hoy 2002). The goal of this framework is to "integrate," "coordinate," and "rationalize" the city's current international activities. This work emerged after a March 24, 1999, recommendation of the Economic Development and Parks Committee to Chief Administrative Officer (CAO), Shirley Hoy, to develop a corporate framework for the international activities of the city. This proposal was adopted by council in its April 11, 12, and 13 decisions and reiterated in a June 26, 2001 resolution. The city's World City Committee reviewed all 37 international partnerships inherited from the amalgamation and set to organize the corporate international activities at the level of the CAO office as part of its Intergovernmental Relations portfolio, with the assistance of the Policy Coordination Team and its various representatives across the municipal departments.

The city defines international activities as

> linkages with international municipal associations, staff membership in international professional organizations, city-to- city alliances, bi-lateral, multi-lateral technical and capacity building partnerships, hosting, presenting and attending international conferences and workshops as well as participating in international research teams and study commissions. International relations are a cross-corporate initiative. Political representatives and staff in the City departments, agencies, boards and commissions assume the role of international ambassadors for the City, as they interact with their colleagues in other cities worldwide. (Hoy 2002:2)

This policy framework sets clear goals for the city. It recommends that the city be positioned as a center for research excellence and knowledge development, a competitor in the global economic marketplace, a city with highly skilled and competent leadership, a compassionate and caring city, and a leading cultural capital.

Those goals have very concrete implications. The city as a center for research excellence leads Toronto to be involved in the resolution of urban management issues in the World Association of Major Metropolises, the International Union of Local Authorities, and the ICLEI. The city also maintains an active working relationship with the World Health Organization through its Healthy City Office. The City is also very active in municipal technical exchange partnerships. This is also part of its goal to promote its Compassionate and Caring City policy. In 2003, it reported 64 such partnerships with cities in the 18 countries of China, Japan, the Netherlands, the United States, Italy, Singapore, Ukraine, Philippines, France, Australia, Mexico, Bolivia, Korea, Botswana, Great Britain, Brazil, Latvia, and South Africa on issues regarding human resource management, training, organizational effectiveness, finance (pensions, debt management, capital borrowing, property tax, user fees) audit, economic development, real estate management, amalgamations, e-government, community services, city planning, transportation, information management, immigration, and settlement and community participation.

For instance, Toronto worked with Istanbul, Turkey, on waste disposal, site preparation, computer services, mapping environmental control, and urban transport; with Lima, Peru, the city brought expertise on emergency services; in Riga, Latvia, and Vilnius, Lithuania, it helped set up a tourism development strategy. Toronto Cares responded to requests to emergencies and crisis situations. It supported the Toronto Fire Department as it supported the New York fire department after the 9/11 tragedy and also mobilized support when Hurricane Mitch hit El Salvador in 2001. The city also participated in research and policy work in the Metropolis Commission of the World Association of Major Metropolises, which focuses on political and administrative governance structures, the participation of civil society in the decision-making process, the coordination between government and agencies, boards and commissions, and municipal services (such as water, wastewater treatment, planning, and public transit).

The City of Toronto as a Competitor in the Global Economic Marketplace brought the city to promote itself through the International Alliance Program, international benchmarking projects, the organization and promotion of key business clusters, trade shows and trade missions, targeted marketing campaigns, business and media editorials, competing for hosting international events and business forums, and the presentation of the economic and quality of life information to the 16 visiting delegations it welcomed in 2003.

Another example of international activism is *Winnipeg, MB,* that has 11 sister city agreements with Setagaya, Japan, Reykjavik, Iceland, Minneapolis, USA, Lviv, Ukraine, Manila, Philippines, Taichung, Taiwan, Kuopio, Finland, Beersheba, Israel, Chengdu, China, Jinju, South Korea, and San Nicolas de los Garza, Mexico. The city is also involved in a partnership with Kampala, Uganda, regarding Kampala's policy initiatives dealing with the HIV/AIDS epidemic. Winnipeg's participation includes the definition of a capacity building strategy, as well as challenges in addressing the epidemic. This work included direct relations with the government of Uganda, international governmental and nongovernmental organizations, the local Makerere University, and The Aid Support Organization.

Hence, the largest Canadian municipalities are very active internationally. All, however, restrain activisms to their specific policy realms. All, nevertheless, describe activities linking them to other municipalities across the world.

2.2 Are the international activities of municipalities a challenge to the gatekeeper position of federal and provincial executives? What means exist for intergovernmental supervision and/or coordination or cooperation regarding international relations among levels of governments?

All provincial level governments report having intergovernmental-international offices, for instance, the provincial government of British Columbia has a 4-staff secretariat for intergovernmental relations that is in charge of BC federal relations, interprovincial relations, and other international relations.[21] Similarly, in Alberta there is a 6-staff department of international and intergovernmental relations, which deals with international relations, Canadian intergovernmental relations, and trade policy and includes the translation bureau.[22] In Ontario, the Ministry of Intergovernmental Affairs with about 20 staff is the most important in the country. Its role is to ensure that Ontario plays "a constructive role in strengthening the Canadian Federation."[23] The international activities of Canadian cities are not included as part of the responsibilities of these offices.

The municipalities surveyed for this research all have small intergovernmental/intergovernmental offices/secretariat, or committees, or both. For instance, the Administrative Transit and Intergovernmental Affairs Committee in *Charlottetown, PEI*, is in charge of liaisons with both the federal and provincial governments regarding transit systems, water waste, taxation issues, or other issues at the discretion of the mayor. Most of their activities focus on transit operations. Similarly, in *Vancouver, BC*, the Greater Vancouver Regional District Board of Directors established an intergovernmental affairs advisory committee, whose focus is sustainable development.[24] In *Halifax, NS*, and *Winnipeg, MB*, there are secretariats for intergovernmental affairs;[25] in *Québec City, QC*, and *Toronto, ON*, the administrative support is much larger, including 11 staff in Québec City, and a large network of municipal employees in Toronto.[26] At the municipal level, there are no offices, secretariat, or committees that actually coordinate systematically municipal international activities to intergovernmental relations.

The emerging picture is that despite the existence of intergovernmental or international coordinating functions, neither the federal government nor provincial governments have in their statutes or as part of their function to either control or coordinate the international activities of municipalities in Canada. One exception to this finding might be the federal invitation to some cities to participate to Team Canada delegations abroad. Actually, most provincial capitals declare having been invited. However, *Charlottetown, PEI, Halifax, NS, and Iqaluit NU*, have never been included in a national delegation, nor do they have any knowledge that their cities' participation has ever been legally required. *Toronto, ON, Vancouver, BC, Winnipeg, MB, and Yellowknife, NT*, have been invited to participate in international trade missions and conventions or international delegations. Winnipeg, however, has turned down participating.

CONCLUSION

The evidence presented in this chapter shows that we cannot argue that in Canada evolving statutes have weakened the federal gatekeeper position in favor of lower level governments. However, the competencies for international relations are not the exclusive responsibility of the federal government; in Canada, they are a shared function of federal, provincial, and local Canadian governments. However, Canadian cities have no say in international treaty negotiation, unless their informal participation to consultations is deemed necessary.

Nevertheless, Canadian cities are active internationally and engage in a multitude of international ventures (justified by economic need, specific need, and specialized needs, and in so doing answer local regional claims), none of which are actually either supervised or coordinated by any systematic mechanisms by federal or provincial governments but in Québec.

Does this mean that Canadian cities could ever be in a position to challenge the statutory gatekeeper position of the federal government in international affairs? No, because according to the constitution and constitutional tradition, municipalities can only act within *the sphere of policies delegated to them by provincial legislatures*. These provincial statuses, which traditionally were prescriptive and limiting, have been reformed recently and greatly enhance the ambit of power of municipalities. Natural person powers within largely defined municipal policy spheres opens wide the door to municipal decision makers.

Ambitious municipal governments are therefore in a position that allows their increased activism internationally and visibility. In this regard, Toronto, Montréal, or Vancouver may be able to take bold initiatives.

NOTES

1. The work of Amen (2011), for instance, presents a wide-ranging review of the literatures available that detail and debate those many discussions on the current rediscovery of the role of cities in the international economy, but also the somewhat limited view from the perspective of the state of those transformations, despite mounting evidence of modest, yet varied and numerous, changes.
2. In this chapter, for rhetorical reasons, the terms *city* or *cities* are used interchangeably with more specific terms such as *municipalities*, *municipal institutions*, and *municipal governments*.
3. Report of the Resolution adopted at a Conference of Delegates from the Provinces of Canada, Nova Scotia, and New Brunswick, and the Colonies of Newfoundland and Prince Edward Island, held at the City of Québec, October 10, 1864, as the Basis of a proposed Confederation of those Provinces and Colonies: www.heritage.nf.ca/law/resolutions.html (accessed December 2013)
4. Report of the Resolution adopted at a Conference of Delegates from the Provinces of Canada, Nova Scotia, and New Brunswick, and the Colonies of Newfoundland and Prince Edward Island, held at the City of Québec, October 10, 1864, as the Basis of a proposed Confederation of those Provinces and Colonies, pp. 8 and 9: www.heritage.nf.ca/law/resolutions.html (accessed November 2003).
5. All of the cities included in the survey maintain sister city relationships, or relationships related to the sister city program. For a list of sister cities, see Appendix 1.
6. European Commission, "Citizenship: Town Twinning," http://eacea.ec.europa.eu/citizenship/funding/2013/selection/selection_action1_11_2013_en.php (accessed April 2013).
7. Sister Cities International, "Fact Sheet," www.sister-cities.org/faq (accessed November, 2013).
8. Sister Cities International, "Mission Statement & Goals," www.sister-cities.org/mission-and-history (accessed May 2013).

9. Benjamin Leffel, "Sino-US Sister City Relations: Subnational Networks and Paradiplomacy," http://american.academia.edu/BenjaminLeffel/Papers/ (accessed December 2013).

10. The City of Victoria, "Twin Cities," www.victoria.ca/EN/main/community/about/twin-cities.html (accessed April 3, 2011).

11. City of Toronto, "International Alliance Program," www.toronto.ca/invest-in-toronto/international-alliance-program.htm (accessed April 8, 2011). Toronto's Partner Cities are Chicago, USA; Chongqing, China; Frankfurt, Germany; and Milan, Italy. Its Friendship Cities are Ho Chi Minh City, Vietnam; Kiev, Ukraine; Quito, Ecuador; Sagamihara, Japan; and Warsaw, Poland.

12. Halifax Regional Municipality, "Media Advisory—" July 4, 2000, www.halifax.ca/mediaroom/pressrelease/pr2000/000704fortressconf.html (accessed April 2013).

13. Halifax Regional Municipality, "Halifax Regional Council—Council Minutes," January 13, 1998, www.halifax.ca/council/Minutes/1998/c980113.pdf (accessed April 21, 2011).

14. Halifax Regional Municipality, "Media Advisory—HRM to Twin with Norfolk, Virginia," August 25, 2006, www.halifax.ca/mediaroom/pressrelease/pr2006/06042HRMtoTwinwithNorfolkVirgina.html (accessed April 21, 2011).

15. Federation of Canadian Municipalities, "Where We Work," www.fcm.ca/home/programs/international.htm (accessed March 2013).

16. FCM, "FCM to Help Provide Basic Services in Haitian Municipalities Hit Hard by 2010 Earthquake," www.fcm.ca/home/programs/international/municipal-cooperation-program-haiti.htm (accessed April 2013).

17. FCM, "Ukraine," www.fcm.ca/home/programs/international/municipal-local-economic-development-ukraine.htm (accessed October 21, 2013).

18. International Association of Peace Messenger Cities, "About the Organization," www.iapmc.org/about-us/ (accessed April 3, 2013).

19. World Energy Cities Partnership, www.energycities.org/ (accessed October 2013).

20. See www.ovpm.org/index.php?newlang=eng.

21. See www.gov.bc.ca/prem/popt/service_plans/srv_pln/prem/intergov_relations_sec.pdf (accessed July 2012); www.gov.bc.ca/igrs/prgs (accessed July 2012); www.gov.bc.ca/bvprd/bc/channel.do?action= ministry&channelID=-8550&navId=NAV_ID_province (accessed July 2012).

22. See http://international.alberta.ca (accessed July 2013).

23. See www.ontario.ca/ministry-intergovernmental-affairs (accessed July 2013).

24. See www.city.vancouver.bc.ca/ctyclerk/cclerk/970527/comm1.htm (accessed April 2012).

25. See www.halifax.ca/IntergovernmentalAffairs/ (accessed July 2013).

26. See www.city.toronto.on.ca/committees/intergovernmental.htm (accessed July 2013).

Appendix 1
Sister City Relationships of Canadian Cities

Table 6a.1

Victoria
- Napier, New Zealand
- Suzhou, China
- Morioka, Japan
- Kharbarovsk, Russia
- Changsha, China (Friendship City Relationship)
- Nanning, China (Friendship City Relationship)

Calgary[1]
- Québec City, Canada
- Jaipur, India
- Naucalpan, Mexico
- Daqing, China
- Daejeon, South Korea
- Phoenix, USA

Regina[2]
- Jinan, China

Vancouver
- Los Angeles, USA
- Guangzhou, China
- Yokohama, Japan
- Edinburgh, UK
- Odessa, Ukraine

Edmonton
- Gatineau, Canada
- Harbin, China
- Nashville, USA
- Wonju, South Korea

Winnipeg[3]
- Setagaya, Japan
- Reykjavik, Iceland
- Minneapolis, USA
- Lviv, Ukraine
- Manila, Philippines
- Taichung, Taiwan
- Kuopio, Finland
- Beersheba, Israel
- Chengdu, China
- Jinju, South Korea
- San Nicolas de los Garza, Mexico

(*Continued*)

Montréal

- Algiers, Algeria
- Amsterdam, Netherlands
- Boston, USA
- Brussels, Belgium
- Casablanca, Morocco
- Bucharest, Romania
- Beersheba, Israel
- Busan, South Korea
- Hiroshima, Japan
- Hanoi, Vietnam
- Lima, Peru
- Lucknow, India
- Lyon, France
- Manila, Philippines
- Managua, Nicaragua
- Milan, Italy
- Paris, France
- Port-au-Prince, Haiti
- Rome, Italy
- San Salvador, El Salvador
- Shanghai, China
- Yerevan, Armenia

Toronto

- Chicago, USA
- Chongqing, China
- Milan, Italy
- Frankfurt, Germany
- Quito, Ecuador
- Ho Chi Minh City, Vietnam
- Sagmihara, Japan
- Warsaw, Poland
- Kiev, Ukraine

Ville de Québec[4]

- Beirut, Lebanon
- Bordeaux, France
- Calgary, Canada
- Namur, Belgium
- Ouagadougou, Burkina Faso
- Paris, France
- St. Petersburg, Russia
- Xi'an, China

Fredericton

- Gangnam-gu, South Korea
- Augusta, USA

Halifax

- Hakodate, Japan
- Campeche, Mexico
- Norfolk, USA

St. John's

- Waterford, Ireland

Whitehorse

- Ushiku, Japan
- Juneau, USA

Yellowknife

- Reno, USA
- Fairbanks, USA
- Yakutsk, Russia

Iqaluit

- Sisimiut, Greenland

[1] Calgary Connect, "Sister City Agreements," Calgary Economic Development, available at www.calgaryeconomicdevelopment.com/about/initiatives/calgaryconnect (accessed April 21, 2011).

[2] "Regina's Sister City Presents Gift," *CBC News*, August 31, 2000 (accessed April 21, 2011).

[3] City of Winnipeg, "Sister City Agreements," *Winnipeg Municipal Manual* (2007), p. 84.

[4] Ville de Quebec, "Ville ouverte sur le monde," available at www.ville.quebec.qc.ca/apropos/portrait/ville_internationale/partenariats.aspx (accessed April 21, 2011).

Appendix 2
Framework for the Interviews

These cities were contacted by e-mail. Each received a letter and questionnaire and were offered to discuss the questionnaire by telephone interview.

Are there specific formal and/or informal agreements that ensure the direct and/or indirect participation of your municipality regarding international matters?

1. What roles, if any, does your municipality play in international matters?

   • It is consulted either before or during the negotiations.
   • It is given information regarding the negotiations.
   • It is present/represented/plays an advisory role.
   • It has delegates present during negotiations.
   • It is among the signatories.
   • Other (please specify)

2. What role, if any, does your municipality have with regards to the process of preference building and implementation of international agreements? Please explain.

3. Are there instances in which your municipality is required to participate either in:

   • The ratification of an international treaty?
   • The implementation of an international treaty? Please explain.
   • They are not involved at any policy stage.

4. What roles does your municipality play in setting foreign policy?

   • It is consulted either before during after the negotiations.
   • It is given information regarding the negotiations.
   • It is a part of the decision-making process.

5. Does your municipality engage in any international activities?
6. Has your municipality ever been included in a national delegation?

7. If yes, are there instances in which your municipality's participation is legally required?

    - What roles does your municipality have within national delegations? Please explain.
    - What limits are set regarding your municipality's involvement? Please explain.

International activities, the federal government and your municipality

8. With regards to international activities, are there instances when the federal government deals directly with your municipality, or an office of your municipality?
9. If yes, are there specific international activities that involve your municipality, or an office of your municipality? Please list.
10. Is your municipality's role formal or informal?
11. With regards to international activities, are there instances when the federal government restricts your participation?

International activities, the provincial government and your municipality

12. With regards to international activities, what is the involvement of your municipality with the provincial government? Please explain.
13. Is your municipality's role formal or informal?
14. With regards to international activities, are there instances when the provincial government restricts your participation?

International activities and your municipality

15. Are there mechanisms of any kind that require consultation of your municipality, or an office of your municipality?
16. If yes, please list those mechanisms.
17. What types of international matters are you most often consulted with regards to? Please explain.

Your municipality's international activities

18. Are there international activities of any kind that lead your municipality to deal directly with other states, cities, provinces, or international bodies?

7 Municipal Bonds and Global Power
Theorizing the Role of Norms

Mark Amen

Cities have played a pivotal role in building, sustaining, and then changing the character of the United States' economic productivity. In each of several distinct stages of growth, from the emergence of a national railway and water system during the 19th century through the rise and decline of the manufacturing era, and now into service-driven forms of growth, local governments issued municipal bonds to finance all kinds of projects, some for the general good and others to satisfy particular private interests. Today, municipal bonds are a critical source of capacity building in the United States. The bond market exceeds $4 trillion (Morgenson 2012) and is comparable to one fourth of the national debt or the current-dollar market value ($15.5 trillion) of the nation's projected output of goods and services in 2012. The municipal bond market is roughly the same size as proposed expenditures ($3.8 trillion) in the fiscal year (FY) 2013 budget. As became evident when the federal government temporarily adopted the Build America Bonds program in 2009, their impact on the global economic position of the United States can be significant. Foreign investors tripled their holdings of municipal bonds, from $29 billion in 2005 to $91 billion in October 2012 (Marlowe 2013). Foreign investors, most of whom do not pay federal incomes taxes, have been willing to enter the municipal bond market even though they do not benefit from the current tax-exempt status municipal bonds have and in all likelihood because they are a safe investment option when global financial markets are volatile. And as documented in a special issue of the journal *Globalizations* (Gills 2010), crisis inheres in unregulated global financial markets. Therefore, foreign ownership of U.S. municipal bonds will most likely continue to grow.

ACCOUNTING FOR BOND MARKETS IN WORLD POLITICS

Globalizing the purchase of U.S. municipal bonds is the latest in a series of developments that blur the former inside/outside divide in interstate relations and theories. At the same time, economic strength has become even more important as a source of state power in the world. Where do Realist and Liberal traditions stand on these claims? Although neorealist accounts (e.g., Waltz 1979; Mearsheimer 2001) rely on systemic/structural factors (i.e., power distributions among states) to explain state behavior/actions in search of survival, they did so by presuming (a) a domestic political hierarchical structure and (b) a national economy as an essential building block of the global economy. These two presumptions provide at least a partial test of realist claims about the sources of state capabilities—that is, the domestic sources of state world power. Furthermore, neorealism relies on rational choice rather than norms analysis to account for the "material security and/or wealth" interests and behavior of states (Finnemore and Sikkink 2001:393). Realists dismiss cities and agency in their explanations by relying so heavily on systemic arrangements and unspecified utilities to account for outcomes in global political economy.

Liberal theory, especially liberal institutionalism, offers more in explaining cities and agency in the global economy. Liberal theory lays out three potential avenues for cities to play a role in world politics—either by importing to them the domestic capacity of the state or as relatively autonomous players in the world economy. First, within the national economic framework, liberals open the state to considering societal interests when adopting trade, monetary, and development policies (Oatley 2012). This opening allows subnational units to affect state capabilities through intergovernmental relations. Second, liberal theory relies on national economic capability. With the emergence of the global economy in the 1970s, liberals claim there is interdependence between the national and the global economy. They see deregulation as a state based practice that is expressed at the national level and extends to the global economy (e.g., Clark 1999; Held et al. 1999). Liberals continue to advise states to "surrender their discretionary economic power to the markets" (Burchill 2009:80). Regime theory or institutional liberalism fits within this linkage. A third avenue emerges with the entry of new players into a heretofore state-based system. Although states have continued to seek mutual gains through free trade between national economies, globalization processes have given other actors (e.g., banks, labor organizations, corporations, cities) additional networks through which to play in worldwide labor, consumer, and financial markets. This avenue requires systemic analysis—one familiar to realists yet not pursued (sufficiently) in liberal theory. Yet liberal theory also falls short when it relies only on changing structural relations (intergovernmental relations and urban autonomy through deregulation) and systemic considerations of financial networks.

In what follows, I make a preliminary attempt to insert what Widmaier and Park refer to as second generation constructivist theorizing, "which stressed the practices employed by agents to promote change" (2012:124). Using this trend within constructivist theorizing (e.g., Finnemore and Sikkink 1998, 2001), I identify norm entrepreneurial behavior in the municipal bond case from the mid-1800s through the 2007 global financial crisis. Some constructivists maintain the inside/outside dichotomy while allowing for an asymmetrical mutual constitution of the domestic and the international (Clark 1999:30–31). I want to go beyond this divide by proposing that "domestic agents" espouse liberal norms that are the basis for the current global economy. As such, these players are global norm entrepreneurs. And their positions on municipal bonds can be generalized to represent their views on all forms and instruments of borrowing and lending because they are rooted in a specific political philosophy of the relation between government and the individual in the economy. I highlight critical points in the case—judicial and legislative decision—where normative and ideational concerns rise to the fore as points of contention, alter outcomes, and thereby reshape the structural parameters of federal-urban, public-private, and domestic-international relations. All levels and divisions of government and the private sector within the United States have woven such a tight-knit and overlapping web of norm-based interactions around municipal bonds that their respective positions are difficult to decipher. Norms become even more important to identify when this mesh of messy relations is further entwined with the blurring of national and global economic life. I begin by identifying what are the norms and interests driving these occasions to see if norms alone "speak for themselves." Or will it be necessary to turn to situation-specific contexts that are more closely related to the current, third constructivist generation's focus on "the affective or sentimental sources of interests and pressures for change" (Widmaier and Park 2012:124) that impact how norms affect municipal bonds? I describe what judicial and legislative "entrepreneurs" claim to be norms guiding the circumstances in which municipal bonds can be issued, what are their legitimate uses, and what is their tax-exempt federal status. The reason for choosing these actions is because institutional status helps to shape the behavior and norms of those engaged in selling and buying municipal bonds. In some instance, norms become apparent by the ways in which various agents ignore or dismiss some pertinent issues—for example, the legitimacy of bond issues for private sector development to promote growth—and result in rulings that privilege some norms over others. I want to use these instances simply to identify what are the norms that may affect financial markets rather than to uncover what are the feelings that affect certain kinds of behaviors in finance (Widmaier, Blyth, and Seabrooke 2007).

What are the norms—expected behaviors about municipal bonds—in question? Within the history of the United States, liberalism has never been effectively challenged by norm entrepreneurs, especially those acting in the municipal bond arena. So variations within the liberal tradition account for norm differences. Hackworth offers a succinct delineation of the tenets of three liberal variants that pose contending constraints on the norm base of economic life in the United States (2007:2–14): (1) classical liberalism—freedom from state involvement in the life of the individual, (2) egalitarian liberalism—autonomy and freedom yet with the government's guarantee of certain basic goods and 'effective demand' in the market to promote the multiplier effect, and (3) neoliberalism—the rejection of egalitarian liberalism with a noninterventionist state only guaranteeing free exchange within the market and for the individual. The widely shared norm differences among these variants of liberalism concerning municipal bonds revolve around three areas: (1) the role of government in growth and general welfare promotion, (2) the autonomy of local government in relation to both state and federal government, and (3) the use of municipal bonds—incurring debt—to promote private sector growth for the benefit of the general welfare. In tracing the history of municipal bonds in the United States, what norms have judges and congressional representatives promoted or rejected in various rulings and legislation? Within the broadly accepted liberal tradition, I look at three norm areas where debates occurred and outcomes tilted behavior: (1) for what can bonds be issued: cities should incur debts to promote the general welfare (including inequities and future generational interests) rather than individual private gain, (2) with what authority do cities issue bonds: cities should be able to issue bonds independent of federal or state regulations (e.g., interest should be immune from federal taxation and state limits), and (3) what is government's role in the economy—the state should allow market forces to guide the economy. I use three Supreme Court decisions as focal points for the case, the first in 1875 about public vs. private gain and the second and third in 1895 and in 1988 about the relative autonomy of cities from federal tax law. I also review Congressional tax legislation in 1894 and the 1980s related to municipal bonds.

DECENTRALIZED FEDERALISM: THE GROWTH OF CITY BORROWING FROM THE 19TH CENTURY TO THE GOLDEN AGE OF GROWTH

Since the creation of the government bond in 17th-century England, its use as a national instrument has been widespread throughout the world. In the United States' decentralized political system, the municipal bond has been an important asset in the growth of the national economy. The urban role in the national economy emerged in two distinct stages. The most significant difference between these two stages is the federal government's efforts, beginning in the late 1960s, to limit the use of intergovernmental tax immunity. I attempt to identify the extent to which this and other changes in intergovernmental relations during the two periods resulted from shifting power relations measured by norm differences about the use of municipal bonds.

The first of these periods extends to the 1960s, corresponds to the emergence of a national economy, and includes the passage from the agrarian based economy and westward expansions of the 19th century through the slow movement to manufacturing and industrialization that finally took off with the outbreak of world war in 1914. This transformation coincided with the rising importance of cities in the national economy. When the issue concerned the authority of cities to incur debt, judicial opinions, court rulings, and state legislatures were not consistent and occasionally at cross-purposes. Their actions were more readily explained as responses to particular situations than as applications of particular political economic theories. In *Clinton v. Cedar Rapids and the Missouri River Railroad* (1868), John Forrest Dillon, a leading jurist of the period and Chief Justice of the Iowa Supreme Court from 1862 to 1869, asserted that states are preeminent over local governments—that cities were 'creatures of the state'. This claim was wholly in line with state constitutions. In what became known as the Dillon Rule, he claimed:

> Municipal corporations owe their origin to, and derive their powers and rights wholly from, the legislature. It breathes into them the breath of life, without which they cannot exist. As it creates, so may it destroy. If it may destroy, it may abridge and control. (24 Iowa 455; 1868)
>
> In an opposing ruling in 1871, Michigan Supreme Court Judge Thomas Cooley established the basis for local self-determination in stating "local government is a matter of absolute right; and the state cannot take it away." (*People v. Hurlbut,* 24 Mich 44, 95; 1871)

Although subsequent legal debates favored the Dillon Rule in principle, the municipal bonds case offers a somewhat more complicated picture of how municipal borrowing allowed cities to become significant forces in building first the national and now the global economy. Municipal bonds were introduced in 1812 to finance canal building (Sbragia 1996:108). State constitutions gave their legislators authority to grant municipalities this power and legislatures routinely did so while setting limits on the total amount of borrowing cities could incur. In the rush to build infrastructures, massive amounts of debt were incurred at both state and local levels through much of the 19th century. As formally constituted government bodies, cities had significant borrowing and debt financing policy autonomy. In the 1840s, property taxes were linked to municipal bonds and became *the* means whereby cities responded to the 'general welfare' of citizens. Yet borrowing authority during this period appears to have been secured mainly through the shifting largesse or distractions of either the federal or state legal-regulatory systems as both were preoccupied with building regional and/or a national economy and transportation systems to stimulate economic growth. In 1840, state debt was seven times larger than municipal debt but 40 years later municipal debt was three times larger than state debt (Sbragia 1996:56).

But did the powers vested in cities—to exercise eminent domain, to tax, to acquire and dispose property, to make contracts and incur liabilities—imply the power to borrow even if not explicitly granted by state legislatures? Court rulings on this question favored implied powers for cities through much of the 19th century, but not without controversy. In his *The Law of Municipal Corporations* John Forrest Dillon expressed serious reservations:

> The dangerous nature of this power by reason of the temptation it holds out to incur needless debts and to make extravagant expenditures, and the facilities it offers for frauds, and the settled and salutary doctrine that such corporations have no powers but such as are expressly conferred, and those which are necessary to effect the objects of the corporations, and those which are incidental to the express grants, the author would be strongly inclined to deny the existence of an *implied power* to power money. But it must be admitted that the few express adjudications on the subject favor the contrary opinion. (1873:200)

Did cities have the right to incur debt to aid in the development of the railway system? When the federal government refused to assume escalating state debts especially in the south after the Civil War, states withdrew their support and conferred powers on municipalities to assist in the construction of railways by purchasing rail company stocks and taxing citizens or property within city limits to pay the indebtedness incurred from the purchases. Initially, court rulings even supported ways to increase the ability of urban officials to maneuver debt limits imposed by their state governments to support the railways. But this was not consistent with previous court rulings about the transportation sector. For instance, in an 1841 case in New Jersey (*Ten Eyck v. The Delaware and Raritan Canal Company*), a river proprietor had taken a canal company to court for obstructing a waterway. The company had claimed it was not liable because it was acting as a public agent of the state. The court disagreed, noting that

> Public corporations are political corporations, or such as are founded wholly for public purposes, and the *whole* interest in which is in the public. The fact of the public having an interest in the works or the property or the object of a corporation, does not make it a public corporation. All corporations, whether public or private, are . . . founded upon the principle that they will promote the interest or convenience of the public. . . . The interest . . . does not determine its character as a public or private corporation. . . . The [canal] corporation itself, the property of the corporation, the object of the corporation are essentially private, subject only to public use, under their own restrictions, and from which use, the company are to derive the profits. (18 N.J.L. 200, 6–7; 1841)

Following this line of reasoning, other justices believed that municipal investment in railway companies violated the "wholly public purposes" principle. In writing against the practice of state and municipal investment in the railways, but acknowledging opposing court decisions, Dillon noted:

Taxes, it is everywhere agreed, can only be imposed for *public* objects, and taxation to aid in building the road of *private railway companies,* even if the use is a public use, is hardly consistent with a proper respect for the inviolability of private property and individual rights. (1873:223)

U.S. Supreme Court rulings (e.g., *Olcutt v. The Supervisors* 1872; *Railroad Co. v. Otoe County* 1872) were not consistent with Dillon's position— that the exercise of eminent domain and use of taxing authority was not justified because a public benefit did not constitute a public use in the legal sense. The Supreme Court rulings supported legislatures authorizing municipalities' to use eminent domain and the power to tax for this purpose based on the judgment that, in Dillon's words:

Highways, turnpikes, canals and railways, although owned by individuals under public grants or by private corporations, are *publici juris;* that they have always been regarded as governmental affairs, and their establishment and maintenance recognized as among the most important duties of the State, in order to facilitate transportation and easy communication among its different parts . . . the use is in its nature a public use, and these works [railways] are subject to public control and regulation. . . . notwithstanding they may be exclusively owned by private persons or corporations. (1873:223–224)

Judicial rulings and opinions in the railway case did not end the debate about supporting private interests. Kansas was no exception to the practice of supporting infrastructure development after it was admitted as a state in 1861 (Wirt 1989; Sbragia 1996:89). Its legislature frequently authorized local governments to issue bonds for such purposes. In the state legislation incorporating cities in February 1872, the legislature gave local councils

power to encourage the establishment of manufactories and such other enterprises as may tend to develop and improve such city, either by direct appropriation from the general fund or by the issuance of bonds of such city in such amounts as the council may determine. (*Loan Association v. Topeka,* 87 U.S. 655, 2; 1875)

A month later, the Kansas legislature passed an act "to authorize cities and counties to issue bonds for the purpose of building bridges, aiding railroads, water-power, or other works of internal improvement" (87 U.S. 655, 1; 1875). The city council of Topeka, Kansas, passed an ordinance on July 17, 1872 to issue $100,000.00 in municipal bonds to finance the King Wrought Iron Bridge Manufacturing and Iron Works Company in constructing a shop that would produce iron bridges. The Cleveland, Ohio–based company was the largest bridge construction company in the United States and had already built its first plant at Iola in southeastern Kansas in 1871. The bonds were payable to the Company, and the plant in Topeka was built at a cost four times that of the one in Iola. The Citizens' Savings and Loan Association of Cleveland held the coupons for interest attached to the city's bonds, and the city began repayment of the interest using taxes imposed for that purpose. After this payment, the Savings and Loan Association purchased the bonds and the coupons. The monetary panic of 1873 resulted in the depreciation of municipal bonds, including those issued for many infrastructure-related projects, and companies like King's bridge-building shops in Kansas failed.

In 1874, the Savings and Loan Association brought suit against the city when the repayments ceased. The Circuit Court for the District of Kansas held that the State legislature lacked authority to authorize the city to issue bonds and therefore they were void. It based its decision on two elements. First, the legislature violated its own Constitutional requirement by not placing a limit on the amount of bonds the city could issue. Furthermore, the Court found that the legislature had allowed cities

> to take property of the citizen under the guise of taxation to pay these bonds, and use it in aid of the enterprises of others which were not of a public character; that this was a perversion of the right of taxation, which could only be exercised for a public use, to the aid of individual interests and personal purposes of profit and gain. (*Loan Association v. Topeka*, 87 U.S. 655, 4; 1875)

The Supreme Court agreed to take up the Savings and Loan Association's request that it review the Circuit Court decision. In affirming the lower court's decision, Justice Miller delivered the majority (8 to 1) opinion. Miller noted the longstanding legal disagreement about what role cities could take in holding stocks in and lending their credit to build railroads. The central issue was to determine if the asset belonged to the public for its use. He found that local government did not control the disposition of the assets for which the bonds were issued, and the public benefit was not satisfied by the jobs and income generated by the company. In so ruling, Miller wrote:

> If it be said that a benefit results to the local public or a town by establishing manufactures, the same may be said of any other business or pursuit which employs capital or labor. The merchant, the mechanic, the innkeeper, the banker, the builder, the steamboat owner are equally promoters of the public good, and equally deserving the aid of the citizens by forced contributions. No line can be drawn in favor of the manufacturer which would not open the coffers of the public treasure to the importunities of two-thirds of the business men of the city or town. (*Loan Association v. Topeka*, 87 U.S. 655, 19; 1875)

The overriding judicial concern about the dangers of government taxing authority limited what cities could do to support the private sector in developing a national economy. And there were other constraints on the urban-private sector relationship during the same period—the monetary crises of 1873 and 1893, the antitrust Sherman Act of 1890, and increased focus on consumer preferences reflected in neoclassical economic thought and summarized in Alfred Marshall's 1890 publication of *Principles of Economics.*

But during the same period, state courts developed the Special Fund Doctrine (Heil 1983), a conceptual framework that allowed courts to approve financing techniques that increased aggregate debt of municipal areas while allowing local government to remain within the state-imposed debt limits. Cities used this framework to create various kinds of local government instruments that were consistent with the 1875 Supreme Court ruling. The first of these were revenue bonds to finance a waterworks system in Spokane, Washington. A special tax had been imposed on property that benefited from improvements financed by borrowing. In *Winston v. City of Spokane* (1895), the Washington Supreme Court upheld the special tax to finance the borrowing and determined that debt restrictions applied to "the general credit or general revenues of a city." (Heil 1983:87). Special taxes did not carry the city's "full faith and credit" as did general-obligation bonds. Subsequent rulings allowed local government to borrow for self-liquidating projects without being subject to debt restrictions as long as loans were repaid with other than tax monies. By 1934, revenue bonds were widely used to finance water systems throughout the United States. Cities came to issue revenue bonds even when debt limit was not a factor because they felt the link between the bond and the user/payer was appropriate. Courts justified their rulings on the basis of "intergenerational equity"—that is, that they were protecting future taxpayers who would not make use of the investment. Capital investment projects were financed by issuing revenue bonds outside state debt limits on the assumption that these projects would not make use of the investments resulting from the bond issues. The revenue bond became the major financial instrument used by local governments in the bond market. They are used for capital investment projects financed by borrowing backed by 'user fees'.

Once local government borrowing was separated from its tax base, cities could create new kinds of financial debt instruments and entities. Encouraged by court rulings, municipalities created three kinds of "special-purpose government" (Sbragia 1996) to circumvent state restrictions on indebtedness:

1. Special districts: Subsets of local government that often charged fees, could levy property taxes, and were generally governed by an elected rather than appointed board. They had the right to issue general-obligation bonds (and sometimes revenue bonds) that might not be subject to the same debt limits as municipal bonds. Issuing bonds required approval of a simple majority of the electorate whereas municipal bonds needed a two-thirds approval.

2. Public authorities: Created to circumvent limits imposed by states, these authorities depended on revenue from their projects rather than taxes. Hence they relied on revenue-bond financing. Normally, public authorities were not governed by a directly elected board but they might include elected officials. Because they were considered semi-independent public entities, their debt did not fall under debt-limitation laws. Most authorities did not need their bond issues approved by city councils or electorates. They relied on user fees to finance themselves. Public authorities were very diverse and differed in their formal independence from parent governments and in their financial base.
3. Authority districts: These were a mix of Special district and Public authorities. They relied for funding on the collection of user charges but could also use special means of taxation (e.g., taxing district related to watersheds, sanitation, hospitals).

Concerns over declining national revenue soon led Congress to consider imposing limits on issuing municipal bonds. The issue was no longer public vs. private sector benefit but rather who had the authority—state or federal government—to generate tax revenue from income earned from issuing these bonds. This debate between 1894 and 1913 secured an important asset for cities: municipal bonds that were exempt from federal taxation. Congress passed the Wilson-Gorman Tariff Act of 1894 to lower trade protectionism by instituting a national income tax to offset revenue losses from tariff reductions. The Act was at odds with the 1875 Supreme Court ruling because it levied a federal tax on income (2% on income over $4,000), including income earned from municipal bonds.

To comply with the tariff act, the Farmers' Loan & Trust Company based in New York announced to its shareholders that it would provide their names to the U.S. Treasury and pay the tax. Charles Pollock, a shareholder from Massachusetts, sued the company. He lost in the lower courts but appealed, and the Supreme Court agreed to hear the case. In April 1895, the Court ruled 5–4 in Pollock's favor (*Pollock v. Farmers' Loan and Trust Co.*). In writing the opinion for the majority, Justice Fuller found the 1894 Act to be unconstitutional because it imposed a tax on income from property— that is, that state and local bond issues and income from them are property. Article I, section 2, of the U.S. Constitution required that direct taxes among the states be apportioned according to population and section 8 required that indirect taxes, such as duties and imports, be uniform throughout the United States. Taxes on property were considered direct taxes and therefore subject to apportionment; taxes on income were considered indirect taxes. The Act had not based the tax on apportionment and was not valid. The majority of the Court held that the distinction between "that which gives value to property, and the property itself" (p. 628) was artificial; it favored treating bonds as property rather than income by arguing that, in adopting the Constitution,

The founders anticipated that the expenditures of the States, their counties, cities, and towns, would chiefly be met by direct taxation on accumulated property, while they expected that those of the Federal government would be for the most part met by indirect taxes . . . Those who made it knew that the power to tax involved the power to destroy. (158 U.S. 601, 620–621; 1895)

It therefore concluded

We have unanimously held in this case that, so far as this law operates on the receipts from municipal bonds, it cannot be sustained, because it is a tax on the power of the States, and on their instrumentalities to borrow money, and consequently repugnant to the Constitution. (p. 630)

The court also used the doctrine of intergovernmental immunity established in *McCulloch v. Maryland* (1819)—that state agencies may not regulate federal government operations in their state—to exempt state and local bonds from federal taxation because, as O'Hara (2012) noted, "a tax on interest would impermissibly burden state government and interfere with its power to borrow money" (p. 226).

The *Pollock* ruling forced passage of the 16th Amendment to the U.S. Constitution in 1913 so that the federal government could establish an 'income tax structure not constrained by apportionment and population requirements'. Because the amendment included the idea that incomes 'from whatever source derived' could be taxed, the U.S. Supreme Court concluded in *Evans v. Gore* (1920) that the words did "not extend the taxing power to new or excepted subjects" but rather were intended to remove the tax apportionment issue (O'Hara 2012:226–227). While the amendment did not eliminate the tax exemption from municipal bonds, subsequent federal efforts to do so have come from both the executive administrative agencies and various members of Congress.

THE FATE OF CITIES AND MUNICIPAL BONDS IN THE PASSAGE TO A GLOBAL ECONOMY

The court rulings and federal and state legislation in the post–Civil War period did not consistently fit the tenets of neoclassical thinking summarized by Marshall in 1890 and in vogue among public intellectuals until the 1929 Depression. Orthodox economists had shifted the focus of wealth generation to consumer preferences and away from the classical emphasis on production and the labor theory of value. Consumer behavior would create general equilibrium as long as government did not interfere. Yet judicial and legislative actions as well as the expanded use of municipal bonds were at odds with the neoclassical belief in laissez-faire economic policies.

Local governments and courts circumvented state limits on issuing debt and found new instruments that expanded urban authority to borrow. Cities did not act in a hands-off manner; and their actions, in a somewhat ironic way, contradicted neoclassical microeconomic premises.

The 1929 Depression befuddled proponents of neoclassical analysis far more than did the inconsistent application of norms by city leaders and state and federal justices and legislators. To account for how to fix persistent high rates of unemployment in the 1930s, Keynes revised the theory in two ways that altered the norms-basis in liberal economic thought. First, the revision required the federal government to play an ongoing if watchful role in the economy and second, it required understanding that there was a national economy and a national government whose behavior mattered in correcting certain business cycles. The Roosevelt Administration became actively involved in policy initiatives consistent with Keynesianism prescription. Through the war effort and then the postwar policies of all administrations, especially those of Kennedy and Johnson, national government policy "fine tuned" the economy to flatten the business cycle and bring about steady-state growth. Cities and the federal government became partners rather than adversaries in the "Fordist" venture of urbanizing the industrial base of the U.S. economy and establishing U.S. dominance over the international economy.

The various kinds of bond issues discussed earlier fueled this "Golden Age of Post-War Growth." As cities developed institutional infrastructures and investment mechanisms on which to base this growth, lines between public purpose and private gain blurred once again. Industrial Development Bonds (IDBs) were the most blatant illustration of borrowing to promote economic development of the private sector rather than to provide capital investment in public goods. Combined with special purpose government entities, IDBs redefined "capital improvements" to lure companies to relocate to or stay put in their locales. This expanded use was part of local government's response to the decline of an urban manufacturing base that had begun with the Vietnam wartime economy—domestic defense production and rising imports for domestic consumption—and followed by transformation of the national economy to post-Fordist, service-driven growth in the1970s.

However, by the late 1960s the United States was in an untenable economic position. Its national economy had overheated as spending for the Vietnam War and the Great Society and Antipoverty programs. Furthermore, it could no longer salvage its key currency position in the international monetary system because U.S. gross national product rates could no longer keep pace with the need for expanded world liquidity. A global economy was slowly emerging from interdependent national economies and governments, including the United States, found it increasingly problematic to regulate money supply and adopt effective fiscal policies. For our purposes here, national efforts beginning with the Nixon Administration included a "domestic" or inside-out effort to shore up rising budget and balance of payments deficits by devolving responsibilities to the local level. Yet as the national government attempted to address its dwindling economic position in trade and finance under conditions of stagflation, investors remained committed to buying municipal rather than corporate bonds even though returns on municipal bonds were about one third lower than returns on corporate bonds.

Congress struggled to find ways to balance Keynesian influenced budget proposals. Beginning in the late 1960s, it passed legislation to limit the volume of tax-exempt bonds and questioned their public purpose (Zimmerman 1991). In 1968, it legislated restrictions on the uses for which IDBs could be issued and still retain the federal tax exemption (O'Hara 2012:229). Sbragia notes that 'of the seventeen tax laws passed by Congress in the period between 1968 and 1989, fifteen had an effect on municipal bonds' (1996:190). The trend in this legislation was to restrict use of the tax exemption in bond issues while allowing cities to continue borrowing for purposes beyond traditional public goods infrastructures like water, sewage, and roads (Petersen 1987). Municipalities continued to make extensive use of bond issues that promoted private activities.

The Reagan Administration espoused a libertarian return to classical economic liberalism, yet its fiscal policies were not clearly recognizable as such. Much of the legislation the Administration supported resulted in a resurgence of federal authority over state and local borrowing. The Economic Recovery Tax Act (ERTA) of 1981 (Amen 1997) included a dramatic reduction in taxes: a phased-in 23% cut in individual tax rates over 3 years, lowered top rate from 70% to 50%, phased-in increase in estate tax exemption from $175,625 to $600,000 in 1987, reduced windfall profit taxes, and IRAs options for all working taxpayers. Yet the following year, Congress responded to the loss of federal revenue by proposing the Tax Equity and Fiscal Responsibility Act (TEFRA), which President Reagan signed in September 1982. The purpose of the legislation was to close tax loopholes and create tougher enforcement of tax rules. The legislation "required most municipal securities to be issued in registered form and conditioned tax exemption on compliance with the registration requirement." (O'Hara 2012:228)

In 1983, the State of South Carolina filed a complaint that, by compelling the state to issue bonds in registered form, the TEFRA violated the Tenth Amendment and/or the doctrine of intergovernmental tax immunity by taxing the interest earned on unregistered State bonds. The financial management organization, the Government Finance Officers Association (GFOA), held that the legislation violated the Sixteenth Amendment. In 1988, the Supreme Court ruled (7–1) in *South Carolina v. Baker* that the U.S. Constitution did not afford state and local governments protection against national regulatory powers (485 U.S. 505). The courts established a new doctrine of reciprocal tax immunity that no longer gave constitutional protection to tax exemptions for municipal and state bonds. This ruling affirmed a normative relationship based on politics and administration rather than law—a relationship among the federal political units that affirmed "a supremely powerful national government and semi-sovereign states" (Wrightston 1989:51). If anything, the new doctrine was more in line with Keynesian neoclassical policy than with the Austrian school of classical liberal prescriptions. The Court found that

> the federal tax immunity has always been greater than the States' immunity. The Federal Government, for example, possesses the power to enact statutes immunizing those with whom it deals from states taxation even if intergovernmental tax immunity doctrine would not otherwise confer an immunity. The States lack any such power. . . . the States have never enjoyed immunity from all federal taxes considered to be "on" a State. . . . The rationale underlying *Pollock* and the general immunity for government contract income has been thoroughly repudiated by modern intergovernmental case law. (p. 520)

The Court also held that the sole purpose of the Sixteenth Amendment was to remove the apportionment requirement from whichever incomes were taxable, not to freeze into the Constitution tax immunity for state bond interests that existed in 1913. Writing for the majority, Justice Brennan concluded:

> The only premodern tax immunity for parties to government contracts that has so far avoided being explicitly overruled is the immunity for recipients of government bond interest. That this court has yet to overrule *Pollock* explicitly, however, is explained not by any distinction between the income derived from government bonds and the income derived from other government contracts, but by the historical fact that congress has always exempted state bond interests from taxation by statute, beginning with the very first federal income tax statute. (p. 522)

An equally significant impact for local governments was the change in tax exempt status for municipal bonds that came with the Tax Reform Act of 1986 (TRA). The Treasury Department had tried for decades to eliminate exemptions for all municipal bonds but it lacked Congressional allies to move reform forward in the legislative process. City officials and national urban-membership organizations, bond dealers, ratings agencies, the U.S. Chamber of Commerce, and the GFOA had developed a web of lobbying efforts and relations with Congress and the Executive Branch with the sole goal of protecting tax-exempt status of bonds. In 1985 Congressman Rostenkowski of Illinois, who had become Chairman of the House Ways and Means Committee in 1981, championed the legislation. He was concerned about rising federal deficits and felt that public purpose bonds had strayed from their original intent. Rostenkowski estimated the loss of tax revenue from the exempt bonds was nearly $14 billion in 1983. (Sbragia 1996:194)

The TRA reflected the impact of constituent interests on those engaged in the legislative process at the time. Petersen (1987) identified four kinds of municipal bond categories established in the TRA: (1) government purpose, (2) private activity: taxable, (3) private activity: capped, and (4) private activity: uncapped. The legislation established a unified volume cap for total borrowing. The formula was based on state population size: capped for 1988 calendar year at $50 per state per capita. It also eliminated some forms of private-purpose borrowing altogether by declaring that 'all bonds whose proceeds are primarily used to benefit private persons or corporations are taxable' (Graham, Shinn, and Petersen 1989:10). Furthermore, it distinguished private activity bonds from government purpose bonds that finance traditional facilities owned and operated by government. To retain tax exempt status less than 10% of the bond could be used for private benefit.

Private activities that lost tax-exempt bond status included industrial parks, sports stadiums, convention centers, nongovernment office buildings, most parking facilities, and industrial pollution control (16% of the bond market in 1984). Those 'capped' included mortgage-revenue bonds, manufacturing small-issue industrial development bonds, student-loan bonds, nonprofit-organization bonds, bonds for local electric and gas facilities, some hazardous waste facilities bonds, mass transit facilities bonds, and multifamily housing bonds (32%). These retained tax-exempt status but had to compete with one another under a cap. Uncapped bonds that retained tax-exempt status included those issued by universities and hospitals and for government-owned airports, docks, wharves, and solid waste facilities (13%). A series of tests was established to ensure that bond issues would benefit "the general public" rather than individuals or economic development. Finally, all tax-exempt private-activity bonds had to be discussed in a public hearing before being issued, and public approval had to be obtained either by voter referendum or the approval of elected officials. Hence most entities charged with economic development lost their authority while those providing infrastructure retained their independence.

Subnational governments took this ruling as a signal to ramp up their political leverage as constitutional protections eroded. They established lobbying organizations for the specific purpose of rolling back the restrictions in the 1986 TRA. Congress established the Anthony Commission, which presented its report on the role of tax-exempt financing in the fall of 1989. Two years later, a congressional caucus on Congressional Infrastructure and Public Finance was formed. The purpose of the caucus was to draw attention to the infrastructure problems of the country and the need to ease restrictions on state and local finance by protecting the tax-exempt status of municipal bonds that were for investment in the nation's future. By the end of the 1980s, private-activity bonds subject to caps had fallen to 20% of the market and all private-activity bonds represented about one third of state and local government's tax-exempt borrowing. Between 1986 and 1989, IDB issues dropped by nearly $10 billion (Sbragia 1996).

The persistence of federal budget deficits contributed to Bill Clinton's election in the 1992. During his administration, federal budget deficits were reduced and the online budget measure moved to a surplus in FY 1999 (U.S. Office of Management and Budget 2013). These surpluses were, however, short lived due to a combination of factors: popping the dot-com bubble in March 2000, post–9/11 policies of the Bush Administration, and the 2007 Great Recession. In response to the overfinancialization of the U.S. economy (Amen 1999; Bardhan 2009) of which the subprime mortgage market was one example, Congress floated policy initiatives that had implications for the tax-exempt limitations set in the 1986 TRA. And as congressional interest revisited the philosophical thrust underlying the TRA restrictions, subnational lobbying ramped up: The GFOA continued to lobby in favor of restoring the tax-exempt status lost in the TRA as did the Public Finance Networks (PFNs), a coalition of groups based in the public sector. From its outset, the PFNs had intentionally excluded banking and bond counseling lobbyists whose efforts they felt had been detrimental to the tax-exempt cause (Sbragia 1996:206–208). The Obama Administration supported Build America Bonds. Although these municipal bonds were taxable, they carried special tax credits and federal subsidies for either the bond issuer or the bondholder. They were created in the American Recovery and Reinvestment Act that President Obama signed into law on February 17, 2009. The program expired December 31, 2010. Senators Wyden (D-Oregon) and Coats (R-Indiana), introduced the Bipartisan Tax Fairness and Simplification Act (TFSA) in 2010, which would have made all new municipal bonds tax-credit rather than tax-exempt bonds. Tax-credit bonds are taxable. The bondholder gets a credit toward its taxes rather than tax-exempt interest (Wyden and Gregg 2010). In November 2010, the Bipartisan Policy Center's debt reduction task force issued its 'Restoring America's Future' report (Domenici and Rivlin 2010). The report recommended no tax exemption for any new private-activity bonds, including bonds for single- and multifamily housing, airports, water and sewer facilities, hospitals, and 'manufacturing facilities. One month later, the President's National Commission on Fiscal Responsibility and Reform made recommendations for deficit reduction "The Moment of Truth" (Bowles and Simpson 2010). Although the commission failed to obtain a supermajority vote, it had recommended there be no tax exemption for new municipal bonds.

Several months later, in September 2011, when President Obama sent Congress his American Jobs Act of 2011, he proposed that it be paid for in large part by limiting the value of tax-exempt interest, other tax preferences, and itemized deductions. This was the first time the Obama Administration proposed such a cap. If passed, the cap would have reduced the incentive for individuals with incomes of $200,000 or more from purchasing municipal bonds. Nearly 60% of the tax-exempt interest reported to the Internal Revenue in 2009 was from these individuals. Lobbyists continued to push lawmakers to support proposals such as the one Senator Bingaman (D-New Mexico) submitted in May 2011 to permanently raise the limit for bank-qualified bonds to $30 million from $10 million. This would allow banks that held tax-exempt bonds to deduct 80% of the cost of buying and carrying bonds sold by issuers whose annual issues are less than $30 million (Hume and DePaul 2011). President Obama's proposal did not pass. The Internal Revenue Code of 1986 continues to exempt interest on municipal bonds "except for arbitrage bonds and certain private activity bonds" (O'Hara 2012:230).

CONCLUSION

How were cities able to rely more and more on borrowing to reach their essential role first in the national economy and more recently in the emerging global economy? Cities on the eastern seaboard were the first to borrow and then, with the westward expansion, cities throughout the country became active in the bond market. The market was indispensable as cities became critical nodes in the development of the United States economy. Various attempts to limit their indebtedness gave way to countervailing interests in support of debt financing to spur more growth. These interests often blurred if not hid who were the most immediate beneficiaries of this debt—the general public or particular private interests. Local government indebtedness expanded because of or in spite of normative opinions and actions of U.S. judicial and legislative institutions that were never wholly consistent with particular versions of liberal economic theory.

As city debt grew, justices and legislators (and presidents) evoked various liberal norms at will in the opinions they rendered and the actions they took. Norms mattered in their rulings and actions because of how they chose to use particular tenets in response to specific political economic contexts. In the end, the situation rather than liberal doctrine—classical, egalitarian, or neoliberal—determined what norms were promoted. It would be difficult, therefore, to align a particular version of liberalism to judicial or legislative decisions about what autonomy cities had (from either state or federal government) to issue bonds, for what purposes they could be issued (public or private gain), or what was the proper role for local government debt in developing the economy (market intervention or laissez-faire). Judicial opinion varied and rulings on occasion even rejected prior juridical decisions.

This pattern—that norm entrepreneurs matter at least as much as the norms—suggests the need for "third generation" constructivist analysis of the subject and the context (Widmaier and Park 2012) to understand how, in this case, norm entrepreneurs affect the applicability of liberal norms to the role cities play in the national and global economy. Such analysis is all the more needed when versions of liberal economic doctrine—classical, egalitarian, or neoliberal—do not align with court rulings, legislative actions, and municipal borrowing. The evidence in support of this pattern is reflected in court rulings and legislative actions on whether municipal bonds could be used only to advance the general welfare and not private gain. The opinions and rulings in *Ten Eyck* (1841), Dillon (1872), *Loan Association* (1875) and the actions taken in ERTA (1981), TEFRA (1982), TRA (1986), and TFSA (2010) sustain that bonds should not be used only for private gain. Because the difference between public and private is not that practicable from rulings and legislation, cities issued bonds more or less continuously from early on in the 19th century through IDBs in the 20th century to build the economy by supporting the growth of private sector interests locally. In sharp contrast to this pattern, classical, egalitarian, and neoliberal versions of liberal economic theory shared a common claim that government should not incur debt for private gain and, in the case of egalitarian liberalism, that government should intervene to correct wealth inequalities.

Several legal cases and congressional actions concerned urban autonomy from state and/or federal government and the right to issue bonds and to do so with immunity from federal taxes. These incidences overlap with the broader question of what role should government at any level play in the economy. The United States has a decentralized federal system wherein cities have significant potential to be players of consequence in building economic life. At the same time, as rulings and legislation document, their authority to incur debt to do so has been arbitrarily granted or denied. With the exception of *Pollock* (1895), the rulings in *McCulloch* (1819), *Clinton* (1868), *People* (1871), *Topeka* (1875), the Dillon Rule, the Special Fund Doctrine (1880s), *Winston* (1895), and *South Carolina* (1988) and the legislation in the Tenth Amendment, Sixteenth Amendment, ERTA (1981), TEFRA (1982), TRA (1986), Internal Revenue Code of 1986, and Buy America Bonds (2009) waffle between, on the one hand, support for urban growth without constraints from state or federal government to, on the other hand, restrictive legislation and rulings in the 20th century, especially beginning in the late 1960s, that limited urban independence in order to resolve national fiscal/monetary instability and balance of payments deficits. This trend is particularly at odds with the emergence of a laissez-faire based global economy and the return to the neoclassical version of economic liberal policies beginning in the late 1970s.

The municipal bond case opens one way for international relations to incorporate municipalities into their accounts by theorizing how traditions like liberalism can be stretched to include a role for norms and norm entrepreneurial behavior. Cities bonds are now part of the global financial market; and cities are centers for various economic activities central to not only this market but also to the production and distribution of goods and services circulating in the world economy. Institutional rulings and legislation impacted how cities dealt with debts and thereby were able to position themselves in this global economy. Our understanding of how this came about can be enhanced by knowing more about who and in what situation-specific contexts norms mattered in promoting this outcome.

8 Johannesburg
Financial 'Gateway' to Africa

Elizabeth Cobbett

> Johannesburg is where the deals are made. It's the most powerful commercial centre on the African continent. There's hardly a major international company doing serious business in sub-Saharan Africa that has not looked to Johannesburg as the gateway. (City of Johannesburg, 2013)

Financial cities are strategic geographical locations that have the necessary infrastructure and market depth to organize and deliver international financial services. Leading financial cities have historically been situated in Europe, the United States, and, in the last decades, Asia. This is changing; there are significant shifts in investment patterns as global investors see the long-term growth possibilities in emerging markets. This relates directly to changes taking place in Africa. The continent has accelerating and broad-based economic growth that is underpinned by links with Asia and Latin America. Johannesburg—Africa's major economic city and powerhouse—is at the heart of these changes. It is being positioned by the South African government as the 'Gateway to Africa'. Along these lines, this chapter discusses the significance of financial cities in the global political economy and studies Johannesburg as an inquiry as to why and how international financial cities are growing outside of historically established centres.

INTRODUCTION

South Africa, as the latest member of the BRIC group (Brazil, Russia, India, and China), is using its new global position to further its goals as a regional power. The government's National Development Plan 2030 (National Planning Commission 2011) identifies the service industry as a key to job creation in the country. Johannesburg links the two: the foreign policy goal of regional power and growth in the service sector. Finance is one of the services sectors in which South Africa excels. This is because Johannesburg is 'one of the critical nodes of Southern Hemispheric capitalism and globalization' (Nuttall and Mbembe 2008:1). Johannesburg is 'Africa's premier metropolis, the symbol par excellence of the "African modern"' (2008:1).

Sub-Saharan Africa has three historical economic hubs: Nigeria for West Africa, Kenya for East Africa, and South Africa for Southern Africa. Of the three hubs, Johannesburg stands out as the leading financial centre. Johannesburg is a financial city. It is an *international* financial city connected to global markets through the country's distinct political economy centred on mining. The rise of an international financial centre is intimately linked to the economic power of the country (Cassis 2010). An important reason why Johannesburg is Africa's leading financial city is because South Africa was part of Britain's empire and international monetary system based on the gold standard (Ally 1994; Cobbett 2010). Johannesburg's wealth and strength comes from historic ties to global capital networks.

Johannesburg has the status of an evolving financial centre within the global economy (Yeandle and von Gunten 2013). Johannesburg is at the centre of an economic and political hub-and-spoke infrastructure. It is the economic 'gateway' for international business and finance into the region. It effectively connects many of its neighbouring countries in sub-Saharan Africa with global actors. Being the 'gateway' to Africa is, as South Africa's President Jacob Zuma (2011) pointed out, a defining feature of South Africa's political economy. South Africa is reinforcing its position as regional hegemon and the gateway provides the country 'with the muscle to increase our economic and trade outcomes' (2011:para. 2).

This vision of gateway is underpinned by the invitation to join the BRIC group of major emerging economies. South Africa was selected in accordance to the priorities of existing BRIC members, namely the need for an African geographic representation in the group (Brooks 2011). Trade and Industry Minister Rob Davies used this concept of gateway at the World Economic Forum to defend the country's new role among the leading emerging economies (Business Day 2011). Davies admitted that South Africa's economy may be small in comparison with other BRIC countries but highlighted its political and economic position on a continent that has considerable growth potential as millions gain consumer power. '"We will be a good gateway for the BRIC countries", said Nkoana-Mashabane, South Africa's foreign minister, to reporters in Pretoria. . . . "we don't just speak for South Africa, we speak for Africa as a whole"' (Conway-Smith, 2011:para. 11).

Several African countries are placing their leading cities as investment gateways into Africa's markets. Kenya is an ancient regional centre by virtue of its location, connected to the Middle East and Asia through sea trade routes and the British Empire. It has excellent infrastructure and political stability that is facilitating the growth of Nairobi as an international financial centre. Mauritius is a key African offshore financial centre; this role is underpinned by its geographical position and its knowledge for doing business in both India and Africa. Mauritius has a business advantage as a gateway into Africa because of its proximity to regional markets, creating lower transport costs, and because there is no exchange control. There is an easy flow of money from Mauritius, which is important in granting loans to African countries. Nigeria, on Africa's West coast, has been at the centre of major investments related to oil drilling. Africa's biggest city, Lagos, is one of the globe's most dynamic and fast-growing mega-cities. MasterCard has recently won a bid to coproduce the country's new national ID card. The card will also be a payments card, sharing a common biometric platform provided by the state. This is part of MasterCard's strategy to bring a significant portion of Africa's underbanked adult population into its global networks.

The need for an African 'gateway' as a base from which investment firms can conduct business operations is accentuated by the fact that foreign investment is no longer concentrated in isolated countries but is spreading throughout the African continent (Lex Africa 2011). *Gateway* is effectively a contemporary term for a longstanding concept of centres of economic and political power. Notable is Braudel's (1982, 1984, 1993) study of what he calls material civilisation—the constraints and possibilities on which the social world is based at any given point in time—which provides an in-depth account of societies, political power, economic modes of production, and the place that capitalism occupies historically and spatially within these contexts. Braudel (1984:21–22; italics in original) makes an important distinction between *the world economy* and *a world-economy*. The former corresponds to the whole world, the market of the universe, the human race or that part of the human race that is engaged in trade and makes up a single market (1984:21). The world economy is analogous to the contemporary concept of globalisation. The latter, world-economy, is a relatively economically autonomous section of the planet able to provide for most of its own needs, a section in which its internal links and exchanges creates an organic unit (1984:22). This concept recognises that other world-economies can exist, that they can overlap, and that they can be governed by different cultural values. A world-economy is not a total unit, thus analytically permitting for the assortment and range of social orders and systems that exist around the world.

Braudel offers an invaluable analytical framework to think about the rise of African cities. The leading economic hubs have been connected to world-economies coming out of Europe and Asia for centuries; they are now once again being positioned as key strategic locations in the changing world order. The global political economy is in a period of transition; its material bases are shifting as production patterns move to and are consolidated in Asia and other locations in the global South, such as Brazil and India. States that were formerly considered as 'Second' and 'Third World' countries, Less Developed Countries, and are now called emerging markets, are at the centre of such changes. Africa is rising, and its cities are part of connections spanning the globe. Johannesburg, the continent's powerhouse and leading financial centre, is a prime example of these global connections.

An essential concern in this chapter is to view these developments from the perspective of Africa. What this means, Nuttall and Mbembe (2008) point out, is to see and read contemporary African cities on their own terms, by provincialising the global city model and understanding how the mega-cities of the South are displacing the old urban centres of the North, not only in terms of population numbers but also through their particular way of being part of globalisation (2008:4). This is an invitation to see how major African cities are, and have been, able to attract and seduce colonial and global capital (2008:5). While much of global capital can be seen as predatory, African cities, the actors within the cities, are part of the processes where global finance seeks profitable opportunities within localised structures and is conversely shaped by local politics, culture, and systems of power. It is in this light that we need to examine in what ways financial centres in the South resemble historical centres in Europe and North America and yet are distinctive as African cities and as centres that reflect the changing world order.

FINANCIAL CENTRES

The empirical importance of financial centres resides in their ability to organize the integration and connection of their domestic economy with the global economy, most importantly by channelling capital flows and thereby spurring economic growth. Why and how financial clustering occurs, as well as the factors that determine the location of financial centres, is an important concern, both for established centres to maintain their competitive position and for emerging economies keen to identify the policy levers necessary to support financial sector growth (Jarvis 2011).

International political economy focuses primarily on state-centric data and the 'international economy', which describes economic relations between states. In contrast, literature on financial centres draws attention to overlapping global political economic networks as well as to the historic materialism of social order and organization in dominant capitalist cities. As mentioned, Braudel (1984:21–22; italics in original) makes an important distinction between *the world economy* and *a world-economy*. A world-economy is a large zone of economic coherence. Certain features define these zones: they have boundaries; they are centred on one particular city—*a world city*—with an already dominant type of capitalism; and they are marked by hierarchies of regional economies, which are, in fact, a type of inequality. In terms of spatial features, they consist of (a) a core: the world city itself and its immediate surroundings; (b) a middle zone: the economic hinterland of the city; and (c) a periphery: colonies and new overseas markets. Shifts in these centres of gravity are significant as they open up new perspectives for world order (1984:32). Braudel's study of capitalism and civilisation traces these shifts as six cities performed the function of urban centres of world-economies: Venice, Antwerp, Genoa, Amsterdam, London, and New York.

When Amsterdam replaced Antwerp, when London took over from Amsterdam, and when New York surpassed London during the 1920s as the new world financial centre, they were accompanying and signalling historical shifts of patterns of accumulation and of production, and interrupting the calm flow of history (Braudel 1984:32). These shifts opened up new and rare perspectives for change. Several authors have built on Braudel's historical approach to civilisations and capitalism but, I argue, they lose sight of the complex ontology that underpins his work. Building on Braudel's progression of world economies, Arrighi (2005, 2010) argues that hegemonic transition and financial expansion are closely linked. Cycles of accumulation relate to century-long or longer periods in which the centre of capitalism resides at the centre of a hegemonic power and goes through the cycle of liquidity, investment, and greater liquidity. While similar to Braudel, Arrighi differs in that he brings the whole world into a single cycle of capitalism. Arrighi (2005:87) sees each cycle of accumulation as expanding further as more territory is brought into the sphere of a hegemonic bloc of governmental and business agencies capitalist interests.

Also working in Braudel's tradition, Wallerstein (1974), privileges an analytical framework that investigates how the market economy and capitalism operate as a world-system. Wallerstein focuses on the world level of analysis as he aims to make a coherent sense of the effects of large structures and processes and move away from the idea that states are all equal and have the same possibilities for development. Wallerstein differs from Braudel in seeing capitalism as progressing in stages. World-systems exist one at a time; they have beginnings, lives, and ends. The argument is that we are now in capitalist world-economy, which has developed a core-periphery division of production and labour. The modern capitalist world-economy is not the first but it is the longest to survive; it did this by becoming fully capitalist (Wallerstein 2005:17).

Arrighi's and Wallerstein's accounts are of single systems of expanding capitalism that analytically reduce the complex ontology apparent in Braudel's work. We lose sight of Braudel's insight that several world-economies can coexist at any one historical period; they can overlap and be governed by different cultural values. A world-economy is not a total unit, thus analytically permitting for the assortment and range of social orders that exist around the world. It is for these reasons that Braudel's analytical framework of civilisations and capitalism evolving in overlapping transnational networks is very rich for thinking about the rise in importance of African cities. These cities can be examined outside of what Ferguson (in Nuttall and Mbembe 2008:5) calls the meta-narrative of modernisation and what I categorise as the story of global convergence to the Western liberal model. In other words, we need to think about African cities in their own histories, contexts, and connections to cities worldwide and to global networks.

Braudel's (1984) historical examination of the role of powerful city-states in world-economies is relevant to this endeavour. What, he asks, would it take for new centres of gravity to emerge within a world-economy? A major shift in production, power, and governance, such as the current change from U.S. super power to a multipolar world order, provokes new alliances, trading networks, and investment patterns. This observation leads into Randall Germain's (1997) argument that we are living in an era of decentralised globalisation and of multiple principal financial centres. Non-Western economies and financial systems are now major components of the global economy (Lavelle 1999, 2004; Germain 2010:65). This decentralisation is provoking a changing balance of state and market authority and denoting a new direction for the organization and governance of finance worldwide, beyond traditional centres of power (Langley 2002).

RISING AFRICA

In spite of these transformations in the global economy and the rise of Africa and its cities, surprisingly little research is being undertaken to understand the institutionalisation of finance and the establishment of financial centres in African economies. This is in good part because financial centres of any global importance have historically been situated in Europe, the United States, and, in the last decades, Asia (Braudel 1984; Cox 1987; Eichengreen 1990, 1996; Helleiner 1994; Germain 1997; Langley 2002; Cassis 2010). Two big changes have encouraged the proliferation of financial centres around the globe: the shift of economic activity and jobs towards China, India, and other developing countries, and the growing demand for natural resources (Klein 2007). Furthermore, the growth of technology, the mobility of capital, and the spread of financial deregulation are deepening the network of connections between financial cities around the globe. Today's financial centres are increasingly dependent on their connections to one another as the number of transactions between them increases.

The 2009 financial crisis took place amid historic shifts in growth patterns around the world. The fallout from crisis amplifies shifts taking place in the global political economy, notably the rapidity with which the emerging economies are 'catching up' to the West. The crisis highlights new patterns of economic growth between the West and the emerging economies, particularly evident in globalising Asia and rising China. We cannot think of the 2009 crisis and ensuing sovereign debt crises and recession without thinking how, in the present conjuncture of shifting political economic power, these events and processes are heralding a changing world order. The combination of these two aspects of current global order—the political and financial crisis and economic recession in Western industrialised economies, and the rise of emerging economies that are increasing their share of world trade and investment—increases the importance of new centres of political economic influence. Emerging powers are 'positioning themselves in relation to the system of global governance, the ideas they articulate, and the extent to which their rise constitutes a counter-narrative to that which is presented by the West' (Qobo 2011:3). There is a new discourse and practice of mutual empowerment cast in terms of South–South relations.

Africa is at the heart of these global political economic transformations. The continent grew faster than most other regions in the five years before the 2009 financial crisis, with more than 40% of its countries enjoying an average annual economic growth rate of 5% or more (Africa Progress Panel 2011). The 5% growth rate is driven by a strong global demand for commodity exports and an emerging African middle class. Only emerging Asian economies register higher growth rates than Africa (World Economic Forum 2013:42). Energetic growth across the continent is being buttressed by the economic presence and investments of leading emerging economies. These countries see opportunities in Africa where many Western economies in the past only saw risk (Sanlam Investment Management 2011:para. 7). They are shaping Africa's global political economy through increased levels of foreign direct investment and development financing:

> The turnaround in emerging Africa is neither temporary nor simply the result of favorable commodity prices. The revival persisted through the global recession of the late 1990s, and these countries weathered the 2009 global economic crisis better than most developing countries. Something deeper is at work. (Radelet 2010:2)

Western business and investment firms are currently shifting their attention to Africa's vast economic potential and abundant opportunities. Financial analysts believe that attention should be given to countries where the powerful emerging economies countries are themselves investing (Sullivan 2011). Africa is the unexpected new destination for global capital flows. These rapid transformations are provoking the emergence of regional financial centres as African states, investment firms, and businesses respond to these new levels of capital inflow and create the necessary institutional framework to control capital flows. These actors are diversifying their financial activities, deepening their lending, and increasing their reach through new products and new technologies (World Bank 2006).

The issue of how African cities are being integrated into this changing world order has largely not been raised or addressed. The rest of this chapter focuses on the central and strategic place that South Africa is carving out amid these transformations as Africa's leading power. South Africa plans to become the main gateway for flows of capital entering the region by supporting and reinforcing Johannesburg's role as international financial centre.

JOHANNESBURG: THE RISE OF
FINANCE IN SOUTH AFRICA

South Africa's historical trajectory has been shaped by its role as world gold producer, its place within the Britain's Empire, and its close ties to the Western international financial institutions for over 100 years. The South African banking and financial industry became, and remains, the most sophisticated in Africa. Its centre is Johannesburg, built around the mining industry when gold was discovered on the Witwatersrand in 1886. The ensuing mineral revolution coincided with the transition of the world financial system to a monetary system based on the gold standard and controlled by the British state and private financiers. The history of banking and finance in South Africa shows the progress from small local banks of the 19th century dotted over the country to the highly concentrated commercial banks of the 20th century (Houghton 1971:46).

The Union State of 1910 secured British economic supremacy in South Africa in spite of it being run by an Afrikaner-dominated government (Ally 1994:139). So while South Africa became politically independent, it remained an imperial dependency directed by Britain's interests in the spheres of banking, currency, and mining (1994:140). The Afrikaans Republican government was seen by the mining magnates as a rural community incapable of managing capitalist industrialisation (Beinart 2001:64).

Fears that the structure of capitalist accumulation would be upheaved by the election of the Afrikaner National Party (NP) in 1948 were unfounded as Afrikaner governments failed to create an 'Afrikaner socialist order' and nationalise the gold mining industry (Terreblanche 2005:302). The NP did not restructure or capture the 'foreign' system of capitalism, and the symbiosis between state and capital was maintained with little adaptation after 1948 and into the era of apartheid. Rather, the relationship between white Afrikaner state and white English capital was reinforced through a common goal of structural subjugation of Black Africans (2005:303). The new Afrikaner political elite relied upon white capitalists' power and networks and the English business class was reassured that their position was not threatened by the change of power when the Nationalists came to power. This collaboration between Afrikaner state and English capital was reinforced through apartheid's racial capitalism from 1949 to 1994.

EGOLI: CITY OF GOLD

Sassen (2012) sees cities as complex systems and incomplete. In that incompleteness lays the capacity of cities to outlive complex political and social systems. This capacity to move through various political systems and scales of governance is clearly evident in financial cities that have been part of city-states, empires, colonies, and the modern international state system.

Johannesburg's history demonstrates this capacity as it moved through Afrikaans rule, British imperialism, apartheid, racial segregation, and the creation of townships around the white core, and now in the postapartheid period as an African metropolis. The province of Gauteng—primarily composed of the cities of Johannesburg, Ekurhuleni (the East Rand), and Tshwane (greater Pretoria)—is fast becoming a polycentric urban region.

Johannesburg is known informally in Zulu as Egoli, place of gold. Gauteng, the province in which Johannesburg is situated, means 'place of gold' in Sesotho. Johannesburg rose on a gold reef on the Witwatersrand range of hills. The world rush sparked by discovery of gold in the 1880s created a city from tent town to wood and iron shanties to bricks and mortar buildings within a couple of decades. Before the gold, the landscape was dotted with African homesteads and farmhouses. This was the land of one of two Afrikaans republics, the South African Republic (later called the Transvaal under apartheid rule), with Pretoria as its capital. The other Afrikaans republic was the Orange Free State. Johannesburg was founded in 1886 as Europeans settled on the East Rand and the Johannesburg Stock Exchange (JSE) was established in 1887 in the wake of the gold rush. The city grew at a phenomenal rate into one of the globe's youngest major bustling metropolises. Intensive building during the 1930s during an economic boom after South Africa abandons Britain's gold standard and its own printed currency is matched by extensive gold reserves.

The underbelly of this system was the growth of segregation and new townships such as Soweto (South Western Township). More than half of Johannesburg's population was black, being made up of migrant labour coming in from rural areas. Most were living in multiracial shanty towns near the gold mines on the East Rand or in mine compounds. But Johannesburg's City Council established racially segregated residential areas, and Johannesburg's black residents were relocated outside of the central business district. One of these new areas for the relocated black population was Alexandra Township, which is now only 6 km away from Sandton, Africa's wealthiest suburb and financial heart.

In the 1950s, Johannesburg's role as financial centre deepened with the emergence of short-term money markets, new financial institutions such as the Land Bank, discount and accepting houses, building societies and the JSE (Houghton 1971:46). The role of South African business and finance was much more limited during the later period of apartheid through international political isolation, sanctions, and self-imposed domestic exchange controls (Verhoef 2011:5). Domestic economic development took place in an incubated space but at the same time as the internationalisation of South African finance and business enterprises was reined in. However, this incubation developed a robust platform for rapid internationalisation of business and finance once political and economic restrictions were removed, as was the case in the early 1990s.

In 2000, the Stock Exchange moved from Johannesburg's central business district to Sandton City, Africa's richest square mile situated in the north of the city. While deeply enmeshed in the transnational economic and capital networks of the country, financial cities obtain a supranational status through connections to global actors and institutional arrangements. Financial centres pool expertise, resources, political power, and capital with the common goal of being part of global capital's infrastructure. Making financial centres international depends on acquiring an exceptional status. Such is the case of Sandton, the heart of Johannesburg's financial centre. The decision to relocate was taken in wake of desegregation as apartheid came to an end and people flooded into Johannesburg. Inner Johannesburg became an international case study in urban decay as the wealth left.

Sandton's financial centre is only 6 km from Alexandra, one of Johannesburg's poorest townships. The very modern and upmarket area of Sandton is separated from Alexandra, or known as Alex for short, by Gauteng's M1 *De Villiers Graaff,* a major freeway that circles Johannesburg. Sandton's financial/township boundary brings together an encounter of the global and the local, international capital and entrenched poverty, technological sophistication in the financial world next to a lack of back services for township residents. Sandton, while fortified by freeways and armed security, exists within a growing African city. Alexandra and the rest of Johannesburg are not kept out of Sandton; township residents sell newspapers on its streets and work in the offices, shops, and coffee bars. They beg on the streets and are part of its everyday social and economic activities. There is a mix of inclusion and exclusion typical of major urban centres. Nuttall and Mbembe (2008:9) suggest that we see the informal as not being outside of the formal; how they end up working together produces unique city forms. For Johannesburg, this form reflects the rise, fall, and reconstruction of a segregated city. This segregation did not stop people moving constantly across lines of segregation and into and out of the city and townships (2008:13).

Building on Asian scholars' framework of 'multiple modernities' of the city, Nuttall and Mbembe (2008:16) propose to move analysis of Johannesburg past habitual stories of the 'rise of apartheid' and racial segregation and to see it as an African metropolis. Johannesburg grew from a frontier city into a metropolis tied to global markets within a century; in less than 15 years after its creation it had all the functional zones and residential patterns in place (2008:18). It is the embodiment of an African metropolis of 'ceaseless metamorphosis'.

A central component of the African National Congress's—South Africa's ruling party—foreign policy is to fortify Johannesburg's role as the leading African financial centre. The country sees its relation to Africa as part of its comparative advantage as gateway. It aims to increase its presence on the continent through manufacturing, financial, and banking services and technology dependent products such as Information Technology. South Africa is one of the leading countries already operating in Africa. In that sense, it is both a gateway for non-African actors doing business in Southern Africa and a competitor with these same emerging economies in other African markets.

'GATEWAY' TO AFRICA

In the last two decades, South Africa has moved from pariah state to new player on the global scene. The vision of gateway arises as shifts in the global patterns of production, trade, and investment create fresh opportunities for the country. China's invitation to South Africa to join the BRIC is about forging political economic connections with the African continent. What the G7 was for the previous world order, BRICS is for the new, and to make it more representative, there has to be an African economy. This economy is South Africa, with its world-class financial sector based in Johannesburg, experience in African markets, and extensive corporate footprint on the African continent. It is already the biggest emerging-economy investor in the continent, and its companies are active in at least half of all African countries. South Africa sees the city of Johannesburg as the continental headquarters for companies doing business in Africa: 'South Africa's location, its strength in financial services and its banking infrastructure make it a potential gateway into Africa. Government proposes measures to enhance this role' (National Treasury 2010:78).

Just 20 years ago, South Africa was a minor, if not irrelevant actor in world affairs, ostracised through economic and political sanctions: 'Africa was little more than an after-thought, or at best the passive object of other nations' foreign policies' (Herbert 2011). South Africa's transition to democracy in the early 1990s took place on the tail of the fall of the Berlin Wall, the end of the Cold War, the transition of the Eastern Bloc countries to democracy, economic boom in the USA, and the rise of the Asian Tigers and their export-oriented economies. It was a period of tremendous change in the world order. In little more than two decades, Africa is coming centre stage on the global political economy as a continent with resources, tremendous market potential and high growth rates.

The undeniable and steady move to a multipolar world order is accompanied by the increasing influence of the BRICS. These developments are having a vital impact on South Africa's domestic and foreign policies. The changing world order is providing important windows of opportunity for South Africa as centres of power of the last century shift, and space for fresh prospects is created. South Africa is using the moment of discontinuity in world order to further its regional power and build its own regional sphere of political economic power. It is doing this by connecting more closely to rising economies in the global South their links to Africa. These developments are conveyed in rhetoric of new alliances, global change, and new opportunities, as is evident in the following excerpt of the South African Minister of International Relations and Cooperation's speech:

> Led by President Zuma, we joined the BRICS formation, just a few years after we co-founded IBSA [India, Brazil, South Africa], as another important formation to champion the cause of the marginalized, and

to bring their voice into the political space that will craft our common future. We have maintained excellent bilateral relations with each of the BRICS countries and our membership binds us in a community of nations that are at the cusp of the wave of change. (Nkoana-Mashabane 2011:para. 32)

Brazil, Russia, India, China and South Africa (BRICS) have formed a bloc to institutionalise their growing influence and augment their bargaining capacity. The new various institutional arrangements being set up by the emerging powers are 'positioning themselves in relation to the system of global governance, the ideas they articulate, and the extent to which their rise constitutes a counter-narrative to that which is presented by the West' (Qobo 2011:3).

While the world is still operating through the set of institutions established under U.S. hegemony after the Second World War, such as the World Bank, World Trade Organization, and International Monetary Fund, the global material bases are shifting as production patterns change. We can also see a different set of norms that offers alternatives to the neoliberal regime that has dominated international relations for the last decades. As highlighted in this chapter, an interesting example of these normative shifts can be seen in South Africa's President Zuma's State of the Nation Address last February 2012, when he reiterated his 'look East' foreign policy. The major component of the Address was that the government is going to bring infrastructure expansion back within state control.

South Africa is placing Johannesburg at the centre of these emerging transnational financial networks in Africa. Domestic growth in South Africa will take place in the service sector (Cilliers 2013), of which finance is dominant. This will reinforce Johannesburg's status as sub-Saharan Africa's leading financial centre. As an established centre, Johannesburg will be buoyed by the rise of financial and economic activity in Africa. For instance, South Africa sees the country as the headquarters for Islamic-based businesses and finance (Cobbett 2011). Finance Minister Pravin Gordhan put in place measures critical for Islamic product development (National Treasury 2010). The state's goals are to encourage global financial actors to use Johannesburg as the springboard into Africa's Islamic communities. The state has revised exchange controls and tax laws pertaining to Islamic finance in order to make the movement of capital through the country and into regional markets smoother. The goal is to harness the burst of Islamic finance that reflects the growth of a global industry based on alternative ideologies and which is growing in African communities. Integration into African markets is critical for South Africa's domestic growth.

In an effort to establish South Africa as this 'Gateway to Africa', South Africa has further changed its tax laws and exchange controls with the hope of providing incentives for investments, not only into Africa, but also in the rest of the world, to be routed to Johannesburg. With interest in African markets on the rise, South Africa offers global actors proximity to these markets, a highly developed legal and financial sector, no language barrier, and excellent infrastructure. However, Johannesburg is not alone. But South Africa is not the only state, and indeed global company, with an African strategy. There is competition between African states, as well as financial actors such as MasterCard, to secure access to niche and mainstream markets. Johannesburg as gateway and financial centre faces competition with leading African cities.

African cities are on the rise. They are increasingly connected to other global cities and hubs of economic activity outside of industrialised Western economies. With over 1 billion people, the African continent presents economic opportunities for global investors. Investment will transit via financial centres and these centres, on the African continent, are the historic hubs of South Africa–Johannesburg, Kenya–Nairobi, and Nigeria–Lagos. Johannesburg is in competition with other rising African financial cities, principally with key offshore financial centres in the Indian Ocean, such as Mauritius, and ancient ports on the coast of Africa, such as Nairobi.

Nairobi, the financial city of East Africa and alternative point of entry for Islamic capital transiting from the Middle East, is at the heart of the Kenyan government's plans to put the country on the global financial circuit. Uhuru Kenyatta, current president of Kenya and the country's former finance minister, launched the all-encompassing Nairobi International Financial Centre (NIFC) plan as part of Kenya's Vision 2030. The NIFC will integrate Kenya's domestic financial sector to others in the region and globally and will act as hub for non-African actors seeking to do business on the continent. For instance, the Kenyan state aims to do business with companies that have established their base in Mauritius or in the Seychelles while operating in African markets (Mugwe 2011). In line with this, Kenya's parliament passed The Nairobi Centre for Arbitration Act, which establishes a dispute resolution centre to administer domestic and international commercial agreements (Wambora 2013).

While South Africa is still Africa's leading economy, Nigeria is set to overtake in the near future. With a population of an estimated 160 million people, the Nigerian federal government has a clear vision for a broad based national development—as set out in its 20:2020 vision—to position Nigeria as one of the world's top 20 economies by 2020. The financial sector is identified by the state as playing a critical role in Nigeria's quest for rapid development by unlocking the growth and development aspirations of the nation (National Planning Commission 2009:7–9). Even Somaliland, a self-declared sovereign state that is internationally recognised as an autonomous region of Somalia, sees itself as gateway to Africa through its port Berbera in the Gulf of Aden (Manson 2013). While Berbera is not considered an international city of great importance, this proclamation gives an indication of the transnational networks being set up in Africa.

CONCLUSION

Over the next few decades, Africa's urban population will grow by more than 300 million people (Cities Alliance 2013). These mega-cities reflect the heightened pace of urbanisation taking place in Africa. High growth in African markets, stalling economic activity in the industrialised economies, and the need to find new lucrative financial markets are pushing global finance to think differently about their activity and reach in African markets. The sheer scale of what is taking place makes it worth global capital's while to expand into these markets. Discourse is shifting from Africa as a hopeless continent to Africa as an emerging pole of growth and as a vibrant new frontier market.

Historic economic hubs in sub-Saharan Africa are being identified as gateways for investment and business into the continent. In spite of these rapid changes, very little research is being conducted to trace and analyse the growth of African financial cities. The reason for this may lay in outdated ideas about Africa as 'the dark continent'. It may be in part because major financial cities are situated in Europe, the United States, and in Asia, and thinking about their rise in Africa calls for a different outlook on what is unfolding.

I am suggesting that a way forward in this for political economy is through a reengagement with Braudel's framework of world-economies. This concept recognises that different world-economies can exist at the same time, that they can overlap, and that they can be rooted in different social orders. This analytical grid enables us to understand that although there is an increasingly global economy, it is not all stemming from a unique place of production. The global economy is not a total unit but a combination of networks and arrangements of trade, investment, politics, and culture. This analytically permits investigation for the assortment and range of social orders and systems that exist around the world. Consequently, it becomes possible to think about African cities in their own historic contexts and examine in what ways financial centres in the South resemble historical centres in Europe and North America and yet are distinctive as African cities and as centres that reflect the changing world order.

References and Further Reading

Abrahamsen, Rita and Michael C. Williams. 2009. "Guest Editor's Introduction." *Security Dialogue* 40(4–5):363–372.

Acuto, Michele. 2011. "Finding the Global City: An Analytical Journey through the 'Invisible College'." *Urban Studies* 4:2953–2973.

Acuto, Michele. 2012. "Urbanizing China-EU Relations?" *CPD Blog*, September 27 (http://uscpublicdiplomacy.org/index.php/newswire/cpdblog_detail/urbanizing_china-eu_relations/).

Acuto, Michele. 2013. *Global Cities, Governance and Diplomacy: The Urban Link*. Abingdon, UK: Routledge.

Africa Progress Panel. 2011. *Africa Progress Report 2011: The Transformative Power of Partnerships*. Retrieved September 9, 2013 (www.africaprogresspanel. org/wp-content/uploads/2013/08/2011_APR_The_Transformative_Power_of_Partnerships_ENG.pdf).

Agnew, John A. and Stuart Corbridge. 1994. *Mastering Space: Hegemony, Territory and International Political Economy*. London: Routledge.

Agyeman, Julian. 2005. *Sustainable Communities and the Challenge of Environmental Justice*. New York: New York University Press.

Ainley, Kirsten. 2012. "The Social Practice of Institutional Responsibility." In *Responding to "Delinquent" Institutions: Blaming, Punishing, and Rehabilitating Collective Moral Agents in International Relations*, edited by Toni Erskine. London: Palgrave.

Albert, Mathias and Lothar Brock. 1996. "Debordering the World of States: New Spaces in International Relations." *New Political Science* 18(1):69–106.

Aldecoa, Francisco and Michael Keating. 1999. *Paradiplomacy in Action: The Foreign Relations of Subnational Governments*. London: F. Cass.

Alfsen-Norodom, Christine. 2004. "Urban Biosphere and Society: Partnership of Cities." *Annals of the New York Academy of Sciences* 10(23):1–9.

Alger, Chadwick. 2011. "Searching for Democratic Potential in Emerging Global Governance." *International Journal of Peace Studies* 16(2):1–24.

Ally, Russell. 1994. *Gold and Empire: The Bank of England and South Africa's Gold Producers, 1886–1926*. Johannesburg, South Africa: Witwatersrand University Press.

Alter, L. 2008. SustainLane ranks Greenest US Cities, Treehugger. Retrieved September 22, 2008 (www.treehugger.com/sustainable-product-design/sustainlane-ranks-greenest-us-cities/page2.html).

Amen, M. Mark. 1997. "Profits Without Growth: Privatizing the U.S. Economy in the 1980s." Pp. 339–352 in *President Reagan and the World*, edited by E. Schmertz, N. Datlof, and A. Ugrinsky. Westport, CT: Greenwood Press.

Amen, M. Mark. 1999. "Borrowing Authority; Eclipsing Government." Pp. 173–193 in *Approaches to Global Governance Theory*, edited by M. Hewson and T. J. Sinclair. Albany, NY: State University Press of New York.

Amen, M. Mark. 2011. *Cities and Global Governance: New Sites for International Relations.* Farnham, Surrey, UK: Ashgate.

Amen, M. Mark, Kevin Archer, and Martin M. Bosman, eds. 2006. *Relocating Global Cities: From the Center to the Margins.* Lanham, MD: Rowman & Littlefield.

Amin, Ash. 2002. "Spatialities of Globalisation." *Environment and Planning A* 34(3):385–399.

Arbour, Louise. 2008. "The Responsibility to Protect as a Duty of Care in International Law and Practice." *Review of International Studies* 34(3):445–458.

Arrighi, Giovanni. 2005. "Hegemony Unravelling—2." *New Left Review* 33:83–116.

Arrighi, Giovanni. 2010. *The Long Twentieth Century: Money, Power, and the Origins of Our Times* (new and updated ed.). London: Verso.

ARUP. 2010a. *Arup C40 Workshop Supports Ho Chi Minh City in Developing Water Management Master Plan* (www.arup.com/News/2010_05_May/12_May_2010_Ho_Chi_Minh_C40_workshop.aspx).

ARUP. 2010b. *Melbourne Smart City.* London: ARUP.

ARUP. 2012. *Zero Net Emissions by 2020* (www.arup.com/Projects/Zero_Net_Emissions.aspx).

Aspinwall, Mark and Gerald Schneider, eds. 2001. *The Rules of Integration: Institutionalist Approaches to the Study of Europe.* Manchester, UK: Manchester University Press.

Balde, Lisa. 2011. *EPA Orders Chicago, Calumet Rivers Cleaned.* Retrieved February 15, 2011 (www.nbcchicago.com/news/local/EPA-Orders-Chicago-Calumet-Rivers-Cleaned-121700494.html).

Bardhan, Ashkok. 2009. "The Twin Excesses—Financialization and Globalization—Caused the Crash." *YaleGlobal,* May 6. Retrieved November 14, 2013 (http://yaleglobal.yale.edu/content/two-views-global-crisis-2).

Barton, Jonathan R. 2006. "Sustentabilidad Urbana Como Planificación Estratégica." *Revista Eure* 32(96):27–45.

Baycan-Levent, Tüzin, Aliye Ahu Gülümser Akgün, and Seda Kundak. 2010. "Success Conditions for Urban Networks: Eurocities and Sister Cities." *European Planning Studies* 18(8):1187–1206.

Begg, Iain. 1999. "Cities and Competitiveness." *Urban Studies* 36(5–6):795–809 (www.kulturplan.lixnet.dk/pdf/litteratur/city-competitive-begg.pdf).

Beinart, William. 2001. *Twentieth-Century South Africa,* 2nd ed. Oxford, UK: Oxford University Press.

Betsill, Michele M. and Harriet Bulkeley. 2004. "Transnational Networks and Global Environmental Governance: The Cities for Climate Protection Program." *International Studies Quarterly* 48(2):471–493.

Bichler, Shimshon and Jonathan Nitzan. 2012. "Imperialism and Financialism: A Story of a Nexus." *Journal of Critical Globalization Studies* 5:42–78.

Bigio, Anthony G. 2003. "Cities and Climate Change." Pp. 91–100 in *Building Safer Cities: The Future of Disaster Risk,* edited by A. Kreimer, M. Arnold, and A. Carlin. Washington, DC: World Bank.

Bigio, Anthony G. and Bharat Dahiya. 2004. *Urban Environment and Infrastructure: Toward Livable Cities.* Washington, DC: World Bank.

Bingaman, Jeff. 2011. *1016 The Municipal Bond Market Support Act of 2011.* Retrieved November 18, 2013 (www.govtrack.us/congress/bills/112/s1016).

Blank, Yishai. 2006. "The City and the World." *Columbia Journal of Transnational Law* 44(3):869–931.

Block, Robert. 2005. "Miffed at Washington, Police Develop Own Antiterror Plans." *Wall Street Journal,* October 10.

Blyth, Mark. 2002. *Great Transformations: Economic Ideas and Institutional Change in the Twentieth Century.* Cambridge, UK: Cambridge University Press.

Bodie, Zvi, Alex Kane, and Alan J. Marcus. 2006. *Essentials of Investments,* 6th intl. ed. London: McGraw-Hill.

Bone, John. 2012. "The Deregulation Ethic and the Conscience of Capitalism: How the Neoliberal 'Free Market' Model Undermines Rationality and Moral Conduct." *Globalizations* 9(5):651–665.

Borja, Jordi and Manuel Castells (with Mireia Belil and Chris Benner). 1997. *Local and Global: The Management of Cities in the Information Age.* London: Earthscan.

Borraz, Olivier and Peter John. 2004. "The Transformation of Urban Political Leadership in Western Europe." *International Journal of Urban and Regional Research* 28(1):107–120.

Bouteligier, Sofie. 2009. "Cities Break New Ground." *The Broker*, November 30. Retrieved November 3, 2013 (www.thebrokeronline.eu/Special-Reports/Special-Report-Cities-of-the-world-unite/Cities-break-new-ground).

Bouteligier, Sofie. 2012. *Cities, Networks, and Global Environmental Governance: Spaces of Innovation, Places of Leadership.* New York: Routledge.

Bouteligier, Sofie. 2013. "Inequality in New Global Governance Arrangements: The North–South Divide in Transnational Municipal Networks." *Innovation: The European Journal of Social Science Research* 26(3):251–267.

Bowles, Erskine and Al Simpson. 2010. *The Moment of Truth.* Washington, DC: President's National Commission on Fiscal Responsibility and Reform. Retrieved November 14, 2013 (www.fiscalcommission.gov/sites/fiscalcommission.gov/files/documents/TheMomentofTruth12_1_2010.pdf).

Brand, Peter. 2007. "Green Subjection: The Politics of Neoliberal Urban Environmental Management." *International Journal of Urban and Regional Research* 31(3):616–632.

Brand, Peter and Michael J. Thomas. 2005. *Urban Environmentalism: Global Change and the Mediation of Local Conflict.* New York: Routledge.

Braudel, Fernand. 1982. *Civilization and Capitalism, 15th–18th Century.* Vol. 2, The Wheels of Commerce. New York: Harper & Row.

Braudel, Fernand. 1984. *Civilization and Capitalism, 15th–18th Century.* Vol. 3, The Perspective of the World. Translated by S. Reynold. New York: Harper & Row.

Braudel, Fernand. 1993. *A History of Civilizations.* Translated by R. Mayne. New York: Penguin Books.

Bremmer, Ian. 2010. *The End of the Free Market: Who Wins the War Between States and Corporations?* New York: Portfolio.

Brennan-Galvin, Ellen. 2002. "Crime and Violence in an Urbanizing World." *Journal of International Affairs* 56(1):123–145.

Brenner, Neil. 1998. "Global Cities, Glocal States: Global City Formation and State Territorial Restructuring in Contemporary Europe." *Review of International Political Economy* 5(1):1–37.

Brenner, Neil. 2004. *New State Spaces: Urban Governance and the Rescaling of Statehood.* Oxford, UK: Oxford University Press.

Brenner, Neil and Christian Schmid. 2012. "Planetary Urbanisation." Pp. 10–13 in *Urban Constellations*, edited by M. Gandy. Berlin: Jovis.

Brenner, Neil and Nik Theodore. 2002. "Cities and the Geographies of 'Actually Existing Neoliberalism'." *Antipode* 34(3):1–32.

Brooks, Sarah M. 2011. "BRIC Gets Built Up: South Africa's Inclusion and China's Response." *Consultancy Africa Intelligence*. Retrieved January 28, 2011 (www.consultancyafrica.com/index.php?option=com_content&view=article&id=641:bric-gets-built-up-south-africas-inclusion-and-chinas-response&catid=58:asia-dimension-discussion-papers&Itemid=264).

Brugmann, Jeb. 2007. "Locating the 'Local Agenda': Preserving Public Interest in the Evolving Urban World." Pp. 331–354 in *Scaling Urban Environmental Challenges: From Local to Global and Back*, edited by P.J. Marcotullio and G. McGranahan. London: Earthscan.

Brugmann, Jeb. 2009. *Welcome to the Urban Revolution: How Cities Are Changing the World*. St Lucia, Australia: University of Queensland Press.

Brütsch, Christian M. 2012. "From Sovereign Prerogatives to Metropolitan Rule? The Anarchical Society in the Urban Age." *International Studies Perspectives* 14(3):307–324.

Bulkeley, Harriet. 2006. "Urban Sustainability: Learning from Best Practice?" *Environment and Planning A* 38(6):1029–1044.

Bulkeley, Harriet. 2013. *Cities and Climate Change*. London: Routledge.

Bulkeley, Harriet and Michele M. Betsill. 2003. *Cities and Climate Change: Urban Sustainability and Global Environmental Governance*. New York: Routledge.

Bulkeley, Harriet and Michele M. Betsill. 2005. "Rethinking Sustainable Cities: Multilevel Governance and the 'Urban' Politics of Climate Change." *Environmental Politics* 14(1):42–63.

Bulkeley, Harriet and Vanesa Castán Broto. 2012. "Government by Experiment? Global Cities and the Governing of Climate Change." *Transactions of the Institute of British Geographers* 38(3):361–375.

Bullard, Robert D., Paul Mohai, Robin Saha, and Beverly Wright. 2007. *Grassroots Struggles to Dismantle Environmental Racism in the United States*. Washington, DC: United Church of Christ Justice and Witness Ministries.

Burchill, Scott. 2009. "Liberalism." Pp. 57–84 in *Theories of International Relations*, 4th ed., edited by S. Burchill, A. Linklater, R. Devetak, J. Donnelly, T. Nardin, M. Paterson, C. Reus-Smit, and J. True. London: Palgrave Macmillan.

Burdett, Richard and Deyan Sudjic. 2007. *The Endless City: The Urban Age Project by the London School of Economics and Deutsche Bank's Alfred Herrhausen Society*. London: Phaidon.

Burdett, Richard and Deyan Sudjic. 2011. *Living in the Endless City: The Urban Age Project by the London School of Economics and Deutsche Bank's Alfred Herrhausen Society*. London: Phaidon.

Business Day. 2011. "We Can Ill Afford to be Complacent." *Business Day*, January 31. Retrieved January 31 (www.businessday.co.za/articles/Content.aspx?id=132907).

Calder, Kent E. and Mariko de Freytas. 2009. "Global Political Cities as Actors in Twenty-First Century International Affairs." *SAIS Review* 29(1):79–97.

Cassis, Youssef. 2010. *Capitals of Capital: The Rise and Fall of International Financial Centres 1780–2009*. Cambridge, UK: Cambridge University Press.

Castells, Manuel. 1996. *The Rise of the Network Society*. Cambridge, MA: Blackwell.

Castells, Manuel. 1997. *The Power of Identity*. Cambridge, MA: Blackwell.

Castells, Manuel. 2000a. *The Information Age: Economy, Society and Culture*, 2nd ed. Vol. 1.,The Rise of the Network Society. Malden, UK: Blackwell.

Castells, Manuel. 2000b. *The Information Age: Economy, Society and Culture*, 2nd ed. Vol. 3, End of Millennium. Malden, UK: Blackwell.

Castells, Manuel. 2001. *The Internet Galaxy: Reflections on the Internet, Business, and Society*. Oxford, UK: Oxford University Press.

Castells, Manuel. 2004. *The Network Society: A Cross-Cultural Perspective*. Cheltenham, UK: Edward Elgar.

CCI. 2010. *Our Approach: Cities* (www.clintonfoundation.org/what-we-do:clinton-climate-initiative/our-approach/cities).

CFCB. 2010. *CFCB Programme: How Carbon Finance Supports Sustainable Development in Megacities in the South* (www.lowcarboncities.info/home.html).

C40. 2007. *C40 Summit Communiqué*. Retrieved April 16, 2010 (www.c40cities/org/docs/communique_2007.pdf).

C40. 2009. *C40 Large Cities Climate Summit Seoul: Seoul Declaration*. Retrieved April 16, 2010 (www.c40cities.org/news/news-20090522.jsp).

C40. 2010a. *C40 Cities* (www.c40cities.org/cities).

C40. 2010b. *C40 Goals for UNFCCC* (www.c40cities.org/about/goals.jsp).

C40. 2010c. *C40 UrbanLife* (www.c40cities.org/initiatives/c40-urban-life.jsp).

C40. 2010d. *Carbon Financing* (www.c40cities.org/initiatives/carbon-financing. jsp).

C40. 2010e. *Clinton Climate Initiative City Programmes* (www.c40cities.org/initiatives/ ccicityprogramme).

C40. 2011. *A "Greener" Mexico City* (www.c40cities.org/C40blog/a-"greener"- mexico-city).

Checker, Melissa. 2001. "Wiped Out by the 'Greenwave': Environmental Gentri- fication and the Paradoxical Politics of Urban Sustainability." *City and Society* 23(2):210–229.

Chenoweth, Erica and Susan Clarke. 2010. "All Terrorism Is Local: Constructing Urban Coalitions for Homeland Security in the American Federal System." *Politi- cal Research Quarterly* 63(3):495–507.

Cilliers, Jakkie. 2013. "SAIIA Podcast 17: South Africa's Economic Future." *South Afri- can Institute for International Affairs*, September 15. Retrieved September 24, 2013 (www.saiia.org.za/multimedia/saiia-podcast-17-south-africas-economic-future).

Cisco. 2011. *Cisco Smart Work Centers: Foster Urban Regeneration, Social Inclu- sion, and Reduced Carbon Footprint* (www.cisco.com/web/strategy/docs/scc/ smart_work_center_solution_overview_us_0725.pdf).

Cities Alliance. 2013. *AFDB: Cities Can Be a Key Driver in Africa's Transformation.* Retrieved September 23, 2013 (www.citiesalliance.org/node/3947).

City of Chicago. 1986. *Building the Basics: The Final Report of the Mayor's Task Force on Steel and Southeast Chicago.* Chicago, IL: City of Chicago.

City of Chicago. 2008. *Chicago Climate Action Plan: Our City, Our Future.* Retrieved November 5, 2013 (www.joycefdn.org/assets/1/7/CCAPFinalReport.pdf).

City of Chicago Department of Planning and Development. 2004. *Calumet Design Guidelines.* Chicago, IL: City of Chicago.

City of Chicago Department of Planning and Development. 2005. *Calumet Open Space Reserve Plan.* Retrieved November 2, 2013 (www.cityofchicago.org/content/ dam/city/depts/zlup/Sustainable_Development/Publications/Calumet_Open_ Space_Reserve/COSR_plan.pdf).

City of Copenhagen. 2010. *The Copenhagen Climate Summit for Mayors.* Retrieved April 22, 2010 (www.climatesummitformayors.dk).

City of Johannesburg. 2013. *Overview: Johannesburgas Business Centre.* Retrieved September 27, 2013 (www.joburg.org.za/index.php?option=com_content&id=410&Itemid=58).

City of Seattle. 2011a. *Getting to Zero: A Pathway to Carbon Neutral Seattle.* Seat- tle, WA. Retrieved November 5, 2013 (www.seattle.gov/environment/documents/ CN_Seattle_Report_May_2011.pdf).

City of Seattle. 2011b. *Swedes Name Seattle as "Greenest City in North Amer- ica."* Retrieved February 22, 2012 (http://conlin.seattle.gov/2011/09/15/ swedes-name-seattle-as-'greenest-city-in-north-america'/).

City of Seattle. 2011c. *The City of Seattle Is Making Progress on Cleanup of Slip 4.* Seattle Public Utilities and the Office of the Mayor. Retrieved February 12, 2012 (www.ldwg.org/Assets/EAA/Slip%204%20Email%20Update%20Dec%20 2011.pdf).

Clark, Ian. 1999. *Globalization and International Relations Theory.* Oxford, UK: Oxford University Press.

Clarke, Susan E. and Erica Chenoweth. 2006. "The Politics of Vulnerability: Con- structing Local Performance Regimes for Homeland Security." *Review of Policy Research* 23(1):95–114.

Clarke, Terry N. 2000. "Old and New Paradigms for Urban Research, Globalization and the Fiscal Austerity and Urban Innovation Project." *Urban Affairs Review* 36(1):3–45.

Clinton v Cedar Rapids and the Missouri River Railroad, 24 Iowa 455 (1868).

Coaffee, Jon and David Murikami Wood. 2006. "Security Is Coming Home: Rethinking Scale and Constructing Resilience in the Global Urban Response to Terrorist Risk." *International Relations* 20(4):503–517.

Coaffee, Jon, David Murikami Wood, and Peter Rogers. 2009. *The Everyday Resilience of the City: How Cities Respond to Terrorism and Disaster*. New York: Palgrave Macmillan.

Cobbett, Elizabeth. 2010. "The South African Reserve Bank and the Telling of Monetary Stories." *Nokoko* 1:67–98.

Cobbett, Elizabeth. 2011. "The Shaping of Islamic Finance in South Africa: Public Islam and Muslim Publics." *Journal of Islamic Studies* 31:29–59.

Cohen, Michael. 2001. "Urban Assistance and the Material World: Learning by Doing at the World Bank." *Environment & Urbanization* 13(1):37–60.

Cohen, R. 1981. "The New International Division of Labor, Multinational Corporations and Urban Hierarchy." Pp. 287–315 in *Urbanization and Urban Planning in Capitalist Society*, edited by M. Dear and A. Scott. London: Methuen.

Collier, Ute. 1997. "Local Authorities and Climate Protection in the European Union: Putting Subsidiarity into Practice?" *Local Environment* 2(1):39–57.

Conca, Ken. 2005. "Old States in New Bottles? The Hybridization of Authority in Global Environmental Governance." Pp. 181–205 in *The State and the Global Ecological Crisis*, edited by J. Barry and R. Eckersley. Cambridge, MA: MIT Press.

Conlin, Richard. 2011. "Let's Make the Duwamish River the Center for a Sustainable City." *Seattle.gov*. Retrieved February 12, 2012 (http://conlin.seattle.gov/2011/11/07/let's-make-the-duwamish-river-the-center-for-a-sustainable-city).

Conway-Smith, Erin. 2011. "South Africa to be a BRIC." *GlobalPost*, January 8. Retrieved February 9, 2011 (www.globalpost.com/dispatch/south-africa/110107/south-africa-be-bric).

Corfee-Morlot, Jan, Lamia Kamal-Chaoui, Michael G. Donovan, Ian Cochran, Alexis Robert, and Pierre-Jonathan Teasdale. 2009. "Cities, Climate Change and Multilevel Governance." *OECD Environmental Working Papers No. 14*.

Coupland, Reginald. 1945. *The Durham Report*. Oxford, UK: Clarendon Press.

Cox, Robert W. 1981. *Social Forces, States and World Orders: Beyond International Relations Theory*. Cambridge, UK: Cambridge University Press.

Cox, Robert W. 1987. *Production, Power and World Order: Social Forces in the Making of History*. New York: Columbia University Press.

Crane, Peter. 2010. *Calumet Connections: Seizing Opportunity and Meeting Challenge. Comments at the Calumet Summit, April 27–28, 2010*. Retrieved November 18, 2013 (www.docstoc.com/docs/60522840/Draftdraft-Sir-Peter-Crane-Comments-at-Calumet-Summit).

Criekemans, David. 2010. "Regional Sub-state Diplomacy from a Comparative Perspective: Quebec, Scotland, Bavaria, Catalonia, Wallonia and Flanders." *The Hague Journal of Diplomacy* 5(1/2):37–64.

Cronon, William. 1996. "The Trouble with Wilderness; or Getting Back to the Wrong Nature." Pp. 69–90 in *Uncommon Ground: Rethinking the Human Place in Nature*, edited by W. Cronon. New York: W.W. Norton and Company.

Curtis, Simon. 2011. "Global Cities and the Transformation of the International System." *Review of International Studies* 37(4):1923–1947.

Davis, Lois M., K. Jack Riley, Greg Ridgeway, Jennifer Pace, Sarah K. Cotton, Paul S. Steinberg, Kelly Damphousse, and Brent L. Smith. 2004. *When Terrorism Hits Home: How Prepared Are State and Local Law Enforcement?* Santa Monica, CA: RAND Corporation.

Davis, Mike. 2006. *Planet of Slums*. London: Verso.

DeAngelo, Benjamin J. and L. D. Danny Harvey. 1998. "The Jurisdictional Framework for Municipal Action to Reduce Greenhouse Gas Emissions: Case Studies from Canada, the USA and Germany." *Local Environment* 3(2):111–136.

de Leeuw, Evelyne. 2001. "Global and Local (Glocal) Health: The WHO Healthy Cities Programme." *Global Change and Human Health* 2(1):34–45.

De Ponte, Giulia. 2002. "The Changing Urban Discourse of Multilateral Aid Institutions." *International Social Science Journal* 54(172):205–216.

Desch, Michael C. 2001. *Soldiers in Cities: Military Operations on Urban Terrain.* Carlisle, PA: Strategic Studies Institute.

Dillinger, William. 1994. *Decentralisation and its Implications for Urban Service Delivery.* Washington, DC: World Bank.

Dillon, John Forrest. 1873. *The Law of Municipal Corporations*, Vol. 1, 2nd ed. New York: James Cockcroft.

Dobrovolny, Peter. 1999. *Salmon, Planning, and the ESA.* Dissertation, University of Washington.

Dodman, David. 2009. "Blaming Cities for Climate Change? An Analysis of Urban Greenhouse Gas Emissions Inventories." *Environment and Urbanization* 21(1):185–201.

Dolowitz, David and David Marsh. 1996. "Who Learns What from Whom: A Review of the Policy Transfer Literature." *Political Studies* 44(2):343–357.

Domenici, Pete and Alice Rivlin. 2010. *Restoring America's Future.* Washington, DC: Bipartisan Policy Center. Retrieved November 14, 2013 (www.bipartisanpolicy.org/sites/default/files/BPC%20FINAL%20REPORT%20FOR%20PRINTER%2002%2028%2011.pdf).

Donnelly, Jack. 2009. "Realism." Pp. 31–56 in *Theories of International Relations*, 4th ed., edited by S. Burchill, A. Linklater, R. Devetak, J. Donnelly, T. Nardin, M. Paterson, C. Reus-Smit, and J. True. London: Palgrave Macmillan.

DRCC. 2009. *Duwamish Valley Vision and Map Report.* Duwamish River Cleanup Coalition. Retrieved February 12, 2012 (www.duwamishcleanup.org/wp-content/uploads/2012/02/Duwamish-Valley-River-Report-2009.pdf).

DRCC. 2012. Retrieved February 12, 2012 (http://duwamishcleanup.org/about/history/).

Duchacek, Ivo D. 1984. "The International Dimension of Subnational Self-government." *Publius* 14(4):5–31.

Duchacek, Ivo D., Daniel Latouche, and Garth Stevenson, eds. 1988. *Perforated Sovereignties and International Relations: Trans-Sovereign Contacts of Subnational Governments.* New York: Greenwood Press.

Edwards, Michael, David Hulme, and Tina Wallace. 1999. "NGOs in a Global Future: Marrying Local Delivery to Worldwide Leverage." *Public Administration and Development* 19(2):117–136.

Eichengreen, Barry J. 1990. *Elusive Stability: Essays in the History of International Finance, 1919–1939.* Cambridge, UK: Cambridge University Press.

Eichengreen, Barry J. 1996. *Globalizing Capital: A History of the International Monetary System.* Princeton, NJ: Princeton University Press.

Eisinger, Peter. 2004. "The American City in the Age of Terror: A Preliminary Assessment of the Effects of September 11th." *Urban Affairs Review* 40(1):115–130.

Elander, Ingemar and Rolf Lidskog. 2000. "The Rio Declaration and Subsequent Global Initiatives." Pp. 31–54 in *Consuming Cities: The Urban Environment in the Global Economy After the Rio Declaration*, edited by N. Low, B. Gleeson, I. Elander, and R. Lidskog. London: Routledge.

Elden, Stuart. 2004. *Understanding Henri Lefebvre: Theory and the Possible.* London: Continuum.

Elden, Stuart. 2009. *Terror and Territory: The Spatial Extent of Sovereignty.* Minneapolis: University of Minnesota Press.

Engels, F. 2006. "Selections from *The Condition of the Working Class in England in 1844*." *Organization and Environment* 19(3):389–402.

Ergazakis, Kostas, Kostas Metaxiotis, and John Psarras. 2006. "Knowledge Cities: The Answer to the Needs of Knowledge-based Development." *Vine: The Journal of Information and Knowledge Management Systems* 36(1):67–84.

Feather, John. 2004. *The Information Society: A Study of Continuity and Change.* London: Facet Publishing.

Federation of Canadian Municipalities. 1979. *Resolution on Constitutional Reform Adopted by the 42nd Annual Conference of The Federation of Canadian Municipalities,* Quebec City, June 3–6.

Ferguson, Yale H. and Richard W. Mansbach. 1996. *Polities: Authority, Identities, and Change.* Columbia: University of South Carolina Press.

Field Museum. 2009. *Engaging Chicago Communities in the Chicago Climate Action Plan, Community #1: South Chicago.* Chicago, IL: The Field Museum Environment, Culture, and Conservation Program.

Finnemore, Martha and Kathryn Sikkink. 1998. "International Norm Dynamics and Political Change." *International Organization* 52(4):887–917.

Finnemore, Martha and Kathryn Sikkink. 2001. "Taking Stock: The Constructivist Research Program in International Relations and Comparative Politics." *Annual Review of Political Science* 4:391–416.

Fischer, Julie E. and Rebecca Katz. 2011. "The International Flow of Risk: The Governance of Health in an Urbanizing World." *Global Health Governance* 4(2):1–17.

Florida, Richard L. 2002. *The Rise of the Creative Class: And How It's Transforming Work, Leisure, Community, and Everyday Life.* New York: Basic Books.

Friedmann, John. 1986. "The World City Hypothesis." *Development and Change* 17(1):69–83.

Friends of the Calumet-Sag Trail. n.d. *Welcome.* Retrieved February 14, 2012 (http://calsagtrail.org/Friends_of_the_Calumet-Sag_Trail/Welcome.html).

Fusfeld, Daniel R. 2002. *The Age of the Economist,* 9th ed. New York: Addison Wesley.

Gaffkin, Frank and Barney Warf. 1993. "Urban Policy and the Post-Keynesian State in the United Kingdom and the United States." *International Journal of Urban and Regional Research* 17(1):67–84.

Galtung, Johan. 1971. "A Structural Theory of Imperialism." *Journal of Peace Research* 8(2):81–117.

Gamble, Andrew. 1994. *The Free Economy and the Strong State: The Politics of Thatcherism,* 2nd ed. Basingstoke, UK: Macmillan.

Garcia, Monique and John Byrne. 2011. "$17.9 Million Boost for Greening of Lake Calumet." *Chicago Tribune,* December 10. Retrieved November 2, 2013 (http://articles.chicagotribune.com/2011-12-10/news/ct-met-calumet-openspace-1210-20111210_1_brownfield-site-lake-calumet-state-funding).

Gebre-Egziabher, A. 2004. "Sustainable Cities Programme: A Joint UN-HABITAT-UNEP Facility on the Urban Environment with Participation of the Dutch Government." *Annals of the New York Academy of Sciences* 1023:62–79.

Geddes, Patrick. 1949. *Cities in Evolution: An Introduction to the Town Planning Movement and to the Study of Civics.* London: Williams & Norgate.

Gerber, Brian J., David B. Cohen, Brian Cannon, Dennis Patterson, and Kendra Stewart. 2005. "On the Front Line: American Cities and the Challenge of Homeland Security Preparedness." *Urban Affairs Review* 41(2):182–210.

Germain, Randall D. 1997. *The International Organization of Credit: States and Global Finance in the World-Economy.* Cambridge, UK: Cambridge University Press.

Germain, Randall D. 2010. *Global Politics and Financial Governance.* New York: Palgrave Macmillan.

Gibbs, David, Andy Jonas, and Aidan While. 2002. "Changing Governance Structures and the Environment: Economy–environment Relations at the Local and Regional Scales." *Journal of Environmental Policy and Planning* 4(2):123–138.

Gills, Barry, ed. 2010. "Globalization and Crisis." *Globalizations* 7(1–2):1–317.

Glaeser, Edward L. 2011. *Triumph of the City*. London: Macmillan.

Government Finance Officers Association. 2005. "Federal Tax Policy and Preserving the Tax-exempt Status of Municipal Bonds." June 28. Retrieved November 18, 2013 (www.gfoa.org/index.php?option=com_content&task=view&id=2204).

Graham, Stephen. 2004. *Cities, War, and Terrorism: Towards an Urban Geopolitics*. Malden, MA: Blackwell.

Graham, Stephen. 2010a. *Cities Under Siege: The New Military Urbanism*. London: Verso.

Graham, Stephen. 2010b. *Disrupted Cities: When Infrastructure Fails*. New York: Routledge.

Graham, Stephen and Simon Marvin. 2001. *Splintering Urbanism: Networked Infrastructures, Technological Mobilities and the Urban Condition*. London: Routledge.

Graham, William, Paul Shinn, and John Petersen. 1989. "State Revolving Funds Under Tax Reform." *Council of Infrastructure Financing Authorities*. Monograph no. 2 (June).

Greenberg, Miriam. 2008. *Branding New York: How a City in Crisis Was Sold to the World*. New York: Routledge.

Hackworth, Jason. 2002. "Local Autonomy, Bond-rating Agencies and Neoliberal Urbanism in the United States." *International Journal of Urban and Regional Research* 26(4):707–725.

Hackworth, Jason. 2007. *The Neoliberal City: Governance, Ideology, and Development in American Urbanism*. Ithaca, NY: Cornell University Press.

Haeck, Tim. 2011. "Cleanup of 'Toxic Soup' in Duwamish River Underway." *MyNorthwest.com*. Retrieved February 12, 2012 (http://mynorthwest.com/11/558660/Clean-up-of-toxic-soup-in-Duwamish-River-underway).

Hall, Peter. 1966. *The World Cities*, 3rd ed. London: Weidenfeld and Nicolson.

Hardt, Michael and Antonio Negri. 2000. *Empire*. Cambridge, MA: Harvard University Press.

Harris, Paul G. 2008. "The Glacial Politics of Climate Change." *Cambridge Review of International Affairs* 21(4):455–464.

Harvey, David. 1982. *The Limits to Capital*. Chicago: University of Chicago Press.

Harvey, David. 1989. "From Managerialism to Entrepreneurialism: The Transformation in Urban Governance in Late-Capitalism." *Human Geography* 71(1):3–17.

Harvey, David. 2003. *The New Imperialism*. Oxford, UK: Oxford University Press.

Harvey, David. 2012. *Rebel Cities: From the Right to the City to the Urban Revolution*. New York: Verso.

Healey, Patsy. 2002. "On Creating the 'City' as a Collective Resource." *Urban Studies* 39(10):1777–1792.

Heil, Dennis J. 1983. "Another Day Older and Deeper in Debt: Debt Limitations, the Broad Special Fund Doctrine, and WPPSS 4 and 5." *University of Puget Sound Law Review* 7(81):81–104.

Held, David, Anthony McGrew, David Goldblatt, and Jonathan Perraton. 1999. *Global Transformations: Politics, Economics and Culture*. Stanford, CA: Stanford University Press.

Helleiner, Eric. 1994. *States and the Reemergence of Global Finance: From Bretton Woods to the 1990s*. Ithaca, NY: Cornell University Press.

Herbert, Ross. 2011. *Dependency, Instability and Shifting Global Power: Influences and Interests in African Foreign Policy in the 21st Century*. SAIIA Occasional Paper No 95, September 2011. Retrieved November 18, 2013 (www.saiia.org.za/occasional-papers/dependency-instability-and-shifting-global-power-influences-and-interests-in-african-foreign-policy-in-the-21st-century.html).

Hodson, Mike and Simon Marvin. 2009. "Cities Mediating Technological Transitions: Understanding Visions, Intermediation and Consequences." *Technology Analysis and Strategic Management* 21(4):515–534.

Hodson, Mike and Simon Marvin. 2010. *World Cities and Climate Change: Producing Urban Ecological Security.* Maidenhead, UK: Open University Press.

Hogan, Trevor, Tim Bunnell, Choon-Piew Pow, Eka Permanasari, and Sirat Morshidi. 2012. "Asian Urbanisms and the Privatization of Cities." *Cities* 29(1):59–63.

Holden, Meg, Mark Roseland, Karen Ferguson, and Anthony Perl. 2008. "Seeking Urban Sustainability on the World Stage." *Habitat International* 32:305–317.

Hood, J. 2010. "Lake Calumet Dumping Ground Declared Superfund Site." *Chicago Tribune*, March 2 (http://ow.ly/qBL4A).

Hoornweg, Daniel, Lorrain Sugar, and Claudia Lorena Trejos Gómez. 2011. "Cities and Greenhouse Gas Emissions: Moving Forward." *Environment and Urbanization* 23(1):207–227.

Houghton, D. H. 1971. "Economic Development." Pp. 1–48 in *The Oxford History of South Africa*, Vol. 2, edited by M. Wilson and L. Thompson. Oxford, UK: Oxford University Press.

Howard, Ebenezer. 1902. *Garden Cities of Tomorrow.* London: S. Sonnenschein.

Hoy, Shirley (with Phillip Abraham and Hilda Birks). 2002. Toronto Staff Reports. *International Policy Framework for the City of Toronto*, presented to council April 25, 2002.

Hubbard, Phil. 1995. "Urban Design and Local Economic Development: A Case Study in Birmingham." *Cities* 12(4):243–251.

humansecurity-cities.org. 2007. *Human Security for an Urban Century: Local Challenges, Global Perspectives.* Retrieved November 2, 2013 (www.eukn.org/E_library/Security_Crime_Prevention/Security_Crime_Prevention/Human_security_for_an_urban_century_local_challenges_global_perspectives).

Hume, Lynn and Jennifer DePaul. 2011. "Tax-exemption Threats Are Still on the Radar." *The Bond Buyer*, December 30. Retrieved November 14, 2013 (www.bondbuyer.com/issues/121_1/tax-legislation-2012-munis-1034777-1.html).

Hurrell, Andrew. 2007. *On Global Order: Power, Values, and the Constitution of International Society.* Oxford, UK: Oxford University Press.

Ikenberry, G. J. 2011. *Liberal Leviathan : The Origins, Crisis, and Transformation of the American World Order.* Princeton, NJ: Princeton University Press.

Jacobs, Jane. 1969. *The Economy of Cities.* New York: Random House.

Jacobs, Jane. 1972. *The Death and Life of Great American Cities.* Harmondsworth, UK: Penguin.

Jacobs, Jane. 1984. *Cities and the Wealth of Nations: Principles of Economic Life.* New York: Random House.

James, Paul. 2006. *Globalism, Nationalism, Tribalism: Bringing Theory Back In.* London: Sage.

Jarvis, Darryl. 2011. "Race for the Money: International Financial Centers in Asia." *Journal of International Relations and Development* 14(1):60–95.

Jessop, Bob, Neil Brenner, and Martin Jones. 2008. "Theorizing Sociospatial Relations." *Environment and Planning D: Society and Space* 26(3):389–401.

Judd, Dennis R. and Randy L. Ready. 1986. "Entrepreneurial Cities and the New Politics of Economic Development." Pp. 209–247 in *Reagan and the Cities*, edited by G. E. Peterson and C. W. Lewis. Washington, DC: Urban Institute Press.

Jun, Jong S. and Deil S. Wright, eds. 1996. *Globalization and Decentralization: Institutional Contexts, Policy Issues, and Intergovernmental Relations in Japan and the United States.* Washington, DC: Georgetown University Press.

Kearns, Ade and Ronan Paddison. 2000. "New Challenges for Urban Governance." *Urban Studies* 37(5–6):845–850.

Keating, Michael. 1995. "Size, Efficiency and Democracy: Consolidation, Fragmentation and Public Choice." Pp. 117–134 in *Theories of Urban Politics*, edited by D. Judge, G. Stoker, and H. Wolman. London, UK: Sage.

Keck, Margaret E. and Kathryn Sikkink. 1998. *Activists Beyond Borders: Advocacy Networks in International Politics.* Ithaca, NY: Cornell University Press.

Keil, Roger and Harris Ali. 2007. "Governing the Sick City: Urban Governance in the Age of Emerging Infectious Disease." *Antipode* 39(5):846–873.

Keiner, Marco and Arley Kim 2007. "City Energy Networking in Europe." *European Planning Studies* 15(10):1369–1395.

Keiner, Marco and Arley Kim. 2008. "City Energy Networking in Europe." Pp. 193–210 in *Urban Energy Transition: From Fossil Fuels to Renewable Power*, edited by P. Droege. Oxford, UK: Elsevier.

Keohane, Robert O. and Joseph F. Nye Jr. 1977. *Power and Interdependence*. Boston, MA: Little, Brown.

Kern, Kristine and Harriet Bulkeley. 2009. "Cities, Europeanization and Multi-level Governance: Governing Climate Change through Transnational Municiple Networks." *Journal of Common Market Studies* 47(2):309–332.

Kjellstrom, Tord, Sharon Friel, Jane Dixon, Carlos Corvalan, Eva Rehfuess, Diarmid Campbell-Lendrum, Fiona Gore, and Jamie Bartram. 2007. "Urban Environmental Health Hazards and Health Equity." *Journal of Urban Health* 84(1):86–97.

Klein, Michael. 2007. "Magnets for Money." *The Economist*. Retrieved August 16, 2013 (www.economist.com/node/9753240).

Kline, John. 1996. "State and Local Boundary-spanning Strategies in the United States: Political, Economic, and Cultural Transgovernmental Interactions." Pp. 329–346 in *Globalization and Decentralization: Institutional Contexts, Policy Issues, and Intergovernmental Relations in Japan and the United States*, edited by J. S. Jun and D. S. Wright. Washington, DC: Georgetown University Press.

Knox, Paul L. and Peter J. Taylor. 1995. *World Cities in a World-system*. Cambridge, UK: Cambridge University Press.

Köhler, Bettina and Markus Wissen. 2003. "Glocalizing Protest: Urban Conflicts and Global Social Movements." *International Journal of Urban and Regional Research* 27(4):942–951.

Krasner, Stephen D. 1978. *Defending the National Interest: Raw Materials Investments and U.S. Foreign Policy*. Princeton, NJ: Princeton University Press.

Krasner, Stephen D. 1999. *Sovereignty: Organized Hypocrisy*. Princeton, NJ: Princeton University Press.

Krippner, Greta R. 2011. *Capitalizing on Crisis: The Political Origins of the Rise of Finance*. Cambridge, MA: Harvard University Press.

Krugman, Paul. 1991. *Geography and Trade*. Cambridge, MA: MIT Press.

Krugman, Paul. 1995. *Development, Geography, and Economic Theory*. Cambridge, MA: MIT Press.

Kumar Sharma, C. 2005. "Why Decentralization? The Puzzle of Causation." *Synthesis* 3(1):1–17.

Lachapelle, Guy and Stéphane Paquin. 2005. *Mastering Globalization: New Substates' Governance and Strategies*. London: Routledge.

Lai, Karen P. Y. 2009. "New Spatial Logics in Global Cities Research: Networks, Flows and New Political Spaces." *Geography Compass* 3(3):997–1012.

Lambright, W. Henry, Stanley A. Chjangnon, and L. D. Danny Harvey. 1996. "Urban Reactions to the Global Warming Issue: Agenda Setting in Toronto and Chicago." *Climatic Change* 34(3–4):463–478.

Langer, Susanne K. 1942. *Philosophy in a New Key. A Study in the Symbolism of Reason, Rite, and Art*. Cambridge, MA: Harvard University Press.

Langley, Paul. 2002. *World Financial Orders: An Historical International Political Economy*. London: Routledge.

Lavelle, Kathryn C. 1999. "International Financial Institutions and Emerging Capital Markets in Africa." *Review of International Political Economy* 6(2):200–224.

Lavelle, Kathryn C. 2004. *The Politics of Equity Finance in Emerging Markets*. New York: Oxford University Press.

Layne, Christopher. 2012. "This Time It's Real: The End of Unipolarity and the *Pax Americana.*" *International Studies Quarterly* 56(1):203–213.

Lecours, A. 2002. "Paradiplomacy: Reflections on the Foreign Policy and International Relations of Regions." *International Negotiation* 7(1):91–114.

Leeson, Howard A. and Wilfried Vanderelst. 1973. *External Affairs and Canadian Federalism: The History of a Dilemma.* Toronto: Hold, Rinehart and Winston of Canada.

Lefebvre, Henri. 1991. *The Production of Space.* Oxford, UK: Blackwell.

Lefebvre, Henri. 2009. *State, Space, World: Selected Essays.* Minneapolis: University of Minnesota Press.

Leitner, Helga and Eric Sheppard. 2002. "'The City Is Dead, Long Live the Net': Harnessing European Interurban Networks for a Neoliberal Agenda." *Antipode* 34(3):495–518.

LexAfrica.2011.*AfricanGatewaysJostleforInvestors'Attention.*RetrievedSeptember21, 2013 (www.lexafrica.com/news-african-gateways-jostle-for-investors-attention-).

Lichatowich, James A. 1999. *Salmon Without Rivers: A History of the Pacific Salmon Crisis.* Washington, DC: Island Press.

Loan Association v. Topeka, 87 U.S. 655 (1875).

Lower Duwamish Waterway Group. 2012. *Executive Summary: Final Feasibility Study.* Seattle, WA (www.epa.gov/region10/pdf/sites/ldw/fs13/final_fs_executive_summary_103112.pdf).

Lydersen, Kari. 2011a. "An Abandoned Area Starts to Hum Again, Raising New Fears." *The New York Times,* July 22, p. 17A (www.nytimes.com/2011/07/22/us/22cnccoal.html?pagewanted=all&_r=0).

Lydersen, Kari. 2011b. "Clean-Coal Debate Focuses on Gasification Plant." *The New York Times,* March 11, p. 21A (www.nytimes.com/2011/03/11/us/11cnctar.html?pagewanted=all).

Lydersen, Kari. 2011c. "Community Is Torn Over Expansion of Oil Refinery." *The New York Times,* September 16, p. 21A (www.nytimes.com/2011/09/16/us/community-is-torn-over-expansion-of-oil-refinery.html?pagewanted=all).

Makkai, Toni. 2006. "Researching Transnational Crime: The Australian Institute of Criminology." *Global Governance* 12(2):119–125.

Mandel, Ernest. 1978. *Late Capitalism.* London: Verso.

Manson, Katrina. 2013. "Breakaway Somaliland Hopes to Become Gateway for Horn of Africa." *The Financial Times,* September 17, 2013. Retrieved September 28, 2013 (www.ft.com/cms/s/0/523ba386–1b93–11e3–94a3–00144feab7de.html).

Marcuse, Peter. 2006. "Security or Safety in Cities? The Threat of Terrorism After 9/11." *International Journal of Urban and Regional Research* 30(4):919–929.

Marlowe, Justin. 2013. "Muni Bonds' Future May Lie in Foreign Investors' Hands." *Governing the States and Localities,* February. Retrieved November 12, 2013 (www.governing.com/columns/public-money/col-muni-bonds-future-in-foreign-investors-hands.html).

Massey, Doreen B. 2007. *World City.* Cambridge, UK: Polity Press.

Mawdsley, Emma. 2009. "'Environmentality' in the Neoliberal City: Attitudes, Governance and Social Justice." Pp. 237–252 in *The New Middle Classes: Globalizing Lifestyles, Consumerism and Environmental Concern,* edited by H. Lange and L. Meier. Dordrecht, Germany: Springer.

Mayer, M. 1992. "The Shifting Local Political System in European Cities." Pp. 255–276 in *Cities and Regions in the New Europe: The Global-Local Interplay and Spatial Development Strategies,* edited by M. Dunford and G. Kafkalas. London: Belhaven Press.

Mayor of London. 2005. *Mayor Brings Together Major Cities to Take Lead on Climate Change.* Retrieved 2007 (no longer available) (www.c40cities.org/news/archive.jsp).

McCann, Eugene J. 2008. "Expertise, Truth, and Urban Policy Mobilities: Global Circuits of Knowledge in the Development of Vancouver, Canada's 'Four Pillar' Drug Strategy." *Environment and Planning A* 40(4):885–904.

McGinn, Mike. 2011. "Major Duwamish Waterway Hotspot Cleanup Effort Begins this Week." *Seattle.gov*. Retrieved February 12, 2012 (http://mayormcginn.seattle.gov/major duwamish waterway-hotspot-cleanup-effort- begins-this-week).

McKendry, Corina. 2011. *Smokestacks to Green Roofs: City Environmentalism, Green Urban Entrepreneurialism, and the Regulation of the Postindustrial City*. PhD dissertation, University of California Santa Cruz.

McKendry, Corina. 2012. "Environmental Discourse and Economic Growth in the Greening of Postindustrial Cities." Pp. 23–32 in *The Economy of Green Cities: World Compendium on the Green Urban Economy*, edited by R. Simpson and M. Zimmermann. New York: Springer.

Mearsheimer, John. 2001. *The Tragedy of Great Power Politics*. New York: W.W. Norton and Company.

Mega, Voula. 2010. *Sustainable Cities for the Third Millennium: The Odyssey of Urban Excellence*. New York: Springer.

Meyer, Carrie A. 1997. "The Political Economy of NGOs and Information Sharing." *World Development* 25(7):1127–1140.

Ministry of Municipal Affairs. 2004. *Ontario Municipal Act, 08, 2001*. Retrieved May 2004 (www.elaws.gov.on.ca/html/source/regs/english/2008/elaws_src_regs_r08105_e.htm).

Moberg, David. 2002. The Accidental Environmentalist. *Chicago Tribune*, September 24. Retrieved November 18, 2013 (http://articles.chicagotribune.com/2002-09-24/features/0209250271_1_scientists-tent-environmentalists).

Moltoch, Harvey and Noah McClain. 2003. "Dealing with Urban Terror: Heritages of Control, Varieties of Intervention, Strategies of Research." *International Journal of Urban and Regional Research* 27(3):679–698.

Morgenson, Gretchen. 2012. "A Fog Warning, Again, for Municipal Bonds." *The New York Times*, February 18. Retrieved November 12, 2013 (www.nytimes.com/2012/02/19/business/municipal-bonds-are-sometimes-still-lost-in-the-fog.html).

Morrison Taw, Jennifer and Bruce Hoffman. 1994. *The Urbanization of Insurgency: The Potential to Challenge U.S. Army Operations*. Arlington, VA: RAND Corporation.

Mugwe, David. 2011. "Nairobi Woos International Bankers." *Business Daily*. Retrieved September 12, 2013 (www.businessdailyafrica.com/Nairobi-woos-international-bankers/-/539552/1117066/-/11r6ee5z/-/index.html).

Mumford, Lewis. 1961. *The City in History: Its Origins, Its Transformations, and Its Prospects*. London: Secker & Warburg.

Murray, Warwick E. 2006. *Geographies of Globalization*. London: Routledge.

National Planning Commission. 2009. *Report of the Vision 2020 National Technical Working Group: Financial Sector*. Retrieved August 29, 2013 (www.npc.gov.ng/vault/NTWG%20Final%20Report/financial%20sector%20ntwg%20report.pdf).

National Planning Commission. 2011. *National Development Plan 2030 Our Future: Make it Work*. Retrieved December 8, 2013 (www.npconline.co.za/MediaLib/Downloads/Downloads/NDP%202030%20-%20Our%20future%20-%20make%20it%20work.pdf).

National Treasury. 2010. *National Budget Review 2010*. Retrieved September 15, 2013 (www.treasury.gov.za/documents/national%20budget/2010/review/default.aspx).

Nichols, Walter J. 2008. "The Urban Question Revisited: The Importance of Cities for Social Movements." *International Journal of Urban and Regional Research* 32(4):841–859.

Nkoana-Mashabane, Maite. 2011. *Budget Vote Speech by Minister of International Relations and Cooperation, H.E. Ms. Maite Nkoana-Mashabane at the National Assembly, Cape Town, South Africa, May 30*. Retrieved January 4, 2012 (www.anc.org.za/caucus/show.php?ID = 1950).

Nuttall, Sarah and Achille Mbembe, eds. 2008. *Johannesburg: The Elusive Metropolis*. Durham, NC: Duke University Press.

Nyden, Philip, Emily Edlynn, and Julie Davis. 2006. *The Differential Impact of Gentrification on Commuities in Chicago*. Chicago, IL: Loyola University Chicago Center for Urban Research and Learning.

Oatley, Thomas. 2012. *International Political Economy*, 5th ed. New York: Pearson.

O'Hara, Neil. 2012. *The Fundamentals of Municipal Bonds*, 6th ed. Hoboken, NJ: John Wiley & Sons.

Owen, David. 2004. "Green Manhattan: Why New York Is the Greenest City in the U.S." *The New Yorker*, October 18. Retrieved November 5, 2013 (www.newyorker.com/archive/2004/10/18/041018fa_fact_owen).

Owens, Susan, Judith Petts, and Harriet Bulkeley. 2006. "Boundary Work: Knowledge, Policy, and the Urban Environment." *Environment and Planning C* 24(5):633–643.

Palmer, John L. and Isabel V. Sawhill. 1986. "Foreword." Pp. xv–xvi in *Reagan and the Cities*, edited by G. E. Peterson and C. W. Lewis. Washington, DC: Urban Institute Press.

Pasotti, Eleonora. 2009. *Political Branding in Cities: The Decline of Machine Politics in Bogotá, Naples, and Chicago*. Cambridge, UK: Cambridge University Press.

Peck, Jamie and Adam Tickell. 1994. "Searching for a New Institutional Fix: The After-fordist Crisis and the Global-local Disorder." Pp. 280–315 in *Post-fordism: A Reader*, edited by A. Amin. Oxford, UK: Blackwell.

Peck, Jamie and Adam Tickell. 2002. "Neoliberalizing Space." *Antipode* 34:380–404.

People v. Hurlbut, 24 Mich 44, 95 (1871).

Petersen, John. 1987. *Tax-exempts and Tax Reform: Assessing the Consequences of the Tax Reform Act of 1986 for the Municipal Securities Market*. Research report. Washington, DC: Government Finance Research Center of the Government Finance Officers Association and the Academy for State and Local Government.

Pieterse, Edgar. 2008. *City Futures: Confronting the Crisis of Urban Development*. London: Zed Books.

Polanyi, K. 1957. *The Great Transformation: The Political and Economic Origins of Our Time*. Boston, MA: Beacon Press.

Polèse, M. 2011. *The Wealth and Poverty of Regions: Why Cities Matter*. Chicago, IL: University of Chicago Press.

Pollock v. Farmers' Loan and Trust Company, 158 U.S. 601 (1895).

Presas, L.M.S. 2004. "Transnational Buildings in Local Environments." Unpublished PhD thesis, Wageningen University, Netherlands.

Province of British Columbia. 1978. *British Columbia's Constitutional Proposal (Presented to the First Ministers' Conference on the Constitution)*, October 1978.

Purcell, Mark. 2002. "Excavating Lefebvre: The Right to the City and Its Urban Politics of the Inhabitant." *GeoJournal* 58:99–108.

Purcell, Mark. 2008. *Recapturing Democracy: Neoliberalization and the Struggle for Alternative Urban Futures*. New York: Routledge.

Qobo, Mzukisi. 2011. "Emerging Powers and the Changing Global Environment: Leadership, Norms and Institutions." *SAIIA Occasional Paper No 91*, September. Retrieved September 12, 2013 (www.saiia.org.za/occasional-papers/emerging-powers-and-the-changing-global-environment-leadership-norms-and-institutions.html).

Rabrenovic, Gordana. 2009. "Urban Social Movements." Pp. 239–254 in *Theories of Urban Politics*, edited by J. S. Davies and D. L. Imbroscio. Los Angeles: Sage.

Radelet, Steven. 2010. *Emerging Africa: How 17 Countries Are Leading the Way.* Washington, DC: Center for Global Development. Retrieved September 15, 2013 (www.cgdev.org/files/1424419_file_EmergingAfrica_FINAL.pdf).

Risse-Kappen, Thomas, ed. 1995. *Bringing Transnational Relations Back In: Non-State Actors, Domestic Structures and International Institutions.* New York: Columbia University Press.

Robertson, Roland. 1994. "Globalisation or Glocalisation?" *Journal of International Communication* 1(1):33–52.

Rodríguez, Arantxa, Erik Swyngedouw, and Frank Moulaert. 2003. "Urban Restructuring, Social-political polarization, and New Urban Policies." Pp. 29–43 in *The Globalized City: Economic Restructuring and Social Polarization in European Cities,* edited by F. Moulaert, A. Rodríguez, and E. Swyngedouw. Oxford, UK: Oxford University Press.

Rodriguez, N. and J. Feagin. 1986. "Urban Specialization in the World System: An Investigation of Historical Cases." *Urban Affairs Quarterly* 22(2):187–222.

Román, Mikael. 2010. "Governing from the Middle: The C40 Cities Leadership Group." Pp. 73–84 in *Rethinking Governance for Sustainability,* edited by A. Midttun. Oslo: CERES 21.

Rosenzweig, Cynthia and Urban Climate Change Research Network. 2011a. *Climate Change and Cities: First Assessment Report of the Urban Climate Change Research Network.* Cambridge, UK: Cambridge University Press.

Rosenzweig, Cynthia. 2011b. "All Climate Is Local." *Scientific American,* August 23. Retrieved November 2, 2013 (www.scientificamerican.com/article.cfm?id=all-climate-is-local).

Salazar, Peggy. 2010. Personal interview, May 19. Interim Executive Director, Southeast Environmental Task Force.

Sample, Hilary. 2012. *Sick City: A Global Investigation into Urbanism, Infrastructures and Disease.* Heijningen, the Netherlands: JAP SAM Books.

Sánchez, Fernanda and Rosa Moura. 2005. "Ciudades-Modelo: Estrategias Convergentes Para Su Difusión Internacional." *Revista Eure* 31(93):21–34.

Sanders, Jeffrey C. 2010. *Seattle and the Roots of Urban Sustainability: Inventing Ecotopia.* Pittsburgh, PA: University of Pittsburgh Press.

Sanlam Investment Management. 2011. *Investor Conference to Tackle China's Growing Interest in Africa.* August 17. Retrieved September 16, 2013 (http://196.36.206.10/wps/wcm/connect/29ceab0047fd8bc1a380e3be04f155b4/Investor+conference+to+tackle+China's+growing+interest+in+Africa.pdf?MOD=AJPERES).

Sassen, Saskia. 1991. *The Global City: New York, London, Tokyo.* Princeton, NJ: Princeton University Press.

Sassen, Saskia. 1994. *Cities in a World Economy, Sociology for a New Century.* Thousand Oaks, CA: Pine Forge Press.

Sassen, Saskia. 1996. "Whose City Is It? *Public Culture* 8(2):205–223.

Sassen, Saskia. 2001. *The Global City: New York, London, Tokyo,* 2nd ed. Princeton, NJ: Princeton University Press.

Sassen, Saskia. 2002. "Locating Cities on Global Circuits." *Environment and Urbanization* 14(1):13–30.

Sassen, Saskia. 2004. "A Global City." Pp. 15–34 in *Global Chicago,* edited by C. Madigan. Urbana, IL: University of Illinois Press.

Sassen, Saskia. 2005. "The Ecology of Global Economic Power: Changing Investment Practices to Promote Environmental Sustainability." *Journal of International Affairs* 58(2):11–33.

Sassen, Saskia. 2006. *Cities in a World Economy.* Thousand Oaks, CA: Pine Forge Press.

Sassen, Saskia. 2006. *Territory, Authority, Rights: From Medieval to Global Assemblages.* Princeton, NJ: Princeton University Press.

Sassen, Saskia. 2007. *A Sociology of Globalization.* New York: W.W. Norton.

Sassen, Saskia. 2009. "Cities in Today's Global Age." *SAIS Review of International Affairs* 29(1):3–34.

Sassen, Saskia. 2010. "Cities Are at the Center of Our Environmental Future." *SAPIENS* 2(3):1–8.

Sassen, Saskia. 2012. *Cities in a World Economy*, 4th ed. Thousand Oaks, CA: Pine Forge Press.

Satterthwaite, David. 2007. *The Transition to a Predominantly Urban World and Its Underpinnings*. London: Institute for Environment and Development.

Saunders, Doug. 2011. *Arrival City: How the Largest Migration in History Is Reshaping Our World*. London: Windmill Books.

Saunier, Pierre-Yves. 2001. "Sketches from the Urban Internationale, 1910–50: Voluntary Associations, International Institutions and US Philanthropic Foundations." *International Journal of Urban and Regional Research* 25(2):380–403.

Savitch, H. V. 2008. *Cities in a Time of Terror: Space, Territory, and Local Resilience*. Armonk, NY: M.E. Sharpe.

Savitch, H.V. and Paul Kantor. 2002. *Cities in the International Marketplace: The Political Economy of Urban Development in North America and Western Europe*. Princeton, NJ: Princeton University Press.

Sbragia, Alberta M. 1996. *Debt Wish: Entrepreneurial Cities, U.S. Federalism, and Economic Development*. Pittsburgh, PA: University of Pittsburgh Press.

Schneider, Keith. 2006. "To Revitalize a City, Try Spreading Some Mulch." *The New York Times,* May 17. Retrieved March 9, 2008 (www.nytimes.com/2006/05/17/business/businessspecial2/17chicago.html?_r=2&oref=slogin&).

Schweller, Randall L. 1994. "Bandwagoning for Profit: Bring the Revisionist State Back In." *International Security* 19(1):72–107.

Sclar, Elliott D., Pietro Garau, and Gabriella Y. Carolini. 2005. "The 21st Century Health Challenge of Slums and Cities." *The Lancet* 365(9462):901–903.

Scott, Allen John. 2000. *Global City-regions: Trends, Theory, Policy*. New York: Oxford University Press.

Scott, Allen John. 2001. "Globalization and the Rise of City-regions." *European Planning Studies* 9(7):813–826.

Short, John R. 1996. *The Urban Order: An Introduction to Cities, Culture, and Power*. Cambridge, MA: Blackwell Publishers.

Sidaway, James D. 2007. "Enclave Space: A New Metageography of Development?" *Area* 39(3):331–339.

Siemens. 2012. *The Siemens Environmental Portfolio: Examples of Sustainable Technologies* (www.siemens.com/sustainability/pool/umweltportfolio/siemens_environmental_portfolio.pdf).

Smith, David A. 2005. "The World Urban Hierarchy: Implications for Cities, Top to Bottom." *Brown Journal of World Affairs* 11(2):45–55.

Smith, Jackie, Charles Chatfield, and Ron Pagnucco, eds. 1997. *Transnational Social Movements and Global Politics: Solidarity Beyond the State*. Syracuse, NY: Syracuse University Press.

Soja, Edward W. 2000. *Postmetropolis: Critical Studies of Cities and Regions*. Oxford, UK: Blackwell.

South Carolina v. Baker 485 U.S. 505 (1988).

Spaargaren, Gert, Arthur P. J. Mol, and Hans Bruyninckx. 2006. "Introduction: Governing Environmental Flows in Global Modernity." Pp. 1–36 in *Governing Environmental Flows: Global Challenges to Social Theory*, edited by G. Spaargaren, A.P.J. Mol, and F. H. Buttel. Cambridge MA: MIT Press.

Spencer, Kenneth, Andy Taylor, B. Smith, J. Mawson, Norman Flynn, and R. Batley. 1986. *Crisis in the Industrial Heartland: A Study of the West Midlands*. Oxford, UK: Clarendon Press.

Stanley, Bruce. 2005. "Middle East City Networks and the 'New Urbanism'." *Cities* 22(3):189–199.

Steger, Manfred. 1999. *Globalization: A Very Short Introduction*. Oxford, UK: Oxford University Press.

Stevenson, Don and Richard Gilbert. 2005. "Coping with Canadian Federalism: The Case of the Federation of Canadian Municipalities." *Canadian Public Administration* 48(4):528–551.

Stewart, Richard B. 2008. "States and Cities as Actors in Global Climate Regulation: Unitary vs. Plural Architectures." *Arizona Law Review* 50:681–707.

Storper, Michael and Anthony J. Venables. 2004. "Buzz: Face to Face Contact and the Urban Economy." *Journal of Economic Geography* 4(4):351–370.

Sullivan, Ruth. 2011. "Emerging Investors Cross New Frontiers." *Financial Times*, July 7. Retrieved September 16, 2013 (www.ft.com/intl/cms/s/0/b2812fa6-a8a7–11e0–8a97 00144feabdc0.html#axzz1USTbNmA1).

Swyngedouw, Erik. 1997. "Neither Global nor Local: 'Glocalization' and the Politics of Scale." Pp.137–166 in *Spaces of Globalization: Reasserting the Power of the Local*, edited by Kevin R. Cox. New York: Guilford.

Swyngedouw, Erik. 2004a. "Globalisation or 'glocalisation'? Networks, territories and rescaling." *Cambridge Review of International Affairs* 17(1):25–48.

Swyngedouw, Erik. 2004b. "Scaled Geographies: Nature, Place, and the Politics of Scale." Pp. 129–153 in *Scale and Geographic Inquiry: Nature, Society, and Method*, edited by E. Sheppard and R. B. McMaster. Malden, MA: Blackwell.

Tarrow, Sidney G. 2005. *The New Transnational Activism*. New York: Cambridge University Press.

Taylor, Paul. 2000. "UNCHS (Habitat): The Global Campaign for Good Urban Governance." *Environment and Urbanization* 12(1):197–202.

Taylor, Peter J. 2004. *World City Network: A Global Urban Analysis*. London: Routledge.

Taylor, Peter J. 2005. "Leading World Cities: Empirical Evaluations of Urban Nodes in Multiple Networks." *Urban Studies* 42(9):1593–1608.

Ten Eyck v. The Delaware and Raritan Canal Company, 18 N.J.L., 200 (1841).

Terreblanche, Sampie. 2005. *A History of Inequality in South Africa 1652–2002*, 3rd ed. Pietermaritzburg, South Africa: University of Natal Press; Sandton, South Africa: KMM Review Publishing.

Thornley, Andy, Yvonne Rydin, Kath Scanlon, and Karen West. 2005. "Business Privilege and the Strategic Planning Agenda of the Greater London Authority." *Urban Studies* 42(11):1947–1968.

Toly, Noah. 2008. "Transnational Municipal Networks for Climate Stabilization: From Global Governance to Global Politics." *Globalizations* 5(3):341–356.

Törnqvist, G. 1993. *Sverige I Natverkens Europa: Gransoverskridandets Former Och Vilkkor*. Malmo, Sweden: Liber-Hermonds AB.

Tsukamoto, Takashi and Ronald K. Vogel. 2007. "Rethinking Globalization—The Impact of Central Government on World Cities." Pp. 15–32 in *Governing Cities in a Global Era: Urban Innovation, Competition, and Democratic Reform*, edited by R. Hambleton and J. S. Gross. New York: Palgrave Macmillan.

Uitermark, Justus. 2002. "Re-scaling, 'Scale Fragmentation' and the Regulation of Antagonistic Relationships." *Progress in Human Geography* 26(6):743–765.

UN-HABITAT. 2006. *State of the World's Cities 2006/2007: The Millennium Development Goals and Urban Sustainability*. London: Earthscan.

UN-HABITAT. 2007. *Global Report on Human Settlements 2007: Enhancing Urban Safety and Security*. London: Earthscan.

UN-HABITAT. 2008a. *State of the World's Cities 2008/2009: Harmonious Cities*. London: Earthscan.

UN-HABITAT. 2008b. *First Announcement: The First Session of the World Urban Forum. Harmonious Urbanisation: The Challenge of Balanced Territorial Development.* Retreived December 12, 2013 (www.unhabitat.org/downloads/docs/5560_72638_2446_2_alt.pdf).

UN-HABITAT. 2009. *Global Report on Human Settlements 2009: Planning Sustainable Cities.* London: Earthscan

UN-HABITAT. 2011. "Hot Cities: Battle-ground for Climate Change." *Global Report on Human Settlement 2011.* Nairobi, Kenya: United Nations Human Settlements Programme.

United Nations. 1992. *Agenda 21: The United Nations Programme of Action from Rio.* New York: United Nations.

United Nations Centre for Human Settlements. 1987. *Global Report on Human Settlements.* Oxford UK: Oxford University Press for the United Nations Centre for Human Settlements (Habitat).

United Nations Centre for Human Settlements. 1991. *Sustainable Cities Programme: Approach and Implementation.* Nairobi, Kenya: UNCHS, UNEP.

United Nations Centre for Human Settlements. 1996. *An Urbanizing World: Global Report on Human Settlements, 1996.* Oxford, UK: Oxford University Press for the United Nations Centre for Human Settlements (HABITAT).

United Nations Centre for Human Settlements. 1998. *Sustainable Cities Programme: Approach and Implementation,* 2nd ed. Nairobi, Kenya: UNCHS, UNEP.

United Nations Centre for Human Settlements. 2001. *Cities in a Globalizing World: Global Report on Human Settlements 2001.* London: Earthscan.

United Nations Development Programme. 2000. *The Challenges of Linking.* UNDP, Management Development and Governance Division, Bureau for Development Policy.

United Nations Human Settlements Programme. 2009. *Planning Sustainable Cities: Global Report on Human Settlements 2009.* London: Earthscan.

Urpelainen, Johannes. 2009. "Explaining the Schwarzenegger Phenomenon: Local Frontrunners in Climate Policy." *Global Environmental Politics* 9(3):82–105.

U.S. Environmental Protection Agency. n.d. *NPL Site Narrative for Lake Calumet Cluster.* Retrieved December 30, 2010 (www.epa.gov/superfund/sites/npl/nar1743.htm).

U.S. Government, Office of the President. 2011. *The American Jobs Act.* Retrieved November 18, 2013 (www.whitehouse.gov/sites/default/files/omb/legislative/reports/american-jobs-act.pdf).

U.S. Office of Management and Budget. 2013. *Historical Tables. Table 1.1: Summary of Receipts, Outlays and Surpluses or Deficits (-): 1789–2018* (www.whitehouse.gov/omb/budget/Historicals).

Valaskakis, Kimon. 2000. *Westphalia II—The Real Millenium Challenge.* Paris Center for New Learning. Retrieved August 2013 (www.paricenter.com/library/papers/valaskakis01.php).

van den Berg, Leo, Peter M. J. Pol, Giuliano Mingardo, and Carolien J. M. Speller. 2006. *The Safe City: Safety and Urban Development in European Cities.* Aldershot, UK: Ashgate.

van der Pluijm, Rogier (with Jan Melissen). 2007. "City Diplomacy: The Expanding Role of Cities in International Politics." *Clingendael Diplomacy Papers No. 10.* The Hague, Netherlands: Institute of International Relations *Clingendael.*

Verhoef, Grietjie. 2011. "'Global Since Gold' The Globalisation of Conglomerates: Explaining the Experience from South Africa, 1990–2009." Working Paper 238. *Economic Research Southern Africa* (www.econrsa.org/publications/working-papers/global-gold-globalisation-conglomerates-explaining-experience-south).

Vettoretto, Luciano. 2009. "A Preliminary Critique of the Best and Good Practices Approach in European Spatial Planning and Policy-making." *European Planning Studies* 17(7):1067–1083.

Vischer, Robert K. 2001. "Subsidiarity as Principle of Governance: Beyond Devolution." *Indiana Law Review* 35(1):103–142.

Wai-chung Yeung, Henry and Kris Olds. 2001. "From the Global City to Globalising Cities: Views from a Developmental City-state in Asia-Pacific." Paper presented at the IRFD World Forum on Habitat-International Conference on Urbanizing World and UN Human Habitat II, New York City, June 4–6.

Walker, R.B.J. 2010. *After the Globe, Before the World.* London: Routledge.

Wall, Ronald and Bert van de Knaap. 2006. "Sustainability Within a World City Network." *GaWC Research Bulletin 2005.*

Wallerstein, Immanuel. 1974. *The Modern World-system: Capitalist Agriculture and the Origins of the European World-economy in the Sixteenth Century.* New York: Academic Press.

Wallerstein, Immanuel. 2005. *World-systems Analysis: An Introduction.* Durham, NC: Duke University Press

Waltz, Kenneth. 1979. *Theory of International Politics.* New York: McGraw-Hill.

Wambora, Joyce. 2013. *Nairobi Centre for International Arbitration Commences Operations.* Retrieved September 28, 2013 (www.internationallawoffice.com/newsletters/detail.aspx?g=23104c54–8be74360-b67a-89a6a3961199).

Warren, Robert. 2002. "Situating the City and September 11th: Military Urban Doctrine, 'Pop-Up' Armies and Spatial Chess." *International Journal of Urban and Regional Research* 26(3):614–619.

Weber, Rachel. 2002. "Extracting Value from the City." Pp. 172–193 in *Spaces of Neoliberalism: Urban Restructuring in North America and Western Europe,* edited by N. Brenner and N. Theodore. Malden, MA: Blackwell.

Wendt, Alexander. 1999. *Social Theory of International Politics.* Cambridge, UK: Cambridge University Press.

Widmaier, Wesley, Mark Blyth, and Leonard Seabrooke. 2007. "Exogenous Shocks or Endogenous Constructions? The Meanings of Wars and Crises." *International Studies Quarterly* 51(4):747–759.

Widmaier, Wesley and Susan Park. 2012. "Differences Beyond Theory: Structural, Strategic, and Sentimental Approaches to Normative Change." *International Studies Perspective* 13(2):123–134.

Wohlforth, William C. 2012. "How Not to Evaluate Theories." *International Studies Quarterly* 56(1):219–222.

World Bank. 2006. *Making Finance Work for Africa.* Washington, DC: World Bank. Retrieved September 13, 2011 (http://siteresources.worldbank.org/INTAFRSUMAFTPS/Resources/MFWfAFinalNov2.pdf).

World Bank. 2009. *Systems of Cities: Harnessing Urbanization for Growth and Poverty Alleviation.* Washington DC: World Bank.

World Commission on Environment and Development. 1987. *Report of the World Commission on Environment and Development: Our Common Future* (www.un-documents.net/wced-ocf.htm).

World Economic Forum. 2013. *The Global Competitiveness Report 2013–2014.* Retrieved September 28, 2013 (http://reports.weforum.org/the-global-competitiveness-report-2013-14).

World Health Organization. 2008. *Our Cities, Our Health, Our Future: Acting on Social Determinants for Health Equity in Urban Settings.* Retrieved December 12, 2013 (www.who.int/social_determinants/resources/knus_final_report_052008.pdf).

Wrightson, Margaret T. 1989. "The Road to South Carolina: Intergovernmental Tax Immunity and the Constitutional Status of Federalism." *Publius: The Journal of Federalism* 19(3):39–55.

Wyden, Ron and Judd Gregg. 2010. "A Bipartisan Plan for Tax Fairness." *The Wall Street Journal*, February 23. Retrieved November 13, 2013 (http://online.wsj.com/article/SB20001424052748704454304575081322884457424.html).

Yeandle, Mark and Chiara von Gunten. 2013. *Global Financial Centres Index.* Retrieved September 20, 2013 (www.geneve-finance.ch/sites/default/files/pdf/2013_gfci_25march.pdf).

Zelinsky, Wilbur. 1990. "Sister City Alliance." *American Demographics* 12(6):42–45.

Zelinsky, Wilbur. 1991. "The Twinning of the World: Sister Cities in Geographic and Historical Perspective." *Annals of the Association of American Geographers* 81(1):1–31.

Zimmerman, D. 1991. *The Private Use of Tax-exempt Bonds: Controlling Public Subsidy of Private Activities.* Washington, DC: Urban Institute Press.

Zuma, Jacob. 2011. "Speech by President Jacob Zuma to the Members of the Abu Dhabi Business Chamber and South African Business Delegation at the Emirates Palace, United Arab Emirates (UAE)." South African Government Information, November 14. Retrieved September 23, 2013 (www.info.gov.za/speech/Dynamic Action?pageid=461&sid=23213&tid=48994).

Contributors

Michele Acuto is Stephen Barter Fellow of the *Oxford Programme for the Future of Cities* in the Institute for Science, Innovation and Society (InSIS) and the Oxford Martin School at the University of Oxford, Fellow of the *Center on Public Diplomacy* at the University of Southern California, and a Member of the Interdisciplinary Global Working Group (IG-WG) on short-lived climate pollutants based at the Institute for Advanced Sustainability Studies in Potsdam. He specialises in diplomacy, global governance, and urban studies. He is editor of *Negotiating Relief: The Dialects of Humanitarian Space* (Hurst) and author of *Global Cities, Governance and Diplomacy: The Urban Link* (Routledge).

Mark Amen is Director of Graduate Studies in the Government and International Affairs Department at the University of South Florida/Tampa and Deputy Editor of *Globalizations*. His research interests are in global governance and finance, globalisation and the nation-state, and globalising cities. His recent publications include coeditor for and contributing author in *Social Movements, the Poor and the New Politics of the Americas* (with H. Haarstad and A. Lera St. Clair), Routledge (2013); *Cities and Global Governance* (with N. Toly, P. McCarney, and K. Segbers), Ashgate (2011); *Cultures of Globalization: Coherence, Hybridity, and Contestation* (with K. Archer, M. Bosman, and E. Schmidt), Routledge (2008); and *Relocating Global Cities: From the Center to the Margins* (with K. Archer and M. Bosman), Rowman & Littlefield (2006). He has been principal investigator for more than $8 million in federal funding from the U.S. Department of Education and the U.S. Department of State to support research and education related to globalisation. Mark received his PhD in Political Science from the Institut de hautes études internationales in Geneva, Switzerland, and has been at the University of South Florida/Tampa since 1982. He was Academic Director of the Patel Center for Global Solutions (2005–2010) and Director of the USF Globalization Research Center (2001–2005).

Sofie Bouteligier conducted her PhD research at the Global Environmental Governance and Sustainable Development Research Group of KU

Leuven, Belgium, after which she was a postdoc researcher at the Environmental Policy Group of Wageningen University, the Netherlands. She is an associate fellow of the Leuven Centre for Global Governance Studies and the author of *Cities, Networks, and Global Environmental Governance: Spaces of Innovation, Places of Leadership*, Routledge (2012).

Emmanuel Brunet-Jailly studied Law and Political Science at Paris IV-Sorbonne and did a PhD in Political Science at the University of Western Ontario, Canada. He has taught at the University of Notre Dame (United States) and is now an Associate Professor of Public Administration at the University of Victoria, British Columbia, Canada, where he is also Jean Monnet Chair in European Urban and Border Region Policy and Director of the Jean Monnet Centre of Excellence. He is the editor of the *Journal of Borderlands Studies* (Taylor & Francis/Routledge). He is the author of 65 articles and chapters and 10 books and special issues of scholarly journals in urban and border studies. His recent publications include *Borderlands: Comparing Borderland Securit in North America and Europe*, University of Ottawa Press (2007), and *Local Government in a Global World: Australia and Canada in Comparative Perspective*, University of Toronto Press (2010). He is currently finishing a monograph called *Vancouver; World City?*

Elizabeth Cobbett is Lecturer in International Political Economy in the department of Political, Social and International Studies at the University of East Anglia. Her research explores the different ways in which global finance seeks profitable opportunities within localised social structures. This amplifies the significance of cultural and social factors that are often ignored by mainstream approaches to the political economy of global finance. Her case study centers on global financial flows in sub-Saharan Africa.

Simon Curtis is Lecturer in International Politics at the University of East Anglia. He was previously Michael Leifer Scholar in International Relations at the London School of Economics and Political Science. His research interests are in international theory and international history. He is currently working on a monograph entitled *Global Cities and Global Order*.

Nik Janos is Assistant Professor of Sociology at California State University, Chico. His work explores the intersection of urbanisation and socio-natural transformations, particularly focusing on Seattle, WA, and New Orleans, LA.

Kristin Ljungkvist studied Political Science at Södertörn University and International Relations at the Patterson School of Diplomacy, University of Kentucky. During 2013, Kristin will defend her doctoral dissertation 'The Global City 2.0' at the Department of Government, Uppsala University. Since 2012, Kristin has been a researcher at the Swedish Institute of International Relations, and her research focuses on global cities as international actors and urban security. During the past few years, Kristin has also been a guest researcher at Fordham University and at Center on Terrorism and the Christian Regenhard Center for Emergency Response Studies at John Jay College of Criminal Justice in New York City. Kristin teaches International Politics at Uppsala University.

Ian Madison, MSc London School of Economics, is a researcher/consultant in international affairs.

Corina McKendry is an Assistant Professor of Political Science at Colorado College, where she teaches courses in environmental politics and political economy in the Political Science Department and for the interdisciplinary Environmental Program. Her primary research interest is the relationship between urban environmentalism and the changing role of cities in the global economy. She is also interested in environmental justice and the social equity implications of urban greening initiatives. She received her PhD from the Department of Politics at the University of California, Santa Cruz in 2011.

Index

Afrikaans Republican Government
    158
Agenda 21 58
agglomeration economies 7, 154
Al-Qaida 45
American Jobs Act 2011 147
American Recovery and Reinvestment
    Act 2009 147
Amsterdam 66, 154
Annan, K. 35, 69
Antwerp 154
Arab Spring 40
arms trade 50
Asian Development Bank 85
authority 42; municipal 114

best practice 64
Bipartisan Tax Simplification and
    Fairness Act (2010) 147
Bloomberg, M. 70, 77, 84
Bloomberg Philanthropies 80
Boeing 94, 96, 97
bottom-up dynamics 18
Braudel, F. 15, 153, 154–156, 164
Brenner, N. 10
BRICs 151, 152, 161, 162
Brundtland report 58
Build America Bonds Programme 132,
    147
Bush Administration 147

Canadian Consortium for Human
    Security 44
Canadian Federation: Constitution of
    112–14
Canadian International Development
    Agency 119
canal building 136
Castells, M. 8

C40 4, 12, 19, 28–9, 42, 49, 57,
    61–6, 77–8, 79, 120; Sao Paulo
    Summit 4
Chadwick, A. 2
Chicago: Calumet 100; Millennium
    Park 93
Chief Seathl 95
Chinese Association of Mayors 75
cities: as actors 33, 52, 73; and
    biosafety 51; and climate change
    mitigation 47–9; economic
    generative power of 3, 27;
    financial districts of 9, 151,
    154–6; foreign policy of 40;
    governance capacity of 77–8;
    independence of 109; as nodes
    60, 148; renaturing of 89, 104,
    105; as sites 44; smart 65, 66;
    US 91
cityspace 5
climate change 12
Clinton Administration 147
Clinton Climate Initiative 12, 28, 62
Cold War 161
constructivism 133–4, 148, 149
core-periphery relations 154, 155
counterterrorism 44–7
creative cities 27
creative class 92, 94

Daly, R. M. 94, 101
Davies, R. 152
debordering 108
decentralization 38, 156
deindustrialization 6, 91
dematerialization 9
deregulation: financial 156
Dillon, J. F. 136–8
Dillon Rule 136

Doyle, R. 4
Durham report 112
Duwamish River Cleanup Coalition 94
Duwamish River Valley 94–100

ecological footprint 90
Economic Recovery Tax Act (1981) 144
emerging markets 151
Endangered Species Act 95
Energie citiés 57
Environmental Protection Agency 91,
    95, 96
EU-China Mayors Forum 74
Eurocities 42
European Commission 71
European Covenant of Mayors 75
European Sustainable Cities and Towns
    Campaign 71
European Union 73, 74

Farmers Loan and Trust Company 141
federalism 135
Federation of Canadian
    Municipalities 72
Fordism 143
Friedmann, J. 9, 19–20

Galtung, J. 8
Genoa 154
gentrification 103, 104, 106
Global City 55; as command and
    control centres 20; concept
    of 18, 21; functions of 20;
    hierarchies of 21; inequality
    within 89; regions 6–7; status 54
global civil society 70
global financial markets 132
global governance 19, 27–30, 76, 157;
    of climate change 2, 91
globalization: economic 7, 153–4
Globalization and World Cities
    Research Network 108
global order 27
global south 14
Glocal Forum 77
gold standard 152, 158, 159
good governance 38
Gordham, P. 162
Great Depression 143
greenhouse gas emissions 90
G7, 161

Habitat for Humanity 82
hegemonic transition 155

hegemony 29
Ho Chi Min City 66
Hong Kong 16
Hoy, S. 122
human trafficking 49
Hurricane Katrina 32
hybridity 81

imperialism: British 15, 112, 152, 158
Industrial Development Bond (IDB) 143
information technology 24–5
International Association of
    Francophone Mayors 120, 122
International Council for Local
    Environmental Initiatives 57, 122
International Labour Organization 60
International Monetary Fund (IMF)
    36–7, 162
International Olympic Committee 116
International Union of Local
    Authorities 2, 120
Islamic finance 162
Istanbul 71

Jacobs, J. 3, 27
Johannesburg 151, 158–61;
    Johannesburg Stock Exchange
    (JSE) 159
Johnson, B. 83
justice: environmental 90; socio-
    ecological 94

Kenya 152, 163
Kenyatta, U. 163
Keynesianism 18, 90, 91, 143–4, 145
Kimberly Agreement 122
King Wrought Iron Bridge
    Manufacturing and Iron Works
    Company 138
Kyoto Protocol 48

Langer, S. 53
Lastman, M. 107
Lefebvre, H. 6, 22–3
liberal institutionalism 133
liberalism 133, 134–5, 144, 148
Lisbon Treaty 39
Livingston, K. 61, 82
Local Governments for Sustainability 42
London 16, 66, 154; bombings 32

Madrid: bombings 32
Mandel, E. 5
Marshall, A. 140, 142

Mastercard 153, 163
Mauritius 152, 163
mayors 12, 40, 69–73; catalytic
    diplomacy of 70;
    internationalization of 79, 185
Mayors Climate Protection Agreement 48
Mayors for Peace 29, 42, 84
Mayors Hemispheric Forum 120
megacities 16, 164
Mega-Cities Project 57
Melbourne 65
Mercocities Network 42
methane capture 65
Metropolis 28, 57, 71, 82, 120
Mexico City 65
M4, 42
Microsoft 95
migration 35
Military Operations in Urbanized
    Terrain (MOUT) 46
Millennium Development Goals
    (MDG) 59
Miller, D. 79
mining 152
multiple modernities 160
municipal bond market 14, 132, 135–49

NAFTA 91
nationalism 1
nature: consumption of 102
neoliberal environmentalism 67
neoliberalism 18, 24, 83, 91, 97;
    discourses of 29, 31
neorealism 133
network society 8, 25, 61
New York City 154; bankruptcy of 16
New York Police Department 11
Nickels, G. 94
Nigeria 152, 153, 163
Nixon Administration 143
Nkoana-Mashabane 152
nongovernmental organizations
    (NGOs) 70
norms: cultural and social 40;
    entrepreneurs 133–4, 149–50;
    human rights 41; international 38

Obama Administration 147
Olympic games 116
Organization of the World Heritage
    Cities 122

Paes, E. 86
paradiplomacy 2, 41, 75, 81, 84

Peace of Westphalia 53
Port of Seattle 94
postindustrial economy 89–93, 100
postmetropolis 5
poverty 8, 36
power: regional 151
prestige projects 92
public health: global 50–2; regulation
    of 90
public-private partnership 92

Québec Conference (1864) 112

Rasmussen, J. 96
Reagan Administration 143
Regime theory 133
regional economy 154
resilience 44
Romanov, R. 113

salmon 95
SARS 32
Sassen, S. 9
Savings and Loan Association 139
scale 10, 92
Seattle: Central Waterfront Plan 93
9/11 32, 45
service sector 151
Shack/Slum Dwellers International
    (SDI) 82
Sherman Act (1890) 140
Sister Cities International 72, 84, 118
slums 36, 50; production of 3, 17, 37
social movements 40
Soja, E. 5
Somaliland 163
sovereignty 26, 30, 109
space: of flows 22, 107; of places 107;
    production of 89
spatial-fix 23
spatial fragmentation 3
Special Fund Doctrine 140
special-purpose government 140
state: agency of 22
State Mode of Production (SMP) 23–5
state-system 17
statism 11; crisis of 18, 22–4
Structural Adjustment Programmes 37
subprime mortgage market 147
subsidiarity 38
Sun Tzu 46
Superfund law 91, 93, 95, 98, 99
sustainability 57, 90
sustainable urbanization 59, 66

Tax Equity and Fiscal Responsibility
    Act (TEFRA) 1982 144
Tax Reform Act (TRA) of 1986 145–6
technology 8; social shaping of 22, 23
territorial centralisation 9
terrorism 45–7
Tibaijuka, A. 34
Topba, K. 71
Toronto 107, 114
transnational crime 49–50
transnational municipal networks 2, 48,
    57, 60–1, 64, 66–7

United Cities and Local Governments 42
United Nations 2, 28, 36; Environment
    Programme 57; International
    Association for Peace Messenger
    Cities 120; Rio Summit (1992)
    57; UN Advisory Commitee
    of Local Authorities 70–1; UN
    Centre for Human Settlements
    35; UNESCO 28, 57;
    UN-HABITAT 3, 6–7, 34, 37,
    39, 42, 48, 57–60, 70
United States: Civil War 137;
    Constitution 141; Supreme
    Court 135, 139
United States Conference of Mayors
    (USCM) 76
Urban Age Project 3
urban entrepreneurialism 92–3, 105

urban environmental governance 105
urbanization 34; planetary 35
urban planning 90
urban security studies 43
urban space: militarization of 46
urban sustainability 80

Venice 154
Villaraigosa, A. R. 76

Washington State Department of
    Ecology 95
water security 72
Westphalian system 53, 107–8
Williams, T. 85
Wilson-Gorman Tariff Act (1894) 141
World Bank 12, 28, 36–7, 57, 71, 73,
    79, 82, 162
world city: concept 154; hypothesis 19;
    networks 3, 8
World Economic Forum 152
world economy 153
World Energy Cities Partnership 120
World Health Organization (WHO) 50,
    123–4
world systems theory 155
World Trade Organization (WTO) 91,
    162

Zoellick, R. 4
Zuma, J. 152, 161–2